FROM THE ECLIPSE OF THE BODY
TO THE DAWN OF THOUGHT

FROM THE ECLIPSE OF THE BODY TO THE DAWN OF THOUGHT

Armando B. Ferrari

Editorial Consultant Anthony Molino
Edited by Paolo Carignani
Translated by Isabella Ghigi

Free Association Books

First published 2004
by Free Association Books
57 Warren Street W1T 5NR

© 2004 Armando B. Ferrari

British Library Cataloguing in Publication Data
A catalogue record for this book is available from the British Library

Printed and bound by Antony Rowe Ltd, Eastbourne

ISBN 1 853437 88 3

To the memory of my father

Publisher's Dedication

This book is dedicated to R. M. Young who founded Free Association Books in 1983. His vision and flair in the early years resulted in the publication of many books which have now become classic psychoanalytic texts, providing the inspiration and material resources for this translation.

I am very grateful to Flavia Donati for her patient help in reading the English version of the manuscript.

I want to express my gratitude also to the Sociedade Brasileira de Psicánalise de São Paulo where I did my training and started my research work.

CONTENTS

FOREWORD

R. D. Hinshelwood

We all start as a fragment of bodily matter, and we remain captive to it as the foundation of our existence. It becomes rapidly an icon of ourselves which we decorate in our own characteristic ways. It becomes a figment of your own thought and mental processes.

I wanted to write something ever so brief about this book, and support its publication because as Armando Ferrari rightly says, psychoanalysts do not concern themselves enough with the mind-brain problem. Psychoanalytic practice and theories have implications for the abstract problems of philosophers, but we rarely pursue them. Of course it is also true that the psychoanalytic neglect of philosophical problems is reciprocated – philosophers tend equally to neglect psychoanalytic data as material for their philosophical work. The neglected interaction is regrettable and this book points a way, like a signpost, towards a more populated territory between the two disciplines. Can there be an experience of the body if there is not a mind? We are so accustomed to think of the representation of things, including representations of the body, that the idea of an experience which is not a representation in the mind, is hard to imagine. And yet . . . there is a persisting suspicion in psychoanalysis, and in many other branches of psychology and philosophy that the body is somehow 'there', even if the mind does not see it. From Descartes time and before, it was a philosophical puzzle that there could be automatic reactions – if a baby's hand goes too near a fire, it pulls it away. We know too of the suckling reflex and the startle response, both present from birth. Even intra-uterine responses are apparent from ultrasound pictures. Are these bodily 'experiences' that can come before a mind?

Ferrari unravels this, but not easily. He creates a complex, interesting model of the earliest state of the infant's experience. As Mauro Mancia concluded, 'This is a rather provocative book, because it forces us to see things from unusual perspectives and to think of our patients on the basis of a model which enables us to understand the interactions between the ego/object and the ego/body relationships' (Mancia 1994, p. 1286). But the book provokes us by nagging away at an issue we should try to master. This is the conception of a primary something to which the earliest ego has to relate at birth. At that moment, the shock of powerful new stimuli creates a primitive awareness of a 'something' we will later call our bodies, or at least sensuous experiences of our bodies. Ferrari calls this primary something an 'object' – actually the concrete original object, or COO). He says the experience is 'a global feeling of *existing* in an environment' (Chapter 1, page 39). He postulates it as the beginning of the ego's relating. Indeed, it is the very beginning of the ego itself, the beginning of a mental self. Yet, it is not clear that this something should really be called an object, since it has such a 'self-ness'. Being the body, it is something of the self. There is no doubt that as development occurs the body becomes an object, and achieves the status of a mental representation. However, it is not an object in the sense of being internalised, it is primary, and might be assimilated into the psychoanalytic notion of primary narcissism. However, the assault of the birth turmoil is to jump-start an awareness that something needs to be attended to. The entire subsequent life is a journey of learning, conceptualisation and abstraction of this something (the COO) that has intruded as an integral sensuous self at the outset.

Ferrari's most central contribution is then to postulate the progressive 'eclipse' of this something, as a new dimension takes over from the COO. The infant's great resource is its mother, who is the first *external* object. She immediately invites a powerful mind-to-mind relationship. The book is an obsessive and vivid cartography of these two dimensions – the vertical between the body and its representation in the mind, characterised as a 'vertical relation', and a horizontal relationship between the infant's mental representation and the maternal one. Or rather, mother's primary function, amongst all others, is to instigate the horizontal relationship in the process of which the infant can begin to establish its COO, and the sensuous turmoil, as a mental representation. This begins a process that is now known as 'mentalisation': if the process of mentalisation progresses satisfactorily, the ensemble of body/mind functions smoothly enough for the experience of body to become unobtrusive, and the body becomes "eclipsed" (Carvalho 2002, p. 159). The process which 'eclipses' the COO is important in Ferrari's scheme as it is in effect the process of generating a mind. In the course of the process the vertical ('body') dimension experienced as unity of self and body (a 'onefold' dimension), is converted into the horizontal dimension experienced as relations with the minds of other objects, and their mental representations (Ferrari terms that the 'twofold' dimension). The external object, mother, begins the eclipse of the primary object. By engaging in a horizontal mind-to-mind relationship mother instigates the development of representations and symbols – the truly mental, non-extended *res cogitans*. The horizontal, i.e. 'twofold', is the inception of thinking, a distancing from the body-self, by representations, which imply others.

The key to the interaction between the two dimensions, onefold and twofold, is the phenomenon of 'feeling'. Feelings are both somatic, having an unrepresented sensuous quality, as well as a representation in the mind. This progressive conversion from vertical to horizontal (or from onefold to twofold) is not absolute, and the body moves as it were into the shadows, eclipsed rather than replaced by its mental representation.

Moreover, the conversion process is far from smooth, and under various circumstances there is a reversion back to the onefold, the bodily dimension. This occurs at crisis stages in life, like adolescence, pregnancy/childbirth, the menopause, or in states of illness (Ferrari, 1992). However, some management of the birth turmoil, with the help of mother's horizontal presence, has to be accomplished. Only then can object-relations (horizontal dimension) properly develop. Without that accomplishment the infant remains fixed in the vertical dimension so that other minds (i.e. reality) lack significance. This condition is psychosis, and remains a preoccupation with the deranged identity arising from the vertical disorder. Insofar as the infant can in its vertical dimension establish a stability against the sensuous turmoil of birth, each infant has to solve the mind-brain problem for itself at the outset before it can properly move on to be a mind.

The notion of the concrete original object is intended by Ferrari to be a solution to the mind-brain problem. The COO is a bodily occurrence, but it is also the primary material of a mental representation. It hovers in a balance between the concrete and the ephemeral, until a clear line is drawn and the split between body and mind occurs. Then, the body subsides into a mental object, a representation, an icon of the self. In its primary state, it is neither mind nor body, and solves the problem by making the conception of mind and brain redundant. It remains, perhaps, for philosophers to confirm whether this is truly a solution to the problem. Certainly, because of his 'solution', Ferrari does not find the usual difficulties. He confirms Spinoza's parallelism between the extensive and non-extensive substances. However, he also suggests a mutuality of influence, the brain affecting states of mind, and mental events resulting in brain states.

> When someone suffers hallucinations . . . the altered mind is actually using the body to develop its own pathological identity and any biochemical alterations are, in such cases, the result of a specific mental state.

Inversely, the body may initiate a mental disturbance, as one might observe in some cases when there is a severe alteration of a body organic function (page 91).

This is a mutual influence between brain and mind. It stimulates a really interesting question: if the brain is in some way responsible for the genera-tion of a symbolic world of representations in which the person lives (instead of pursuit of basic sensual satisfactions), then can that epiphenomenon achieve a partial autonomy so that its symbolic interactions reverberate back upon its physical basis? Ferrari does not go so far, but points forwards for someone to make a more extensive analysis of such interaction between foundation and symbolic superstructure. There is something profound about the possibility that the relations between a neurophysiological world and a symbolic world, are rooted in sensuous bodily experience.

For the British reader, the idea of a primary 'object' formed of bodily sensations, might strike a cord with the central organising effect of skin sensations as proposed by Esther Bick (Bick 1967; and see Briggs 2002). Ferrari suggests the turmoil of the birth trauma is the origin of the need for a mind, and this correlates with Bick's designation of skin sensation is the primary bodily container. Both are inherent and primary, they are exam-ples of a concrete original object. Skin sensation is not an internalised object, but in the same category as Ferrari's COO.

Ferrari has described the transition from the sensuous apprehension of the body to the symbolic awareness of another mind. To a remarkable degree he is considering the baby's dependence initially on the interocep-tors – that part of perception which is concerned with awareness of body states, such as hunger, cold, falling, etc. His model – from vertical to hor-izontal – in effect plots the move to the exteroceptors, or distance percep-tion – the eyes and ears that can identify a three-dimension world around, outside and separate. And, what is there in between these two dimensions, intero- and exteroceptors? Well, it is the skin and skin sensation. Following Bick's work, is not skin sensation the transitional moment, or bridge, from the vertical relation with the body to the horizontal relation with the 'other'? Skin sensation, like Ferrari's COO could equally be that crucial internal object that was never internalised.

Ferrari has made a challenging venture into psychoanalytic philosophy, taking us on a tour that orbits a foreign planet, the unknown world of our infantile experience at birth. The book challenges with continual reap-praisals of what psychoanalysts can so easily take for granted. It is an extended hypothesis for understanding the primary origins of what is essen-tially human, our symbol-using mind. Would that our philosophy col-leagues might come to mine Ferrari's work, and return stimulated by him. They might find the rest of psychoanalysis a useful test bed for doing the philosophy of mind.

NOTES

Bick, Esther 1968 The experience of the skin in early object relations. International Journal of Psycho-Analysis 49: 484–486.

Briggs, Andrew 2002 (ed) Surviving Space: Papers on Psychoanalysis. London: Karnac.

Carvalho, Richard 2002 Psychic retreats revisited: Binding primitive destructiveness of securing the object? British Journal of Psychotherapy 19: 153–171.

Ferrari, Armando 1992 L'Eclissi del Corpo. Roma: Borla.

Mancia, Mauro 1994 Review of L'Eclissi Del Corpo. Una Ipotesi Psicoanalitica. (Eclipse of the Body: A Psychoanalytical Hypothesis.). International Journal of Psycho-Analysis 75:1283–1286.

INTRODUCTION

Paolo Carignani

This book is a collection of some of Armando B. Ferrari's writings published as books, in Italy and in Brazil, between 1992 and 2000[1]. These essays are a meaningful novelty in psychoanalytic thinking as they carry significant theoretical and technical innovations originating from Ferrari's intense clinical practice. The eight chapters of this book are assembled in three sections that were originally published separately. In the first section the Author's main psychoanalytic hypothesis is presented together with some clinical vignettes. In the second section there is a revision of some psychoanalytic concepts following and enlarging the line of thought that goes from S. Freud to K. Abraham, M. Klein and W. R. Bion. In the third and last section the initial hypotheses are applied with special reference to work with adolescents. All the chapters have been expressly revised by the Author for this English edition: they have been adjourned in the light of his more recent research work and edited to become a book, rather than just a selection of essays[2].

It may prove useful to relate Ferrari's research and findings to his life and personal history. Ferrari was born in Montreal in 1922 and went to live in Italy as a child. At the end of World War II, after visiting Brazil as correspondent of several Italian newspapers interested in South America, he moved to Brazil and lived there for more than thirty years. In this country he studied sociology, anthropology and psychology and became a Professor of the University in São Paulo. He then started a long anthropological research work, mainly on the subject of death, with Brazilian tribes in Mato Grosso. In the same period Ferrari initiated his analytic training, coming close to Freudian theories (both through Freud's books and through work

15

with Freudian analysts who had emigrated to South America during the Nazi period) and later to Kleinian theories when the latter were introduced in Brazil by Argentine analysts. The training at the Psychoanalytic Society in São Paulo, several years of work in the Psychiatric Hospital in Juquerì (São Paulo) and in other psychiatric units together with an intense psychoanalytic practice enabled Ferrari to gain a vast and multifaceted experience in the clinical field. His first significant written contribution was a revision of the concept of Death Instinct seen both from a psychoanalytic and an anthropological perspective[3].

Ferrari's most significant encounter was with W.R. Bion who became his mentor and with whom Ferrari worked for a long period of time, becoming one of his most assiduous and constant scholars and collaborators in South America.

In the mid-Seventies, interested in investigating the subject of the Analytic Relationship, Ferrari came to Europe and lived in Rome. Here, in the Eighties and Nineties, he gave birth to his more significant hypotheses, bearing the strong influence of his studies and experience (Bion's last years' contribution and teaching above all) but also introducing a totally new perspective both on the theoretical and clinical level and opening the way to a completely original line of research.

Ferrari's main hypothesis is that the *body* – long excluded from the field of psychoanalytic research – has a fundamental role in the birth, development and realisation of mental functions. The body is not regarded, one should notice, as the body that is the object of medical investigation – an anatomical aggregation provided with and kept together by a number of physiological systems – but rather as the body that is perceived and experienced by the subject himself. This model relates closely to Freud's *Studies on Hysteria* and *Project for a Scientific Psychology*[4] as well as to all metapsychological essays in which he investigated the link between somatic experience and psychic representation[5]. Freud, as Jones (1962) pointed out, was always greatly attracted by the ancient problem of the relationship between body and mind and hoped that he could determine the physiological ground of psychic functions[6].

Several psychoanalytic authors have dealt, some occasionally others at length, with the subject of the relationship between body and mind. Freud's writings show a constant concern for the relation between somatic experience and psychic representation but, after him, one can think of K. Abraham, S. Ferenczi, G. Groddeck, E. Jones, M. Klein, S. Isaacs, P. Heimann, H. Segal[7]. All these authors regard the somatic experience as fundamental and believe it is closely correlated with the first psychic experiences (unconscious phantasies, somatic memories, body-mind problem). It is also worthwhile to mention P. Schilder, W. C. M. Scott and A. Aberastury[8] for the notion of construction of the body scheme and D.W. Winnicott, E. Gaddini and J. McDougall[9] for the notion of relationship

16

between psyche and soma. In conclusion it should be said that the body with its sensory manifestations is also a great silent protagonist in Bion's writings though it may be somewhat concealed in the complexity of his contribution. And yet none of these authors has placed – as Ferrari does – the body at the origin of the development of thought and at the centre of the psychoanalytic process.

The founding element of Ferrari's hypothesis is that the body is the one "object" of the mind as well as its primary reality; hence the notion of the Concrete Original Object (COO), a notion which aims to introduce the body in the field of psychoanalytical theory and originates, as a result, a totally new and different understanding of the term "object". By COO Ferrari describes a kind of primeval nucleus, present since birth, of somatic functions (sensory, physiological, metabolic etc.) that interact articulately with the primary mental functions of registration and containment. The COO imposes itself as the first object amidst the turmoiling sensations that start in the body and reach out towards the mind – a mind that is just beginning to take shape – but this object is also, and at the same time, experienced as the subjective nucleus that enables the recognition of the individual's psycho-physical existence. Thus the COO should not be regarded as an introjected object but as a nucleus that exists before any kind of introjection, the original matrix of the physicality expressed through sensations and emotions. Finally, the COO includes the physical body, the compound of sparse sensations and emotions coming from the body, the mental apparatus which has the functions of perception and notation.

The body is understood as having the first and essential functions of the mind, and the mind as emerging from the body and never separate from it. At the beginning of life the child is first of all in relation with this COO since, before any other event takes place, the child lives and experiences his body. The differentiation from the Kleinian model is therefore quite marked. Ferrari writes: «In M. Klein's theoretical model there are two objects: one is the child, the other is the mother. Klein describes the interaction between these two objects and delineates how the latter, the mother, becomes an internal object causing the child to acknowledge that there is also an object that is external to him. This is a satisfactory description at an operative level but it is insufficient when it ends up expressing a spatial division. I think it is necessary to think of a different theoretical model: first of all an entity that perceives itself as corporeality (Onefold) and as symbolicalness (Twofold). It is not just a breast that offers itself to the mouth of the child, it is a completely different condition; the child offers himself, through corporeality, to himself.» (*infra*, p. 13). This perspective has vast clinical consequences since the attention is not focused so much upon the analysand's relationship with his "objects" (internal or external) but rather upon the dialogue which the analysand has with himself, that is with his sensations, perceptions, emotions, desires etc. Ferrari's psychic object is therefore quite different from Klein's, Winnicott's or even Bion's models of object.

An example can clarify some of the differences: it is about the prototype of *a newly born baby crying because he is waiting for mother to feed him.*

1. According to the Kleinian theory the object is the breast with its characteristics and its potentialities, offering or denying the food and love which the baby needs. The "breast psychic object", characterised by its positive and negative qualities, is introjected by the baby and the baby develops more or less intense emotions and feelings towards it. This experience provides a fundamental pattern for the development of the child's mental capacities. External reality is of fundamental importance for M. Klein but the characteristics of the process of introjection (and the feelings relating to it) are determinant to the qualities and potentialities of the introjected object.

2. Reality is more important for Winnicott: the harmonious psychic development of the child is seen ad deriving from the possibility of having good gratifying experiences. The capacity of the mother to look after her child and to adapt to his needs is the main condition for the formation of a good object and, therefore, for the establishment of a stable psychic apparatus. A *good enough mother* is necessary for a healthy growth.

3. Bion's model is again different: the psychic object isn't anymore the real breast expected to become experience or the breast as an introjected object. The psychic object, enabling the emergence of thought and providing it with its foundations is, paradoxically, the absence of the breast, or, in Bion's more precise words the *non-breast.* The child's capacity to tolerate this absence or rather this negative presence, to tolerate, in other words, frustration, is the source of his capacities for thought. If the child tends to evade frustration he opens the way to psychotic processes; if, on the contrary, he tries to tolerate and modify the state of frustration he develops the *alpha function* and creates the conditions for thought to become possible.

4. Ferrari's point of view is once again different. The psychic object isn't, in his hypothesis, neither the breast nor the non-breast, neither gratification nor frustration, neither the mother nor the mother's functions. The child's psychic object is the child's *hunger* since when the child feels hungry that is what he has to deal with. Hunger isn't seen as the product of a betrayal on the part of the breast, and isn't therefore related to the breast, and it isn't seen as a sheer experience of frustration. Hunger (same as the sense of being well fed, warm, cold, sleepy or all other possible sensations that the human being can experience) is a datum, an information coming from the body which the whole living organism has to take into account. Each sensation can have, in itself, a pleasurable or a painful element, but the element's function is much more ample than that as it supports the biological process of protec-

tion both of the individual and of the species. The child has the tasks of discerning and recognising each specific sensation from all the others, of experiencing the emotional impact without being overwhelmed, of learning to express such an experience so that he can communicate it to himself and to others. In order to be able to perform these tasks he needs the help of his mother's function of *rêverie*. Thus the object of the mind (continuosly present and unexcludable) is the body with its infinite and unforeseen manifestations.

This theoretical perspective leads, needless to say, to significant differences in the clinical approach. The task of the analyst could be described (according to the metaphor of the newly born baby) as that of directing the analysand's attention towards the sensation of hunger rather than towards the breast or the breast's absence (regarding the 'breast' both as a real introjected object and as a model). The analysand's attention should also be directed towards: the mode in which the above mentioned sensation of hunger can be dealt with by himself (harboured, refused, evaded etc.), the emotions which it originates (acknowledgement and respect or rather hatred, fear, anxiety etc.), the possible integrations with other physical perceptions. With this approach the analysand is encouraged to take responsibility for his mode of using and dealing with data originating from his body.

It becomes thus possible to soften (when they are excessive) or to intensify (when they are perceived as scarce) the tension and conflict intrinsically belonging to human life: the basic strain originated by the impossibility of fully knowing about, and dealing with ourselves; by the unreachable *otherness* that is inside all of us and that constantly turns us into subject and object of our own experience of living.

When after birth the mental functions begin to emerge from the COO (initially it is just registration) the dialogue between the registering subject and the registered object (COO) may start. Ferrari states that in this dialogue one can observe the essential conflict of the human being. This notion is not distant from Matte Blanco's conceptualisation of a fundamental antinomy of human beings;[10] though in Ferrari's theoretical model the central paradox or insoluble dyad is not seen, in the *intrapsychic* domain, between the unconscious and conscious levels (and the correlated symmetrical and asymmetrical modes) or between the Ego and the Id, or the internal objects and the self, but rather, in a *biologically* significant domain, between the body and the mind. The founding otherness of human experience is seen as originated by the experience of being a living body that incessantly emanates sensations and emotions and also a mind that has the task of registering and dealing with such data. The two different moments though closely related, cannot actually join because there is an unbridgeable gap – not only temporal – between sensation and registration, just as between sensation and perception, or between emotion and thought. We observe ourselves in a way that is similar to the way in which we can observe the sky and the stars: when we perceive an astronomical event (a comet, the birth or the explosion of a star, the movement of a constellation, etc.), the phenomenon in itself belongs already to a distant past. The same happens when we perceive the emergence of a sensation, of an emotion or of a state of mind: the phenomenon in itself is extinguished though we may perceive it as still actual. Furthermore, when we observe ourselves, we lack the distance between observer and observed that is necessary for discernment and discrimination between the two. We are in fact the aim of our observation and find ourselves in the insoluble discord of being both the instrument and the object of our search.

In this perspective the psychic object is understandably regarded as a concrete inevitable presence not as a pure *imago* representing an aspect of external reality. The object is not understood as Klein's symbol: it is a *concrete object* because it is the body we live in, and provides, furthermore, an insoluble paradox for it presents itself, at the same time, as the object (since we *have* a body) and as the subject (since we *are* our body)[11]. Ferrari's hypothesis therefore defines the *mind as a function of the body*[12] and sees the nucleus of human experience in the relation between these two poles.

In order to make it clear that he did not wish to reproduce – except for the necessities of the scientific investigation – the ancient dichotomy between *res cogitans* and *res extensa*, Ferrari chose the language of mathematical concepts to indicate the two functional areas of the organism and suggested that one might use the term Onefold (in Italian: Uno) to define the body as active presence and Twofold (in Italian: Bino) to define a primary, almost 'physical' function of perceiving, registering and subsequently containing the sensations originating from Onefold. One could then say that Onefold gives life to Twofold and that Twofold then includes the Onefold and develops to reach the most refined mental activities never losing, except at the risk of becoming mad, the original physical roots. In the simultaneous presence of both Onefold and Twofold two interesting areas are further defined: the area mainly related to Onefold is named by Ferrari the entropic area while the area mainly related to Twofold is called negentropic. The former, as its name suggests, is based on an unstable equilibrium, generating a kind of disarray, tending to other forms of non-equilibrium; the latter, on the contrary, tends to order and equilibrium, to containment and organisation. In the tension which originates from the overlapping of the two areas dialogues, communications and encounters are generated but also all internal contrasts, difficulties and conflicts that are characteristic of the human being.

The relation between Onefold and Twofold is named *vertical relation*. This relation can be expressed and signified when the Twofold progressively includes the catalysing functions of maternal *rêverie* and of cultural linguistic surroundings, originating the *horizontal relation*: thus the body becomes a symbol and enables representation. The body-mind relationship is founding for individual development but needs, in order to express itself, the horizontal relation which is where experience of the vertical relation takes up shape and meaning. Here the Twofold progressively acquires the capacity to register, contain, discriminate, acknowledge and employ the vast range of sensations and emotions coming from the COO. The appearance of these functions relates to Ferrari's main hypothesis: when the mind takes form (in the manner that has been described) the mental functions throw a shade and cool down intense sensations and emotions. The Eclipse of the COO takes place enabling the child to come out of the original turmoil of sensations and emotions when, as stated by Ferrari: «the shadow of the mental activity projects itself upon the COO.» (infra, p. 18).

In this hypothesis, as it has been said, the mental domain is closely connected with the physical domain and depends upon it directly; this outlook introduces a highly dynamic vision of the individual since it implies that the dialogue between body and mind is in continuous movement and transformation and that the task of the analyst is that of investigating the level of harmony or of disharmony existing between body and mind, in each moment, using dynamic rather than structural co-ordinates. This implies, for instance, that a child's mental motions should be functional to a process leading to approach and knowledge of a body as yet mostly unknown but that a pregnant woman's motions should be investigated in relation to her capacity at harbouring pregnancy's physical transformations (just to mention two extremely different cases). In childhood, latency, adolescence, young age, adulthood, old age, illnesses, traumas, pregnancies etc. the mind should be prepared to receive the body's communications and needs and to configure itself in relation to the latter. This is an often difficult task because the incessant physical transformations require the mind to follow and to adapt itself continuously to the body's new needs by means of a remarkable flexibility. When this mental elasticity is missing disharmonious movements take place and the mind hinders and fights the body instead of attending it.

This perspective introduces a concept that is essential in Ferrari's theoretical model: the temporal dimension. Because the dialogue between body and mind can only take place in the frame of space/time co-ordinates, Freud's idea of a timeless unconscious is not shared by Ferrari who believes that no domain of the mind should be regarded as unrelated to the passing of time. The body-mind dialogue can therefore only follow the direction of time, from birth towards death, and the notion of regression is unacceptable, in Ferrari's opinion, both theoretically and clinically: the vertical relation cannot ever revert to the past as it constantly responds to, the needs of the present and the analyst who is observing it should be concerned only with the degree of functionality and harmony in the hic et nunc of the session. The body-mind dialogue has but one irreversible direction and all varying forms of equilibrium reached during the whole span of life should be regarded as incessant and more or less functional adjustments to the needs of the moment. In his recent research Ferrari[13] regards Freud's unconscious as a notion bearing the characteristics of a process, more related to time than to space, in which time, far from being absent, is present in a continuous form. At each moment – Ferrari states – we produce unconscious and consume it.

Moreover, the emotional experience, one of the most archaic and essential levels giving birth to the mental area, should be understood as a phenomenon that takes place in time. It has a beginning, it lasts and it eventually finishes. Clinical work should have, between other things, the function of recognising this evolution in time. Emotions are regarded as an actual bridge for the passage from the corporeal to the psychic level. Ferrari suggests that they should be regarded as «an intermediate domain between the field of bare sensations and the area of initial thought, composed of physical qualities and of psychic potential qualities» (infra, p. 21). The close relationship between sensation and emotion is thus seen as the foundation of any kind of thought, since both sensations and emotions characteristically tend towards thought.

The very specificity of this hypothesis has led Ferrari, as one can see in the second section of the book, to delineate a new understanding of some fundamental psychoanalytic concepts in the light of his initial assumption. If the never ending tension and conflict of the human being are not to be understood as interpersonal or intrapsychic phenomena but as the inevitable result of the irredeemable challenge between body and mind this notion can cast a different light on the main psychoanalytic findings. The reader will find new suggestions, in the understanding of concepts such as the Oedipus Complex and the Ego, opening the way to new theoretical and clinical perspectives. If the dialogue/conflict between body and mind is ever present and, above anything, ever actual, then the elements that are responsible for the foundation of psychic processes must be actual as well and what changes is the mode and form in which any given phenomenon manifests itself.

Thus Ferrari acknowledges both Freud's view and M. Klein's innovation in the concept of Oedipal Constellation (a term which he prefers to 'Oedipus Complex' as it highlights the composite and ever changing character of the 'Ego, Mother, Father' triad) but he also adds that the Oedipal constellation doesn't end with latency[14], and continues during the whole life. This has to do with the Oedipal Constellation responding to the triangular Ego/Mother/Father experience but also, and more directly, to the child's need to harbour and compose in himself the aspects of masculinity and of femininity contained in the body-mind dialogue. This concept isn't very distant from Freud's understanding of infantile bi-sexuality[15] except that Ferrari extends it to the entire life. Aspects of masculinity and femininity are ever present in each individual and they can be easily represented and visualised in family dynamics but their tension can't be solved (or

22

reduced to an infantile context) and it assumes different configurations in the different moments of life. This view is coherent with the model: if the body is the object of the mind, constantly and in many ways unexpectedly changing then the *choice of the object* can't be perpetual and it must be characterised by innumerable variations. During adolescence (see section three) for instance, in the long or even never ending process of formation of identity one can observe that masculinity and femininity combine in a way that is quite different from the one that characterises childhood, for instance, or adult age.

The subject of identity and the Ego is also discussed at length in this book. Ferrari prefers the term *Ego configuration* to the term *Ego*, of Cartesian origin, employed by Freud to refer to the *structure*, and focuses rather on the *functional aspects* highlighting the continuous dynamicity and elasticity of all the psycho-physical movements of the individual. His point of view derives from an acknowledgement of the extreme difficulty of establishing the boundaries of the Ego, since these boundaries continuously vary, incessantly expanding and decreasing according to different situations in the dialogue between the body and its mental functions: puberty, adolescence, pregnancy, illness etc. produce significantly different psychic states of organisation, though in preservation of the continuity of individual experience.

Other clinical and technical points are developed in chapters 7 and 8 of the book through detailed presentations of clinical material concerning work with adolescents and adults. The clinical illustrations provide several samples of technical approaches adopted and formulated by Ferrari in the course of his work. We would like to mention briefly the one that concerns the quality of the analytic dialogue. In previous papers[16] Ferrari had critically discussed the concept of psychoanalytic interpretation, seen as the instrument by which the analyst could translate, in a language accessible to the conscience, the analysand's unconscious communications. Ferrari had suggested, in his papers, that the analyst's communications could be seen as simple propositions, offered to the analysand, referred to the modes in which the analysand adjusts his mind in relation to the products and demands that come from his body. He therefore preferred the term *Analytic Proposition* to signify an instrument in the hands of the analyst, an instrument for the construction of a dialogue with the analysand rather than a description or a translation of something that happens *in* the analysand. One can see, in this book, that Ferrari further develops his ideas and implicitly suggests that the task of the analyst is that of translating his own thoughts in an accessible language for the analysand, to have access to, in that moment, rather than translating the analysand's unconscious thoughts. This understanding originates, as its development, the notion of *language register,* a kind of specific dialect, spoken by the analysand who, though he may be sharing aspects of the common tongue, can often employ an emergency language strongly and characteristically featured by obsessional, paranoid, delusional, phobic traits, depending on the needs of the moment. Analysands are often compelled to use just one of these dialects as they are unable to switch from one language register to the other. The analyst's task is that of learning to speak that specific dialect and its syntactic and semantic rules, so that he can establish a communication with the analysand and start proposing the first significant variations to the patient's theme. It is possible to sense, in this approach, the influence of Ferrari's anthropological experience, of the research work he did in the fifties, as he firmly believes that it is necessary to learn about the communicative modes and rules of the community one is approaching, before acquiring any kind of active role towards it. The analyst differs nevertheless from the anthropologist, because he isn't just there to learn and understand but aims at fostering the production of transformations and, more specifically, at facilitating the analysand's task of learning other 'dialects', other language registers, so that he can gain more freedom and come out of the prison engendered by the impossibility of establishing a dialogue with his own anxiety.

One can see from the subjects that I have mentioned, and essentially from reading the book, that Ferrari's hypotheses, though firmly rooted in the main pathway of psychoanalytic tradition, suggest several innovations both on the theoretical and on the clinical level therefore fully justifying this first English translation.

NOTES

1 The original volumes have the following titles: Ferrari A.B. (1992), *L'eclissi del corpo*, Roma: Borla; Ferrari A. B. (1994), *Adolescenza. La seconda sfida*, Roma: Borla; Ferrari A. B. e Stella A. (1998), *L'alba del pensiero*, Roma: Borla.

2 The reader can find book reviews and papers on A. Ferrari's work in English. Reviews of two of the books appeared in IJPA: *L'eclissi del corpo* reviewed by M. Mancia (*IJPA*, 1993, 75: 1283–1286) and *L'alba del pensiero* by P. Bria (*IJPA*, 2000, 81: 609–612). Two papers on Ferrari's work appeared in IJPA as well: R. Lombardi (2002), «Primitive mental states and the body: a personal view of the Armando B. Ferrari's concrete original object», (83: 363–381) and R. Lombardi (2003), «Mental models and language registers in the psychoanalysis of psychosis», (84: 843–863). A third paper on Ferrari's theory appeared in *Psychoanalytic Quarterly* (R. Lombardi (2003), «Catalyzing the dialogue between the body and the mind in a psychotic analyzand», LXXII, 1017–1041). A paper by R. Carvalho appeared: Carvalho R. (2002), «Psychic Retreats Revisited: Binding Primitive Destructiveness, or Securing the Object? A Matter of Emphasis», *British Journal of Psychotherapy*, 19 (2): 153–171.

3 Ferrari A. B. (1967), «Instinto de morte: contribução para uma sistematização de seu estudo», *Revista Brasileira de Psicanálise*, 1, 3: 324–350 (primeira parte), 1,4: 487–525 (segunda parte).

4 Freud S. (1892–95), *Studies on Hysteria*, S. E., 2, London: Hogarth Press; Freud

24

S. (1895 [1940]), *Project for a Scientific Psychology*, S.E., 1, London: Hogarth Press.

5 Freud S. (1911), «Formulation of the Two Principles of Mental Functioning», S.E., 11, London: Hogarth Press; Freud S. (1915), «Instincts and Their Vicissitudes», S. E., 14, London: Hogarth Press.

6 Jones E. (1953), *The Life and Work of Sigmund Freud*, New York: Basic Books, Inc.

7 Abraham K. (1912), «Notes on Psycho-Analytical Investigation and Treatment of Manic-Depressive Insanity and Allied Conditions»; (1913), «A Constitutional Basis of Locomotor Anxiety»; (1924), «A Short Study of the Development of the Libido, Viewed in the Light of Mental Disorders»; (1925), «Psycho-Analytical Studies on Character Formation», in *Selected Papers on Psycho-Analysis*, London: Hogarth, 1927. Ferenczi S. (1913), «Stages in the Development of the Sense of Reality»; (1913), «The Ontogenesis of Symbols», in *Contributions to Psycho-Analysis*, Boston: R.G. Badger, 1916; (1917), «Disease or Patho-Neuroses», in *Further Contributions to the Theory and Technique of Psycho-Analysis*, London: The Hogarth Press and the Institut of Psycho-Analysis. Reprinted New York: Brunner/Mazel, 1980. Jones E. (1946), «A Valedictory Address», *International Journal of Psycho-Analysis*, 27. Klein M. (1921), «The Development of a Child»; (1923), «Early Analysis»; (1930), «The Importance of Symbol-Formation in the Development of the Ego» «Symposium_on_Child_Analysis»; (1931), «A Contribution to the Theory of Intellectual Inhibition», in *Love, Guilt and Reparation and Other Works*, London, Virago Press, 1988. Isaacs S. (1948), «The Nature and Function of Phantasy», *International Journal of Psycho-Analysis*, 29, pp. 73–97. Heimann P. (1958), «Notes on Early Development», in *About Children and Children-No-Longer. Collected Papers 1942–1980*, London: Routledge, 1989. Segal H. (1964), «Phantasy and Other Mental Processes», *International Journal of Psycho-Analysis*, 45, reprinted in *The Work of Hanna Segal. A Kleinian Approach to Clinical Practice*, New York: Jason Aronson, 1981.

8 Aberastury Pichon Riviere A. (1958), «House Construction Play. Its Interpretation and Diagnostic Value», *International Journal of Psycho-Analysis*, 39. Scott W.C.M. (1948), «Some Embryological, Neurological, Psychiatric and Psycho-Analytic Implications of the Body Scheme», *International Journal of Psycho-Analysis*, 29. Schilder P. (1935), *The Image and Appearance of the Human Body*, New York: University International Press.

9 Winnicott D.W. (1949), «Mind and its Relation to the Psyche-Soma», in *Collected Papers: Through Paediatrics to Psycho-Analysis*, London: Basic Books, 1958; (1963) «Fear of Breakdown»; (1964–1969), «Psycho-Somatic Disorders; (1970), «On the Basis for Self in Body», in *Psycho-Analytic Explorations*, London: Karnac Books, 1989. Gaddini E. (1980), «Notes on Mind-Body Question», *International Journal of Psycho-Analysis*, 68, 1987. McDougall J. (1974), «The Psychosoma and the Psychoanalytic Process», *International Revue of Psycho-Analysis*, 1; McDougall J. (1989), *Theaters of the Body*, London: Free Association Books, 1989.

10 Matte Blanco I. (1975), *The Unconscious as Infinite Sets: an Essay in Bi-Logic*, London: Duckworth.

11 This insoluble paradox has been highlighted by early psychological researchers: W. James in *The Principles of Psychology* highlighted the extreme difficulty in establishing a relation with one's body and the consequences of this difficulty for the development and understanding of the concepts of self-conscience and identity: «Our bodies themselves, are they simply ours, or are they *us*? Certainly

men have been ready to disown their very bodies and to regard them as mere vestures, or even as prisons of clay from which they should some day be glad to escape. We see then that we are dealing with a fluctuating material. The same object being sometimes treated as a part of me, at other times as simply mine, and then again as if I had nothing to do with it at all». James W. (1890), *The Principles of Psychology*, New York: Holt, reprinted by Encyclopedia Britannica, Chicago-London, 1952, p. 188.

12 In some neuro-scientific hypotheses concerning the mind-brain relationship the mind is also seen as a function of the body, originated from and permanently relating to it. See Damasio A. (1994), *Descartes' Error. Emotion, Reason and the Human Brain*, New York: Putnam.

13 See Ferrari A. B. *Il pulviscolo di Giotto*, about to be published, in particular the first chapter 'La freccia del tempo' (The Arrow of Time).

14 As, on the contrary, suggested by Freud and in substance accepted by M. Klein. See: Freud S. (1924), «The Dissolution of the Oedipus Complex», S.E., 19, London: Hogarth Press and Klein M. (1932), *The Psycho-Analysis of Children*, London: Hogarth Press.

15 Freud S. (1905), *Three Essays on the Teory of Sexuality*, S.E., 7, London: Hogarth Press and Freud S. (1908), «Hysterical Phantasies and their Relation to Bisexuality», S. E., 9, London: Hogarth Press.

16 Ferrari A. B. (1983), «Relazione analitica: sistema o processo?», in *Rivista di psicoanalisi*, 29, 4: 476–496 and Ferrari A.B. (1986), «La proposizione analitica», in AA. VV. *L'interpretazione psicoanalitica*, Roma: Bulzoni.

SECTION I

The Eclipse of the body

1

INTRODUCING THE HYPOTHESIS OF THE CONCRETE ORIGINAL OBJECT

The analytic relationship, mode and form of the analysts' daily contact with their analysands is not a one way relationship. The development of the mental capacities of the analysand is often accompanied by an enrichment of the analyst's thoughts. Furthermore these thoughts are sometimes expressed and made public, or even configured as hypotheses. The Eclipse of the Concrete Original Object (COO) is an example of this.

Several years of research with the philosopher Emilio Garroni gave as a result, in 1979, a first paper on the study of the analytic relationship[1]. The paper focused on the dynamic aspects of the encounter between analyst and analysand where interpretation was regarded as the proposition made by the analyst to the analysand, an Analytic Proposition. A further development of this theoretical model was presented in Brasilia in 1982 as one of a series of lectures on the "Analytic Relationship". A more complex version, with the contributions of Giuliana Milana and Luisa Tirelli was given in Milan in 1984 at the 6th National Conference of the Italian Psychoanalytical Society. In 1985 it became a paper and was published in the *Revista Brasileira de Psicanálise*[2].

The subject of this section is the relation between body and mind, a subject that hasn't been much focused upon by psychoanalytic literature, except on rare occasions. The reason for this might well be found in the general nature of the context of western culture. In "Cratilus" Plato thus describes the Orphic conception of body and soul: "Thus some people say that the body (*sôma*) is the tomb (*sêma*) of the soul ..."[3]. Plato himself had no doubts on the subject, and in expressing his opinion he actually originated a doctrine that was to become extensively popular in the western world. One could almost say the he signed the act of birth of western culture: "Lovers of knowledge recognise that . . . it (the soul) has been veritably bound and glued to the body, and is forced to view things as if through a prison, rather than alone by itself, and that it is wallowing in utter ignorance"[4].

The mind has henceforth been constantly regarded as predominant while the nature of the physical body has been all too often disregarded by researchers of the mental area.

In this work I am therefore endeavouring to focus upon and highlight this area of knowledge that, although sometimes intuitively understood and signalled, hasn't as yet achieved a definite formulation of its own. I have come to the conclusion that such a formulation is indeed possible, after having thoroughly and accurately analysed the clinical observations that I have carried on over several years, while investigating the Analytic Relationship.

My hypothesis requires that psychoanalytic research on mental functioning be somehow related to the biological and ethological disciplines, so that mental functioning might be observed in its relational features, that is in the interactions between the individual and his surroundings (including animate *and* inanimate objects). My suggestion is that mental activity might actually originate from an ethological context by means of ongoing composition of internal and external stimuli.

I do realise that my opinion raises several, yet unanswered, epistemological and psycho-physiological problems. The epistemological aspect of the matter, was nevertheless utterly investigated by K. R. Popper and J. C. Eccles[5] who had the further task of delineating and discussing exhaustively the relation between body and mind, a subject which, as we have seen, has been considered significant from the Orphic conception onwards. As for the psycho-physiological aspect of the matter I am referring to D.O. Hebb[6] for an integrated view of contemporary contributions. Finally, I am referring to J. von Neumann[7] for what concerns cybernetics and for a cognitive approach to U. Neisser[8].

In the field of clinical psychoanalytic research my main point of reference is in the work of W.R. Bion[9].

Although the actual state of knowledge and research doesn't allow for definite answers upon the subject of the relation between body and mind, I nevertheless hope to facilitate further clarification of the subject, by offering a hypothesis resulting from extensive clinical work and investigation of primitive mental functioning.

Furthermore, the elaboration of my theoretical model, centred upon the relation between body and mind, can be compared, in mode and form, to the model of psycho-physical interaction in which the body-mind duality is overcome through a conjoint investigation of mental and somatic aspects, regarded as differentiated but complementary levels of functioning.

My hypothesis is based upon and relates to some specific aspects of the ontogenetic development; mainly the organisational and adaptive aspects of mental functioning and the progressive reduction of the primitive area of experience, initially exclusively occupied by turmoiling[10] sensations.

In this theoretical model I acknowledge the importance of intersubjective relationships in promoting individual growth and I am therefore distant from the New York post-Freudian theoretical developments as well as from neo-analysts such as Rado, Abraham, Kardiner.

In my hypothesis the "environmental" aspect of the relationship doesn't actually include, any cultural notion like Marx' "super-structure" or Popper's "World 3". It mainly refers instead, to situations in which growth can be regarded as a strict biological endowment, while learning and the organising of mental functioning are seen as utter psychological features.

In mentioning the base and the super-structure Marx delineates, I believe, a concept that is similar to the one developed in Popper's World 3 and suggests that learning processes have cultural components in themselves, such as language, to which the baby is exposed since the beginning of life. The linguistic competence starts early and the immersion of the baby in World 3 is immediate. In Popper one can notice an obvious conflict between the two opposite poles of the mental and bodily areas. An immediate splitting of some kind is hypothesised, at least implicitly, and expected, as well as a consequent problem in placing the two aspects. So the mode of being of any child seems to include, even theoretically, an anticipation of a mind-body conflict.

The somatic area, that I name Concrete Original Object (COO) should, in my theoretical model, be understood neither as the "environment" of the mental functioning, nor as its support but rather as a complex of functions (sensory, metabolic etc.) that join and interplay with mental functions. The development of mental functions and the containment (registering) of confusing sensations occurs through progressive mental "distancing" from the Ego's corporeal nature, the corporeality, therefore through the establishment of a relationship between the Ego regarded as the site of representations (Twofold), and the body (Onefold), in other words between the individual person and the mind.

It is easy to forget that sensations are grounded on the body functioning since the prevailing tendency is to regard them as related to the perceptual apparatus rather than to the somatic processes. As an example of this we might be reminded, for instance, that Locke called "ideas" the products of physical sensations.

My hypothesis is, on the contrary, that mental activity initiates with the primary function of containing and organising the sensations of the newly born baby. I think that it is mainly the mind that performs this task but, obviously, this is a complex matter. The aim of containing and organising sensations is reaching a state of widespread adaptation, staying

31

alive in any specific form that evolution may have assigned to us.

An interesting book on this subject is "The Mind's I" by D.R. Hofstadter and D.C. Dennett[11]. The authors present and discuss several papers by scientific and philosophical researchers investigating the fascinating subject of Artificial Intelligence. The mind is here mainly regarded as a kind of system of representations, physically located in the brain, and capable of self-organisation. But there must be some yet "incomprehensible" element, for Hofstadter comments: "We all fluctuate delicately between a subjective and objective view of the world, and this quandary is central to human nature"[12].

W. Heisenberg in *Philosophical Problems of Quantum Physics* suggested that physicists had to give up the idea of using a common objective time scale and of believing in the existence of events that are independent from our capacity to observe. He also emphasized that laws of nature don't deal with elementary particles but with our knowledge of the particles, in other words with the content of our minds[13].

H. J. Morowitz maintains that: "... a complex system can only be described by using a probability distribution that relates the possible outcomes of an experiment. In order to decide among the various alternatives, a measurement is required. The measurement is what constitutes an event, as distinguished from the probability, which is a mathematical abstraction. However, the only simple and consistent description physicists were able to assign to a measurement involved an observer becoming aware of the result. Thus the physical event and the content of the human mind were inseparable"[14]. Finally Nobel Prize E. Wigner in "Remarks on the mind body question" writes: "It was not possible to formulate the laws of quantum mechanics in a fully consistent way without reference to the consciousness"[15].

The integration of the theoretical positions of researchers from different areas such as psychology, biology, and physics uncovers a global, wholly unexpected pattern that could be summarized in three primary issues:

a) human mind contains consciousness, the states of reflection upon mental operations should therefore be explained through activity of the central nervous system. The activity of the C.N.S. should then be related to biological structures and, furthermore, to the physiological functioning of the system;

b) biological phenomena should be at all levels understood in terms of atomic physics, that is, in terms of action and interaction of the atoms of carbon, nitrogen, oxygen, etc. that originate the biological phenomena;

c) contemporary atomic physics in order to gain precision and understanding, rely upon the mechanics of quantum, and should, for this reason, be exclusively formulated considering the mind as one of the primary components of the system.

These three issues or grades of elaboration formulate a kind of global integrated approach. Outside this approach there can be only two widely opposed models. One physical, assuredly ample, since it describes everything that is in nature, one psychological, comprehensive as it deals with the mind, which is the only means for knowledge of the universe.

This is a kind of epistemological vicious circle. On the one hand it deprives us of any absolute certainties and on the other it raises anew the problem of the mind-body relationship that psychoanalysts, as theorists of psychology, cannot elude. The human being cannot be regarded as capable of thought but devoid of emotion. It is impossible to differentiate emotions from thoughts since emotions are a collateral automatic production of the capacity to think. Emotions are part of the essential nature of thought. Furthermore, they originate the capacity for thought.

Any conscious system uses symbols to represent the state of the brain. The symbols are part of the brain that they symbolize, for consciousness requires a remarkable degree of self-consciousness. The latter is a kind of bizarre experience consisting of the feeling of being aware that one is the centre of a representation, a necessary experience since without such feeling there would be no such thing as consciousness. Self-consciousness couldn't exist in its turn without consciousness, as it depends on representations. Kant stated this point quite clearly when asserting that the phrase "I think" is an element of synthesis not of analysis, in other words that it can be grasped as an isolated analytic datum just because it is the condition for representations. This might be true of all animals, human beings included, and, mainly of the latter, through language, since language represents – as stated by F.Ponge[16] – a kind of environment that surrounds the human being, an environment in which life begins, develops and eventually ends.

Self-consciousness isn't just essential as a system of representations, it is also, one could say, the area in which the representations take place. For this reason and in a different sense from Plato's, we all are undeniably bound, as if by chains, to being ourselves.

This is the notion of self-consciousness to which I refer in my research.

One might regard a system as endowed with symbolic capacities or levels, or, better, one might regard it as a system of representations, that is as an active system composed of differentiated structures that allow for permanent self-modification and for adaptation to the continuous external transformations. It then becomes possible to understand how intricate and self-involved any system might become when reacting, at different levels, both to external stimuli and to aspects of its own internal configuration. It is of course almost unthinkable to discriminate, in a system of this kind, reactions to the external world from self-involved responses, since any minimal external perturbation unclenches an enormous amount of interwoven events, the latter unclench another myriad of events, and so forth.

Nor can self-perception be differentiated from perception. In the case of the brain it is, for instance, impossible to trace any structures that might, at a high level, supply a description of the linguistic or aesthetic human beliefs actually contained in the brain. This model confirms an opinion that is by now widely spread. The mind is a configuration that is perceived by the mind. Hofstadter writes: "Perception resides at the level of the full system, not at the level of the self-symbol"[17]. Furthermore he states that the self-symbol shouldn't be characterised by its aspect but by its potential functions.

In this perspective the mind-body dualism could be considered a mere mystic residue. In this respect we might be reminded of the well known Cartesian substances and of the differentiation between the "res cogitans" and the "res extensa" that Descartes tried to overcome by inventing an almost ineffable point of conjunction, the pineal gland that might enable the contact between the two substances.

One could hypothesise that the magic of the human mind might be originated by the closure of a kind of symbolic link of causality in which the symbolic and neurophysiological levels are somehow bound together. The link being of the sort that enables the representational system to perceive its own state by means of a kind of directory of its own concepts. Not as connections between neurones and neuronal discharges but as a storehouse for beliefs, feelings, ideas.

In another of his essays Hofstadter writes: "Not only does our conscious mind activity create permanent side effects at the neural level; the inverse holds too: our conscious thoughts seem to come bubbling up from subterranean caverns of our mind, images flood into our mind's eye without our having any idea where they came from! Yet when we publish them we expect that *we* – not our unconscious structures – will get credit for our thoughts. This dichotomy of the creative self into a conscious part and an unconscious part is one of the most disturbing aspects of trying to understand the mind"[18].

It is extremely difficult to imagine what it is that anyone feels in particular states of the mind such as, for instance in total darkness when external stimuli are drastically reduced. It is of common knowledge that when the organ senses stop transmitting, the human brain progressively disintegrates. If the current of impulses from the external world is interrupted the psyche tends to deteriorate.

Consciousness is nevertheless the real insoluble problem of the mind-body relationship, in addition to our as yet complete ignorance about the physical basis of any mental phenomenon. There is enough there to make a complex pattern. Without consciousness, the mind-body relationship would therefore be of no interest, but this doesn't authorise us to deny reality or the logic of phenomena that we might never be able to describe or understand, for such a denial would convey the blindest refusal of any potential knowledge.

T. Nagel writes ". . . an organism has conscious mental states if, and only if, there is something that it is like to *be* that organism – something it is like *for* the organism"[19]. Whatever the experience of being a human being or of being a bat, the experience apparently expresses a specific viewpoint accessible just to one unique individual being.

All this relates directly to the mind-body issue since, if the events of subjective experience – events concerning the feelings felt by the organism that has the experience – are accessible from a unique viewpoint, it is then impossible to discern how the real nature of subjective experiences might be revealed in the physical functioning of that organism.

The problem stands as follows. If mental processes are physical processes, this means that something is experienced when such processes take place. The quality of this experience is, nevertheless, as yet unknown.

The mode in which a mental and a physical issue might relate to the same thing is as yet unknown, and the usual analogies with theoretical identifications from other areas of research don't really provide much help. Nagel asserts that if one considers the reference of mental terms to physical occurrences the result is:

a) a reappearance of subjective events

b) a false explication of how mental terms refer to physical objects, that is a kind of behaviourist causal explanation.

Nagel also writes "Donald Davidson has argued that if mental events have physical causes and effects, they must have physical descriptions. He holds that we have reason to believe this even though we do not – and in fact *could* not have a general psycho-physical theory[20]. His argument applies to intentional mental events, but I think we also have some reason to believe that sensations are physical processes, without being in a position to understand how. Davidson's position is that certain physical events have irreducibly mental properties, and perhaps some view describable in this way is correct. But nothing of which we can now form a conception corresponds to it. Nor have we any idea what a theory would be like that enabled us to conceive of it"[21].

Something similar is suggested by Nagel himself when he asserts that: ". . . whether or not this guess is correct, it seems unlikely that any physical theory of mind can be contemplated until more thought has been given to the general problems of subjective and objective. Otherwise we cannot even pose the mind-body problem without side-stepping it"[22].

Nagel does not define the word "physical" for it obviously doesn't just apply to phenomena that might be described by the concepts of contemporary physics but rather by the concepts that will be originated by future developments: ". . . some may think there is nothing to prevent mental phenomena from eventually being recognised as physical in their own right. But whatever else may be said of the physical, it has to be objective. So if our idea of the physical ever expands to include mental phenomena, it will have to assign them an objective character – whether or not this is done by analysing them in terms of other phenomena already regarded as physical. It seems to me more likely, however, that mental physical relations will eventually be expressed in a theory whose fundamental terms cannot be placed clearly in either category"[23].

I am extensively relying on these quotations to emphasize that the phenomena usually called physical belong to systems that, for their constitutional essence, do not allow for an explanation of mental phenomena. This might be due to the fact that the actual concept of mental functioning, although it might have been hinted for instance by the Italian philosopher Giambattista Vico as the reason that acknowledges itself in the activity of reasoning (something like the contemporary concept of self-consciousness), is only a quite recent discovery.

Up to this moment I have dealt with and discussed models referring to mere partial conceptions of the world. Models that are still representational and not yet self-representational. If we hypothesise a potentially unified theoretical formulation it might result in a completely different theory from the one we have dealt with up to now when relating to great physical phenomena and to the vastness of mental events.

I have earlier mentioned, nevertheless, that in my opinion the thought of an integrated theory is, at least for the moment, an arduous thought, as human beings seem to function actually just on the ground of this dissociation.

One should also keep in mind, when investigating the possibility of integrating theoretical models, that dissociation and conflict might well be structural and that it might not be by chance that psychology and physics both exist separately. Further developments of an integrated theoretical model are of course always possible (chemistry and physics have recently undergone essential transformations) but it seems hard to believe that, at least for the moment, a solid conjunction might come about. On the contrary, one might think that a unifying theoretical model isn't possible because it is the separation that actually grants our capacity to function as human beings.

My suggestion, therefore, is that the hypothesis of the Concrete Original Object (COO) might help us to investigate the nature, meaning, and functions of the object that is the central focus of our research and interest. One might wonder whether the COO should be regarded as a symbol or as a representation, I will endeavour, first of all, to answer such a question. In observing a child (using for instance the theoretical instruments provided by Melanie Klein) it is easy to think about the child's mental development as the development of representations. The position of psychoanalysis is nevertheless more complex than that as it attempts to describe the child's psychic functioning and also to follow the developmental process that enables the child to become capable of representations, that is of thought, in adult life. The word 'representation' isn't completely correct when a child's mental activity is concerned. It may be functional for anyone who investigates the child's psychic life but, in fact, the child doesn't have any representations of the functioning of his own body or mind. He just simply and directly experiences them. We, the adults, don't know how that can be done, because we aren't children anymore, but something of that condition remains and enables us to have a rough representation of our own corporeality.

We can indeed have representations that are separate from our functions and that we try to correlate, in order to reach a whole complex representation of our body but, before that, we have a kind of global enigmatic representation of our physical essence that we can't really or adequately think about or delineate. It is a kind of "something" that tends towards representation. It is our "feeling of ourselves now" probably similar to what children feel about themselves. One might call it a symbol, not in the psychoanalytic meaning of a substitutive formation, because one is experiencing the symbol of one's body or, in other words globally "feeling that one is a body". So this isn't a datum and it isn't as yet a precise representation. It is something that tends to emerge as a representation.

The meaning of the word symbol corresponds therefore, in this context, to the capacity to create a kind of distance from the pure physical essence of the objects.

In turning one's attention from the body to the mind, one might question the attitude of the mind towards the body. The truth is that the mind can't ever get rid of this symbolic root. Bodily perceptions will never be completely transformed into absolute representations. Before anything else there is a perception that isn't a simple vision but on the contrary is a kind of being inside, of living. The *symbolicalness* is, in other words, the *corporeality*.

Corporeality might remind one of what scientists of the past used to call raw material. Such material exists but it is a kind of abstraction that isn't part of any human deep experience. "Symbol" is also a dangerous word, since, if otherwise understood, it might dissolve the body inside its own symbol.

My hypothesis is that *the body is the main object of the mind and its primary reality*.

When the body loses its symbolical value, the corporeality, then the global feeling that one is that one body, that specific, constant and concretely defining emotional tone, isn't any longer present. The body in many disharmonious conditions[24] is just a body and nothing else, an object, a physical thing, other than oneself. There is no corporeality left unless one understands this concept as a universal concept or as an *ideal* of some unreachable perfection. The body in these cases is just a mere object with exclusively physical qualities, it can't be represented, it can't feel or express itself. On the contrary, it becomes a kind of battlefield upon which the mind performs, exercising the power of its strength and deriving an exalted feeling of triumph. As the mind refuses to acknowledge reality it doesn't enable the body to acquire its own symbolical value, the lack of symbolical value hinders furthermore the establishment of a functional relationship between body and mind, between Onefold and Twofold, and what is left is just a body FOR the mind.

The question could be whether the mind deals with an object that can be, and actually is, represented in many ways or with the several forms of the object's symbolicalness. It is my belief that the mind establishes a relationship both with the object and with the object's symbolicalness.

Representations always presuppose a more global vision to make them possible. The symbol, on the contrary, is the body that becomes significant, revealing its direct physical essence, communicating something. This is why I believe the body should be considered more of a symbol than of a representation and suggest that the word symbol should be used for the representations that are susceptible of being eventually defined, clarified and delimited.

In M. Klein's theoretical model there are two objects, one is the child, the other is the mother. Klein describes the interaction between these two objects and delineates how the latter, the mother, becomes an internal object causing the child to acknowledge that there is also an object that is external to him. This is a satisfactory description at an operative level but it is insufficient when it ends up expressing a spatial division.

I think it is necessary to think of a different theoretical model, first of all an entity that perceives itself as corporeality (Onefold) and as symbolicalness (Twofold). It isn't just a breast that offers itself to the mouth of the child, it is a completely different condition. The child offers himself, through corporeality, to himself.

We all are, paradoxically, all things considered, living symbols. Symbols because the symbol is concrete, it lives and, somehow, can be felt living.

If one were to ask, once more – what is the *object*? – the answer would certainly include the corporeality but also the mind's representations, as the objects are both material and immaterial and any object is always correlated to a representation or to something that is communicated through representation.

I believe it is appropriate to name the object *concrete* to emphasize that this isn't one of the many possible objects, in other words, the object that anyone might observe at any specific moment. Concrete *object* signifies that it is an object inside which one stays and is. It isn't a proper object but it will become an object for anyone who represents it to himself, first of all, for the mind. It can therefore be named object from a theoretical point of view so that then there will be a description of a something that would otherwise inexorably escape. Finally I have named it object and concrete because it is the only concrete object that seemingly belongs to a global perception of oneself in the world. Proper objects are actually interactions that we build up, as we live in the world and we tend to determine the objects that surround us.

Certainly the mind can represent the body as a kind of masterpiece since this would be a representation and the body would also, in this case, become a representation. On the contrary this isn't possible in the meaning conveyed by the definition of *Concrete Original Object*, which I have described as a global feeling of *existing* in an environment.

Finally, the word "object" may be used, but always keeping in mind that the term is employed to represent something that wouldn't otherwise be representable. It is possible to use "concrete" because it isn't a real object but rather the origin of all possible objects and because from this object all representations are originated along with the possibility of determining physical and non physical objects.

All objects are potentially abstract but the one thing that one can't ever exhaustively comprehend is oneself, one's corporeality. There is such a global quality in the perception of one's body that it can't ever be extinguished, not even by actual self-observation.

NOTES

1 Ferrari A. B., Garroni E. (1979), "Schema di Progetto per uno Studio della Relazione Analitica" in *Rivista di Psicoanalisi*, 25, 2, 282–322.
2 "O eclipse do objeto originario concreto: O.O.C." *Rev Brasil. Psicánal.* 19, 2:281–290.
3 Plato(1998), *Cratilus* translated and edited by C.D.C. Reeves, Hackett Publishing Company, Indianapolis,p. 30.
4 Plato (1993), *Phaedo* translated and edited by D. Gallop, Oxford University Press p. 35.
5 Popper K., Eccles J. (1977), *The Self and its Brain*, New York: Springer-Verlag.
6 Hebb D.O. (1980), *Essay on Mind*, Hillsdale N.J: Lawrence Erlbaum Associates.
7 von Neumann J., Burks A.W. (1966), *Theory of Self-Reproducing Automata*, University of Illinois Press, Urbana Il.
8 Neisser U. (1967), *Cognitive Psychology*, New York: Appleton-Century-Crofts. Neisser U. (1976), *Cognition and Reality. Principles and Implications of Cognitive Psychology*, San Francisco: W.H. Freeman and Company. Gibson J.J. (1979), *The Ecological Approach to Visual Perception*, Boston: Hoghton Mifflin.
9 Bion W .R. (1962), *Learning from Experience*, London: Heinemann. Bion W.R. (1965) *Transformations*, London: Heinemann . Bion W.R. (1970) *Attention & Interpretation*, London: Tavistock Publications.
10 The Italian terms "marasma" and "marasmatico" are translated as "turmoil" and "turmoiling" to convey the meaning of a state of undifferentiated confusion and turbulence.
11 Hofstadter D. R., Dennett D. C. Eds. (1981) *The mind's I*, London: Penguin Books, 1982.

12 Ibid. p. 33.
13 Ibid. p. 38.
14 Ibid. p. 38.
15 Ibid. p. 39.
16 F. Ponge, *Entretiens*, Paris: Le Seuil 1970.
17 Hofstadter D. R., D. C. Dennett Eds. (1981) *The mind's I*, London: Penguin Books, 1982 p. 200.
18 Ibid. p. 283.
19 T. Nagel, (1974) "What Is It Like to Be a Bat?" in D.R. Hofstadter, D.C. Dennet Eds. (1981) *The mind's I*, London: Penguin Books, 1982, p. 392.
20 "See Davidson (1970) though I do not understand the argument against psychophysical laws" (D. Davidson, (1970) "Mental Events" in L. Foster and J.W. Swanson Eds. *Experience and Theory*, Amherst, Univ. of Massachusetts Press).
21 T. Nagel, (1974) "What Is It Like to Be a Bat?" in D. R. Hofstadter, D. C. Dennett Eds. (1981) *The mind's I*, London: Penguin Books, 1982 pp. 401–402.
22 Ibid. p. 403.
23 Ibid. p. 403 (footnote).
24 One might think of anorexic patients, of drug addicts etc.

2

THE HYPOTHESIS

1.1 A DEFINITION

By selecting the denomination Concrete Original Object I aim at focusing on and emphasizing the existence of a unity composed of a mental apparatus that has a capacity for perception and notation, and a physical body, and the sparse sensations that come from it.

Although it is nowadays assumed by almost all scientific communities that these three components, the mind, the sensory apparatus and the body in its physicality (the physicality that makes the body an object of the mind-subject), constitute a unity and are the elements of a whole, nevertheless the three components are still thought of as totally divided and separate on a cognitive and clinical level. This separation is in fact a necessity unless one conceives the grandiose project of founding a new theoretical model (or paradigm in Kuhn's terms) capable of hosting and integrating the several different sciences concerning the human being. I think however that it might be useful to emphasize anew the existence of the above mentioned unity and to regard it as a concept of constant importance in psychoanalytic practice, a necessary model for the analyst's internal endowment when observing psychic phenomena.

1.2 THE COO AS AN ANALYTIC INSTRUMENT

The hypothesis of the Eclipse of the Concrete Original Object is meant to enlarge this internal endowment of the analyst and may contribute to throwing a new light upon some well known psychic states that are usually interpreted according to other different psychoanalytic categories.

The Eclipse of the Concrete Original Object (COO) isn't a new principle or theory but it rather belongs to the area of psychoanalytic instruments and is offered as a model for the acquisition of knowledge and for clinical work.

1.3 POINTS OF REFERENCE FOR THE COO:
FREUD, KLEIN, BION

In the progress of psychoanalytic thought I believe it is possible to trace two main theoretical positions, related to two of Freud's most relevant papers, considered with good reason to be the milestones of the development of psychoanalysis. The papers are: *Three Essays on the Theory of Sexuality* [25] and *Formulations on the Two Principles of Mental Functioning*[26].

The central core of the *Three Essays* is the concept of instinct, a concept that is half way between the physical and the mental areas[27] and that provides the evidence of Freud's purpose and effort towards keeping physical and mental aspects closely related to each other: instinct, affects, character formation and symptoms.

In his 1911 paper, Freud is only concerned with the mental functioning so that the primary and secondary systems are discussed and developed. He is exclusively investigating the psychic world and is obviously fascinated by it, the physical area and the related physical sensations are seldom and only indirectly referred to.

These two essential conceptual aspects are henceforth both present in the development of psychoanalytic theory and they alternate in either coming close to each other or in gaining reciprocal distance.

There is a substantially important moment in which they come close and that is when Melanie Klein[28] outlines the concept of epistemophilic instinct. According to Melanie Klein the sensations that are provoked in the child by the contact with the maternal body, continuously strengthened by internal instinctual drives and combined with the activity of phantasy life, constitute the raw material through which, by progressive elaboration, the desire and capacity for knowledge are acquired. A consistent line unites therefore the sensory perceptions to the most sophisticated procedures of thought.

Bion's grid follows, one could say, this developmental trend, beginning with a primary confused sensory experience and reaching the sophisticated essence of the utmost abstraction. Nevertheless in creating the grid, although he indicates a broad developmental span, Bion does not situate the different levels of mental elaboration in a fixed progression from the beta elements to the algebraic calculus but rather seems to imply the existence of a transformational motion going both ways. This is actually what we encounter also in clinical work.

1.4 THE COO AS A CONSEQUENTIAL CONSTRUCTION

This transformational motion, facing two directions, is one of the essential features of the model of the Eclipse of the COO. The sequence that goes from sensory perception to emotion and to thought, regarded as a continuous line that can be followed in the two directions, enables a large quantity of possible combinations. Furthermore it facilitates the observation of the specific route chosen by any single analysand allowing for the necessary outlining of these unique modes of progression and of the corresponding specific symptoms, object relations, thought formation.

It has been possible, thanks to this model, to trace some very distinctive links, relating phenomena that are apparently very distant from each other such as physical symptoms, emotional inclinations, manners of feeling and treating one's own body, modes of thought.

1.5 THE COO AND ANALYTIC "REVERIE"

In clinical work the model of the Eclipse of the COO, besides adding coherence and organisation to phenomenological data – as any model should do – might facilitate the development of a capacity for analytical "reverie". It is an instrument for the exploration of new vertices, for observation, and aims at opening new perspectives rather than setting forth at all costs a new systematization.

1.6 THE ECLIPSE OF THE COO AND THE ORIGIN OF MENTAL FUNCTIONS

I have already mentioned the unity of body, emotions and mind that I named COO but I would now like to describe the events that cause the occurrence I have called the Eclipse. To do so, presuming that the activity of perceiving sensations is different from the activity of recording them (which is related to the *system of notation* described by Freud in "The two principles of mental functioning") I will assume that the mind begins to function with its first recording of a sensory perception.

There is a subject, the apparatus that registers, and an object that is registered. I name the latter "Concrete Original Object" and maintain that it is formed both of the physical body and of the sparse sensations originating from it (corporeality).

Close to the COO is the mother, that is an ethologically anticipated presence.

Under the pressure of violent and turmoiling sensory perceptions, endangering the harmonious physical functioning (i.e. the co-ordination of the nervous, endocrine and vascular systems), in the presence of the mother, of her mind and of the essential function of 'reverie', the child's mental apparatus begins to fulfil its own functions, that is recording and containment. The recording takes place, presumably, because it is necessary to create a distance from the sensory perceptions that would otherwise be completely invasive and also because it is necessary to provide them with meaning. In this process the Eclipse of the COO begins to take place and, at the same time, the mental area is established. In terms of the model one could say that the shadow of the mental activity projects itself upon the COO. I name it a shadow because it causes the light to diminish and a beneficial cooling to take place. When the light becomes less dazzling and the whole situation less intense it is possible to discern the more delicate and complex profiles, the lights and the shades, the thinner and more articulate sensations.

The whole mental activity is therefore regarded as the answer of a containing function of sensations and emotions that, for their nature, can only be experienced.

1.7 THE TWOFOLD RELATIONSHIP

The violence of the sensory perceptions that need containment, and the presence of maternal reverie immediately reveal that the eclipse of the COO takes place in a double and dual relationship. The first external, including mother and child and the second internal, intrapsychic, including the mind and the COO.

Since the beginning of extra-uterine life each individual person establishes a Twofold relationship, that is the relationship between his physical and psychic internal areas and an external relationship with the ethologically anticipated object, the mother.

In clinical practice one can find that the two relationships are often phenomenologically connected with each other when mother's phantasies correspond to the child's own representations of his physical and psychic selves.

1.8 THE CHILD AND THE ENVIRONMENT

I am, indeed, considering the psychic presence of the child not as a separate entity but as related to another physical presence, the mother.

As I have said before, I am hypothesizing that psychic activity initiates during the passage from uterine to extra-uterine life. I have assumed this hypothesis because it functionally helps our model although I know that opinions of a different nature have been developing on the subject in recent years. For the moment, I will therefore assume that the cutting of the umbilical cord, the experience of caesura, is the first encounter with loss, and that it cannot be compared with anything that happened before.

Onefold and Twofold contain both the physicality and the psychic essence. In an extended way they also contain body and mind. The physical wholeness or system may (and should!) transform itself and become corporeality, so that it can become a symbol, join the Twofold and establish, as far as possible, a harmonious relationship. This corporeality is sensitive to any eventual vicissitudes or dearths of the mother-foetus couple since intra-uterine life. The corporeality continues to have this function (Onefold) in postnatal life until the Twofold function is established. When the Twofold is unable to accomplish its functions of perceiving and registering, the corporeality (mind of the body) then acts as a substitute of the missing function. I do realise that, in this context, the use of the word "mind" might create some confusion, as it immediately evokes the notion of awareness and of self-awareness, implying a kind of strong hypothesis that isn't really justified at the present state of my research. I am therefore using the word as a mere indication. By *mind of the body* I wish to indicate a fundamental aspect of the complex organisation of the body (= corporeality) that has the aim of establishing a relation with the mind, focusing also upon the thick pattern of operative events (well beyond molecular exchanges and endorphin production) and creating a transformative movement, leading either towards life or towards death.

The aim of such events is either of saving the person's life or of giving it up. The psychic system is of course also involved. Corporeality has its own "vocabulary" which may offer, both in harmonious and in disharmonious situations, something more than just mere informations for the psychic apparatus. I am gathering all such functions under the name of Onefold system. The nucleus of its functioning is the relationship with the Twofold system, to which the Onefold turns and from which it takes, making all limits and needs quite evident. Furthermore the specific essence of the contributions of the Onefold to the Twofold is the dynamic construction of a *unity in the identity*. This is only possible if the two systems neither oppose each other nor become fused or prevail one upon the other but if they manage to generate functional antitheses, according to different necessities and different contexts. This implies that Onefold and Twofold enjoy great autonomy, an autonomy that isn't unfortunately limited by the laws of survival. Both areas are constantly threatened by the menace of being overwhelmed by states of turmoil.

Inside the uterus, in fact, any foetal modification or suffering could be considered as dearth rather than as actual loss. Birth, with its sharp separation and consequent turmoil, seems to have the power to put in motion the slow construction of a dam, a kind of vital container capable of giving "shape to the turmoil". This great enterprise can, nevertheless, only take place in the presence of a functioning maternal reverie, an already established capacity for thought, orientated towards the turmoil experienced by the child.

1.9 COMMUNICATION

This initial clutter is translated by the child into signs, like crying, and into other modes of communication, weak, obscure, different kinds of communications only understood by mindful reverie.

This introduces another question in a wider and more complex perspective. What kind of an influence does the child have as a Concrete Original Object upon the mother's capacity for reverie? Is maternal reverie to be considered as the varying capacity to understand the child's signals or should it be considered a mental presence endowed with other specific features? One might think of the different modes in which a mother may gain perception of her child. Either by focusing upon his physical existence or upon his mental functioning.

Finally, one last question: is maternal reverie fostered mainly by the mother's processes of thought or is it rather sustained by her sensory perceptions?

2.1 APPEARANCE AND FUNCTION OF EMOTIONS

In my hypothesis I shall consider, at first, the emergence of emotions as the appearance of an intermediate domain between the field of bare sensations and the area of initial thought, composed of physical qualities and of psychic potential qualities. The process of modification seems to be caused by a biological necessity: the perception that something is missing, or lacking. The gap between the child's perception of something insufficient or missing and of mother's catalysing presence is what enables the survival and establishment of the internal composite relationship between the physical and psychic domains.

I believe that the moments in which the child perceives that there is something that is not there or that is insufficient, are the forming elements out of which the rudimentary pattern of an emotion springs. One can see them archaically expressed by the newly born baby in frantic movements, losses of breath and cyanosis, crying, vomiting, discharging of faeces or urine. This primitive emotional quality is, possibly, also an essential component of ethological drives and therefore may well allow for the functional specificity of instinctual responses.

2.2 SENSORY ORGAN AND PSYCHIC CO-ORDINATOR

By observing babies attentively one can see that most babies seem to privilege one of their senses in some peculiar way. This choice of one sense might become an indication of the specific mode of development of each person. It is well known that, since birth, the baby has an autonomous capacity for some kind of mental activity. It should furthermore be considered that it has an incipient capacity to evaluate its sensations. The baby has, in other words, a discriminating mental function, aiming at preserving life and originating the mature mental activity. A mental function that tends to establish a first correlation between different and sparse physical sensations (corporeality). Often, when this happens, one of the senses prevails, co-ordinating different sensations as well as the other senses, and supplying a point of reference in the initial turmoil. I will name the organ of sense that is *selected* by the baby for this function the *"psychic co-ordinator"*. In some cases it can preserve its primary importance during further development, in other cases it loses its pre-eminence as well as its archaic properties.

From the original unique physical nucleus each child develops his own personal sensations and emotions. The emotional phenomena appear and are expressed, as I have mentioned, when there is a conflict between the child and the world.

2.3 MODES AND FORMS OF MENTAL BEHAVIOUR

When a baby is born and confronts the world he needs to face a trauma, that is the revolutionary experience of entering a state in which one is at the same time 'biologically' independent and physically dependent.

I have hypothesized the existence of an internal twofold relationship between the mind and the body. This assumption enables the observation in clinical practice of many different and organised connections of this same internal relationship, above all the mode in which the mind behaves, lives and elaborates the relationship with its sensations and its emotions. One could say that the internal duality seems to be just as insurmountable as the external duality (the relationship between mother and child), since birth it characterizes intrinsically the functioning of the mind as the mind exists to contain the turmoiling sensations emanating from the perceptive-sensory apparatus. I believe, for this reason, that the experience that each individual person has of him/ herself is only and always in terms of a relationship. A relationship that can be characterized by a dialogue, a conflict, a confrontation, an overpowering by feelings of hatred or love and so forth.

2.4 INITIAL INTERNAL RELATIONSHIP

At the beginning of life the relationship is established between the initial functioning of the mind and the physical essence of each person. During growth, as the data of experience progressively increase, the problems which the mind has to solve become more and more complicated.

The internal aspects with which the mind entertains a relationship are therefore manifold. The initial internal relationship keeps being a basic reality or even a sort of model. An original model with unique characteristics that reflect upon the relations which the mind subsequently establishes with its different aspects, the outcome of a specific internal experience.

The initial internal relationship doesn't just reflect upon the following relationships by analogy. A mind, for instance, that fears the physical sensations coming from its own body doesn't necessarily fear its own thoughts. There might nevertheless be a connection between the mode in which different internal aspects relate to each other.

The COO represents each individual person in its original aspects and not in its relation to the world. I feel I can therefore assert that it is not related to the process of introjection and that it is not formed from external contributions that give the psyche its shape while they occupy it. It can rather be described as the original specific nucleus, differentiating since birth each individual person from all other human beings.

It is an *Object* because it *is there*, it isn't made, it isn't the result of a development (of a process, for instance, of introjection-projection) but it is the child himself, and is bound to last, since the original nucleus will survive all subsequent mental operations.

The object is *concrete* because its primary quality is physicality. Physicality consists of being a man or a woman, and ever more, of being that man or that woman with that specific instinctual cathexis and endowment of a bodily apparatus.

2.5 THE COO AND THE MENTAL AREA

The developmental trend that goes from physicality to the progressive establishment of mental activity is a kind of line joining Onefold and Twofold. In going from Onefold to Twofold the COO begins its Eclipse. It is an Eclipse, rather than a disappearance or a transformation – just a kind of shading, or in other words a progressive reduction of the place that was occupied by the COO.

2.6 SENSORY PERCEPTION, FEELING OF ONESELF, EMOTIONS AND OTHERNESS

The first sensory perceptions may provide the child with a feeling that he is himself, while the first emotions may well be related to a perception, although rudimentary, of another entity external to himself.

The COO is the datum. The mind begins to function on this datum-presence. A relationship is established, characterised by a never appeased tension. The datum-presence remains, day after day, as a permanent unsolved problem for the mind inasmuch as the core of physicality can't be reached by perception since it is contemporaneous to it.

The history of the development of any psyche – its functioning and its eventual involutional aspects – may be seen as the vicissitude of a mind that permanently endeavours to comprehend its own physical essence. The parable of the Eclipse has to do with this essential unattainability.

The mind can't contain a concrete object without transforming it into a symbol. The symbol requires some abstraction and some degree of permanence. Furthermore it needs to gain and establish some distance from the thing it represents. How can this happen with this datum-presence? The body, with its continuous stimuli, interferes with, contrasts and disturbs its own process of symbolization.

The human mind permanently faces this problem, a problem but not necessarily a conflict, as there might well be a dialectic relationship between a mind that tries to project a shadow upon the COO to "cool it down" enough so that it is then able to think it and a COO that is constantly present with its luminousness and warmth.

These aspects don't necessarily contrast each other. They sometimes even mutually potentiate each other, for instance when the sensations feed the emotions and the latter support thoughts. In other cases the two aspects ally. This happens when the sensations supplant emotional feelings and concrete actions consequently supplant symbolic operations.

For example one can see occasionally that when the capacity for thought is overwhelmed an individual might use representation in the attempt of avoiding passage to action. The representation is, nevertheless, so saturated with physicality or emotion that it doesn't allow the mind to proceed to any further levels of elaboration. In such cases the only way-out is the development of some phantasy-expedients, that are, however, still closely linked to an impelling need for psychic containment. Clinically we might distinguish two kinds of such phantasies:

1) Very elaborated mainly abstract phantasies;

2) Mainly bodily phantasies with a relevant amount of crammed physical sensations and a narrow space for symbolic play.

From this perspective one might disagree with the idea that people suffering from severe mental disturbances act instead of thinking. Actually thought processes are, in such cases, strongly hindered by the concreteness of the representations and can't be employed to accomplish mental consequential operations. Repetitive stereotypes are therefore necessarily introduced as rigid pre-formed containers, only apparently similar to logical mental operations. This procedure corresponds to the phantasies of the first kind, the second kind of phantasies relates to states in which sensations and emotions both spatially and temporally saturate any capacity of the mind.

In spite of what has been said usually there is an area, except in extremely severe cases, to which the individual may refer, although minimal, an area potentially capable of thought. Analysts encounter difficulties in these cases, either because analytic propositions are used pre-eminently to establish a kind of pseudo-thinking, exclusively oriented towards the external world and devoid of any relation with the internal needs, or because analysis itself is transformed into an instrument that is alien to any personal necessities.

The cases I have outlined are just some of the innumerable "casualties" that may occur along the announced route developing from sensations to emotions and to thoughts. I will discuss some of such casualties later.

2.7 CORRELATION BETWEEN INTERNAL RELATIONSHIP, EXTERNAL RELATIONSHIP, CLINICAL WORK

All these difficulties, impediments, deviations, parallel and substitutive formations are related to both lines of development of individual human beings, the line of the intrapsychic relationship that the mind entertains with its own physicality and the line of the interpersonal relationship that the child establishes with the ethologically anticipated object, the mother. It is therefore obvious that the two lines are in strong mutual correlation.

The correlations are useful in clinical work since the relationship that the analysand has with the analyst supplies information about the primary relationship with the mother (it supplies the data but doesn't identify with it) and this links with the internal line of development, that is with the relation that the analysand entertains with his sensations, emotions and thoughts, the relation between Onefold and Twofold.

One can easily observe that people entertain complex and differentiated relations with the area that I have defined as the sequence sensations-emotions-thoughts, and that, indisputably, such intrapsychic relationships aren't limited to the mind-body relation.

This is just one part, or maybe an excessively simplified version, of the rich complex internal dynamics that may cause, for instance, a mind to take notice of its sensory perceptions but be unable to place them, by giving them a meaning and a function, or it may cause a mind to idealize its emotions therefore disdaining its thoughts, or vice-versa.

2.8 A HYPOTHESIS ABOUT THE ORIGIN OF MENTAL FUNCTIONING

In short, although it is hardly possible, especially in psychological sciences, to ascertain for sure any definite beginnings, I am suggesting a hypothesis which might explain the origin of mental functions.

I am using the word Concrete because the Object is solid and real. It has the physical qualities from which the child may develop its mind.

I say it is Original because it is unique since the beginning. Every individual person has, from birth onwards, a specificness that is retained throughout life.

I use the word Object because I refer to the child's body which eventually becomes an object and later object and/or subject in relation to the child's mind.

Finally, I call Eclipse the phenomenon which I think is important to emphasize at this point, the progressive decrease of the place initially occupied by the turmoil of sensations, the area that can always be invaded anew, all throughout life, by sensations and emotions. The Eclipse consists therefore of this progressive reduction and containment, aiming at facilitating the development of more functional forms of adaptation of the individual person to its environment.

2.9 THE NATURE OF THE COO

It is necessary to clarify that the COO is originated by a relationship and that it isn't just a datum. This assertion has significant consequences in clinical work as it implies that not all internal relationships are derived from sedimentations of relationships with the external world.

Things aren't, of course, as sketchy as this. No analyst would expect to discern the analysand's introjected relationship and to be able to differentiate it from the relationship that is originated by the COO. This conceptualisation offers, nevertheless, ample clinical possibilities as it enables the analysts to organise further their observations and interpretative hypotheses.

The function of the Eclipse of the COO is easily forgotten. It is a model and when the capacity for symbolization is achieved the physical datum seems to fade away, almost as if concealed. Yet when a situation that alters the equilibrium between the physical and psychic systems arises, there is a sudden invasion of sensations and emotions (the COO emerging from its Eclipse). The invasion may be caused both by an excess or a lack of tension, or by frustrations, fears, desires etc. Furthermore, the Eclipse shouldn't be considered as an exclusively developmental straight-forward evolution. It is a continuous process and may therefore occur an innumerable amount of times in any individual life.

3.1 ENTROPIC AND NEGENTROPIC AREAS

The hypothesis of the Eclipse of the COO is clinically significant. If Onefold and Twofold are simultaneously present, two areas co-exist, an entropic[29] area, mainly related to the Onefold and a negentropic area (as defined by W.R. Beavers[30]) mainly related to the Twofold. The two areas are somehow complementary but dynamically related so that, if one or the other prevails, there can be either evidence in mental production of a capacity for containment and therefore for thought or, on the opposite, of an incapacity for both. In my hypothesis, the dynamic relationship between the two areas seems to imply that the unconscious is configured as the moment in which things are distanced from perception or can't find their way towards it.

When the two systems succeed in operating harmoniously, the physical system can then be contained by the psychic system and therefore slowly initiate its Eclipse.

3.2 MATERNAL REVERIE AND THE DYNAMIC RELATIONSHIP BETWEEN THE TWO AREAS

For the establishment of this harmonious state, maternal reverie – hypothesised in its ideal state, i.e. positive, nourishing, capable of metabolizing the child's experiences including the painful ones – should anyhow be considered fundamental. Yet one could imagine the child trying to elaborate frustrations on his own, using his own resources. That he might try to control the frustrations and contain the pain they are provoking, or on the contrary that he might endeavour to cope resorting to an attitude in which impotence and omnipotence prevail.

In the first case the child succeeds in establishing for a moment a *kind of unity* of Onefold and Twofold, an experience that is functional for growth. This process is usually protected and facilitated by the mother but when the mother is unable to achieve this purpose (maternal reverie can't transmit what it doesn't have) then the child needs to function by himself, in order to survive.

When the child's functioning and elaboration fail, which is highly possible since his means are scarce, the result is a kind of one-way procedure. Either through the body, by mainly privileging the physical experience, or through an eminently psychic elaboration. In both cases, as there is no unifying experience, a conflict may arise, heavily influencing either the physicality or the psychic area.

One can find an example of this process in very severe cases, when the eclipsing is interrupted and muscular activity becomes very evident, while thought isn't but is a reminder of action.

In order to deal with the problems of life the activity of thinking needs to establish some stable though not static points of reference. The mind has to construct anew its thinking instruments each time. One can only hope that it will be able to do so, since the process is felt to be risky and often requires painful efforts that therefore make thinking difficult.

3.3 HORIZONTAL AND VERTICAL RELATIONS

The hypothesis of the COO therefore implies two kinds of primary relations. *Primary horizontal relation:* child – external world / mother. *Vertical relation* (the other primary relation): mind – COO.

In the vertical relation the COO shouldn't be identified with the body as an objective datum but with the body emanating sensations, a living body, or corporeality, continuously and actively present, an object for the mind that registers it but a subject in relation to the external world.

The COO has both objective and subjective qualities. The mind has to deal with something that belongs to it and is an integral part of its individual entity but also with a contrasting, almost foreign presence. The otherness is sometimes dramatically experienced, when severe illness or a death threat originate from the COO.

The two primary relations initiate simultaneously at birth and continue throughout life. Their development, far from being straightforward, permanently oscillates with continuous connections and correlations.

It is therefore possible to isolate and distinguish, among different personality aspects, symptoms, attitudes and actions, the issues that relate to the primary vertical relation and the ones that have to do with the horizontal relation not for their origin but rather – and more usefully – for their actual specific dynamic vicissitudes.

The distinction is sometimes rather hazardous, a fact that is well known to anyone operating in the clinical field. It is possible to represent the two relations as co-ordinates, an abscissa and an ordinate, so that the different moments of any individual life and the different aspects of personality can be then regarded as the points of encounter of the segments coming from the two co-ordinates.

3.4 OBJECT, INTERNAL OBJECT, INTROJECTION

The clinical relevance of an approach that doesn't just regard the analysand's mental phenomena and actions as manifestations of the relationships between internal objects is quite evident by itself. This perspective implies, in fact, that one is regarding the internal world as a unique precipitate of external relationships although heavily influenced by the projections emanating from the subject. Furthermore, while Klein interprets the internal object as the result of introjection of the maternal object, my hypothesis implies the existence of an internal object that pertains both to the Onefold and to the Twofold systems of the infant.

Furthermore, in the Kleinian notion of introjection, the maternal object retains the characteristics of a separate object although it is introjected. In the hypothesis of the COO, Onefold and Twofold have a common matrix relating to both, while the mother, rather than being the introjected object, is regarded as the catalysing element. The object is therefore present since the beginning and its presence enables the world of internal object relations, facilitated by mother's catalysing presence.

I don't mean to say that physicality should be regarded as an internal object (physicality just exists) but I do believe that it has the characteristics of an object and that it becomes all the more an object when the mind progressively operates the functions that are necessary for survival.

The mind gradually drives the physicality into the shade (Eclipse of COO) and so configures its mental quality and becomes a subject. *Physicality therefore becomes the phenomenological reality of the mind.*

Clinically as well as theoretically, Klein's hypothesis suggests a system in which there is one object confronting the other party "devoid" of an object and should therefore introject it. My hypothesis, on the contrary, suggests confrontation with another that is also subject-object and with whom one may establish a relationship, seen as a process in which both parties have a chance of illuminating the object that is internal to each of the two.

The mother-child model implies a dual relationship while the Onefold-Twofold-Mother model suggests a triadic relationship. As a consequence of this and besides the area of internal objects and of acquisition by introjection there is an area, just as relevant, connected with *the relation between that specific mind and that specific COO*. It is doubtless that any specific mind has to form a specific mode of containing and dealing with the sensations that come from that specific body. It has to find daily appropriate answers to the needs of that unique body.

This area concurs greatly, although maybe not exclusively, in determining a strong perception of identity, of a unique, personal, indestructible, inaccessible nucleus that characterises human beings and that is more significant than the area of internal objects, also belonging to subjectivity, but perceived as less central, almost fluid, mobile, in contact with the external world.

I believe that I can now go back to the notions of entropy and negentropy which I have, up to now, kept separate but only with the aim of clarifying my hypothesis.

Entropy and negentropy describe specific functional moments or equilibriums of the entropic and negentropic potentialities. When one or the other prevails it is a sign of the individual's capacities to supply more or less adequate answers to his own psychic and physical necessities. The negentropic area extends to occupy the sector of the exchanges with the external world, including the osmotic section of introjections and projections.

3.5 PERCEPTION OF THE INTERNAL NUCLEUS AND IDENTITY

The central area, that one could describe as the high-density area – somehow comparable to the nucleus in the molecular structure – and that is mainly related to the vertical relation, is sometimes perceived by the subject as dramatically unattainable and unmodifiable. In fact, clinical experience has many times shown that the absence of subjective perception of this central core or solid nucleus, endangers the construction of the sense of identity.

Some authors describe autistic nuclei that may continue being encysted and are therefore somehow contained in the personality. These nuclei are hardly reached by the analytic process. Still I don't think these nuclei might be identified with the internal nucleus of the vertical relation, though they certainly are closely related to it and, maybe, have their roots in the area of personality that unfolds around the COO.

In describing autistic nuclei F. Tustin ("black holes")[31] and D.W. Winnicott ("fear of breakdown")[32] mention the powerful defensive barriers that have the task of circumscribing and restraining strong self-destructive impulses, because the area that is encircled and excluded from the circuit is supposed to contain death. Winnicott writes for instance that some analysands seem only to bother with: ". . . sending the body to death which has already happened to the psyche"[33]. For them suicide isn't an answer, it is just a desperate act.

Autistic nuclei are described, in this perspective, as containers of a high potential of destructiveness, that is extremely dangerous areas, therefore not only kept separate from the rest of the personality but hard to grasp since they seem to elude both the relationship with the other and the possibility of thought and understanding by the individual subject.

In the vertical relation the sense of unattainableness is intrinsic to the nature of the COO, and it is not originated by the defences. The COO may be shaded when the Eclipse takes place but it can't ever be completely understood or reached and can't furthermore be ignored.

The essential point is that in the relationship between the mind and the COO the latter can't be driven out of the psychic or confront the mind-subject as if it were an external "other". The duality is never completely attained or established and there is therefore the perception of a "something" which belongs so originally that it feels both indestructible and abysmal, an abysmal hole that it will never be possible to really explore or become familiar with.

3.6 THE COO AS SOURCE OF LIFE AND DEATH

In the relation with the COO one approaches, in my opinion, one's personal source of life as well as one's personal source of death. It is therefore highly probable that, whenever one of these two aspects of the COO prevails upon the other, it may originate the basic characteristics, and maybe personal history and destiny of illness or good health, both physical and mental.

I therefore believe that there is a precise and remarkable difference between the unattainableness that is the result of the defences from self-destructive impulses, and the difficulties in reaching the sector that I have been discussing, a sector which I don't regard as belonging to highly disturbed areas. The definition of this difference opens the field for further clinical thoughts.

3.7 ADOLESCENCE: A NEW MANIFESTATION OF THE COO

I wish to emphasize the importance of a phase of life, Adolescence, that has been undervalued for a long time by psychoanalysis albeit I will not discuss it in detail for the moment. Adolescence is a time of life in which one can see a new and different manifestation of the Eclipse of the COO. The process is the inverse of the one I have delineated for the beginning of life. Then, it was the mind which presented itself to the body, now, in adolescence it is the body that violently presents itself to the attention of the mind. One could say that, while the child ignores his body, except when it suffers a handicap or severe malformation, the adolescent has to deal with a body that has ceased to belong to him. Therefore he reacts by developing a state of panic, caused by ignorance. This happens because the body of the adolescent changes and while it changes it becomes the object of knowledge, and immediately it changes again and again it becomes unknown and embarrassing.

The daily physiological and aesthetic changes of adolescence belong to reality and not to phantasy any more as in childhood. While the child has magical and fantastic theories of the world, the adolescent hasn't any and can therefore only encounter his phantasies, an ideal world represented by his projections. With time his phantasies are replaced by experiences, since for adolescents *knowing and doing* coincide.

This is a moment in which the individual history is determined by the acceptance or the refusal of the integration between the physical and the mental aspects. Here, in this constructive and necessary phase, the elaboration of the conflict begins, a conflict that can have highly disturbing outlets, such as anorexia and bulimia in girls and other severe pathological manifestations in boys.

3.8 INTEGRATION AND UNITY. OMNIPOTENCE AND UNIFICATION

The dynamic exchange between the mind and the COO creates therefore an alternating internal history. There is a tendency towards integration, a continuous tension towards unity which is never completely achieved but it is a constant aim and a point of reference.

This tension is also easily observed in the cases in which unity is, so to speak, obtained by eliminating or rather by attempting to expel one of the terms of the relationship.

For a short moment omnipotence and unification appear to be the same thing but if one considers the aims and functions of the two, it is immediately evident that omnipotence appears to unify the Onefold and therefore doesn't unify at all, while an actual unification can only take place when Onefold and Twofold are both present at the same time.

If one relies upon the notion of the Eclipse of the COO, it becomes possible to follow step by step the vicissitudes of the complex relationship between body and mind, as observation of the specific area involved in the eclipse enables understanding of the relationship and of the functions of the mind versus the COO and vice-versa. It is just this kind of internal relationship that gives evidence of the connections between the two areas and their alternating influence on modes of thought and on the connections with the external world and objects.

3.9 PRIMARY CONFIDENCE

Clearly, when the child's primary confidence, which is provided by the mother, is lacking or is scarce and inadequate (inadequacy relating also, eventually, to the child's specific anxieties), the child then may tend to privilege the relationship and dialogue with his Onefold-Twofold system, leaving both the mother and the external world to themselves.

I regard this latter as a possible hypothesis as I think that the initial act of the newly born baby is dealing with himself, his vital dynamism and his necessity to survive. I believe that the child tries hard, with great pain and anxiety, to enforce his presence, specificity and uniqueness by overcoming the turmoil.

When satisfactory relationships are present, the baby has the opportunity to develop the Onefold and Twofold relationships between the COO and the mind, the latter included and protected by the influence of a state of primary confidence. When this protection is missing the baby develops instead, several different and specific modes of introjection as opposite substitutes of the above mentioned internal relationships.

4.1 SEDIMENTATION OF PHYSICAL EXPERIENCES AND INTROJECTION OF THE BREAST. DIFFERENT CONCEPTUALISATIONS OF ENVY.

Klein describes, as I have said, the act of bringing inside the breast and then the mother. I suggest, on the contrary, that at the very beginning, there might be a physical experience, the sedimentation of an experience that is originated by the body rather than by an introjection of an external object. For Klein it is therefore consequential to assert the hungry child experiences the breast as owning all the desirable things but keeping them for itself and that the above phantasy is the source of primary envy. I believe, on the contrary, that such an experience relates mainly to physical sensations, of being hungry or cold etc., and that, therefore the psychic correlate to it is an anxiety of annihilation and death.

Obviously the idea of the breast – food is, at least when the object is absent, central in an archaic functioning that aims at avoiding the anxiety of disintegration and at enabling some kind of self-integration.

For this reason in my model envy is a co-ordinating function rather than a primary mechanism as suggested by Klein. It is an organising principle such as identification. Envy may originate confrontation and emulation and not just competition and it may even be considered as the source of gratitude.

Finally Klein regards envy as an original feeling, related to death anxiety, my hypothesis, on the contrary is that envy derives from death anxiety but rather as a kind of organiser, with the aim of trying to avoid disintegration.

This process has an eminently archaic structure. It isn't casual that Bion[34] mentions a primitive rudimentary consciousness (the term consciousness has the Freudian meaning, i.e. the sense-organ with a capacity for perception of psychic qualities) and suggests that when reverie is absent or inadequate an excess of projective identification might take place. In this respect, when maternal reverie is absent, envy could be said to acquire a cohesive quality.

4.2 PHYSICAL ORGANISER AND PSYCHIC CO-ORDINATOR

One might therefore assume that some developmental steps are absolutely necessary and that the more archaic mechanisms can only be replaced when there is an initial organisation of emotions and feelings and, therefore, thought becomes possible. The area of physicality is wholly and entirely present and available since the beginning, while the mental area only gradually structures itself. The initial answers of the COO may therefore originate from physical organisers, which gradually lose their importance and eclipse in favour of psychic co-ordinators which substitute, at least partially, the phylogenetic responses and eventually succeed in organising functional ontogenetic responses. The meaning attributed to the mother-object could therefore be said to originate from what the child has provided for himself *by means of,* or *through,* the relationship with himself.

The Twofold necessitates the function of reverie in order to be able to develop while corporeality is independent from reverie as it relates to a phylogenetic imprinting. Corporeality may well be considered a *physical organiser* inasmuch as the Twofold, and the senses that depend from it, enable the selection of a psychic co-ordinator. While for the psychic co-ordinator the five senses are needed as well as the initial development of an incipient Twofold, for the physical organiser the corporeality alone is needed, in its final pre-natal modifications. The answers of the Twofold (senses = psychic co-ordinators) therefore depend from the specific moment and circumstance. There could be an overdetermining of the selected sense or no selection of the sense at all. When the selected sense fails in co-ordinating it seems therefore to be extremely difficult to operate a substitution. On the contrary, as the consequence of a failure, *islands of physicality* seem to proliferate. These islands are incapable of unitary action and representation towards the Twofold system as they are supposedly originated when a trauma-dearth or other situations, take place – before or after birth – in a violent offensive manner, at a time when the Twofold hasn't yet reached some kind of organisation.

Corporeality originates, in other words, as the harmonious or disharmonious result of all the activities which concur in the formation of the physical system and of all pre and post-natal data.

I would like to emphasize once more that it is the Onefold, just the Onefold, that originates the Twofold, not vice-versa. If any serious casualty takes place while the functions of the psychic co-ordinator are being established – before, during, or after birth – the psychic co-ordinator doesn't reach its expected level of functioning. In other words the selected sense doesn't become capable of co-ordinating or aggregating the other senses. As I have mentioned, at this stage of observation and research I believe that when this happens whilst no other sense is able to substitute the co-ordinating function, one can observe interestingly the phenomenon of the appearance of physical islands of mere sensory experience that are unable to reach the Twofold through psychic co-ordination. It is a sensory experience that is somehow enclosed in itself. The corporeality can only harbour these sensory phenomena (visual, auditive, tactile, etc.) never reaching the stage in which they can be registered and become significant for the Twofold system. Clinical work supplies evidence of the impasse and it should therefore be possible to detect signs of this physical situation at the psychic level.

The problem is, nevertheless, actually quite complex as it isn't often that one can uncover expressions of such situations, through an attentive observation of the analytic material. When the Twofold registers and transforms sensations into meanings-symbols it tends to include them into the more ample context of the pleasure-displeasure dyad. It seems therefore quite arduous to detect visible signs of these registrations. If corporeality isn't reached, the Onefold can't adequately relate to the Twofold. The latter tends therefore to consider the Onefold as a compound of physical aspects, as a bodily (physical) concreteness, void of any specific meaning and therefore unrepresentable.

In the actual vertical axe the corporeality offers some indication of the limits, needs, dearths etc. to the Twofold, thus signalling the physical possibilities of the living system. The mind is thus able to deal with that specific corporeality instead of relating to an undetermined hypothesis of a body, something that unfortunately happens all too often, to most of us, whenever there is an inadequate representation of the body.

When the psychic co-ordinator is absent because it hasn't developed, or when it fails and is unable to co-ordinate, the physical organiser is left with the task of answering on an exclusively physical level to bodily experiences. It is important to isolate and recognise the phenomenon (e.g. breathing/asthmatic disorders, convulsive disorders in infancy etc.) so that it won't be regarded as something that is connected with memory. The phenomena we are discussing are mere physical sensations that can't proceed further ... and therefore mark *physically* some stimulus-response circuits. The sensations which determine the phenomena are sometimes regarded as senseless repetitions in children, adolescents and sometimes even adults but they are the physical matrix of an answer to a traumatic situation. By the word *trauma* (although I do have in mind the Freudian concept) I mean an event that has a physical effect and that stays physical, not an event that eventually determines psychic consequences.

4.3 PANIC AND ANXIETY: A DIFFERENTIATION

I suggest that one might name a situation of this kind a situation of *panic*, limiting the use of the concept of panic to aspects of corporeality related to the answers of the Onefold. I also suggest that one might use the word *anxiety* for the answer of the Twofold when it includes the Onefold and is able to elaborate a global individual answer to specific situations of internal or external danger. Panic isn't therefore characterised by the impossibility of expressing oneself in the horizontal axe but rather by a kind of refractory impossibility of expression, related to the islands of physicality and to their origin – an answer to danger originated from the body's need for survival.

4.4 KLEIN'S PHYSICAL STIMULI, BION'S SENSE DATA. COMPARISON WITH THE HYPOTHESIS OF THE COO

I believe, moreover, that further comparison of aspects of the hypothesis of the COO with Klein's and Bion's theoretical postulates may allow for a possible inclusion of my hypothesis and for an investigation of its possible clinical relevance as my interest mainly focuses on the technical and clinical fields.

In Klein's view physical stimuli always have their correlate in phantasy. Bion's notion of sense data, on the contrary, is the point of departure of a process which either reaches the realisation or the non-realisation. The thought that derives from this process may therefore express elaboration or evacuation. Bion, in other words, regards the sense data as the point of departure of thought. My hypothesis investigates the question more extensively as the notion of eclipse suggests a continuous endless process in which the aspect of sensory perception may be partly or totally eclipsed by the activity of thinking or vice-versa.

The peculiarity of this model is that it enlightens these possible different courses, but at the same time constantly focuses upon the two extreme opposites, the area of sensory experiences and the area of thought and the mode in which the two intertwine and influence each other.

Psychic reality, for instance, is easily inclined to drop sensory data, since it is essentially limited by the latter, but the transgression of signals conveyed by the sensory apparatus tends to endanger life.

4.5 VICISSITUDES OF THE ONEFOLD-
TWOFOLD RELATIONSHIP

Clinical observations supply the elements that are necessary to estimate the points of equilibrium or of conflict between the two areas.

The psyche is, as I have already mentioned, strongly involved in communication and in exchanges of information from and towards the external world. It would be unable to employ its remarkable potentialities if the eclipse of the physical area didn't happen. When sensory perceptions and their emotional correlates haven't undergone a sufficient eclipsing there can be no space for thought.

The observation of the vicissitudes that characterise the Onefold and Twofold relationships is relevant for the investigation and understanding of severe disturbances and for the comprehension of the personal history of any individual human being. Hatred and love are fixed points in any ontogenetic individual development. There is no substantial difference between the infant and the adult, in what concerns the emotional sphere, except in the use that they make of it and that it may originate a container, which we name mind.

4.6 LINEAR TIME, CIRCULAR TIME

I wish to illustrate some considerations, which may be useful at this point, which I have formulated during clinical work and that seem to be relevant both from a theoretical and a practical viewpoint.

It is necessary that I state in advance that the Onefold-Twofold relationship is ruled by a variety of different characteristics in its mutual distinct modes. The Twofold presupposes continuous development which usually enriches it of knowledge and experience. One can therefore apply the concept of *linear time* to this kind of development.

The Onefold, on the contrary, and for its peculiar characteristics, seems to express a kind of *circular time* that is coherent with the concept of eclipse. This implies that the Twofold modifies itself and progresses while the Onefold reveals, when it emerges, the same (or almost the same) emotional characteristics that it has always manifested. As there is no *progress*, we may say that there is no possibility of *regression*.

4.7 CLINICAL MANIFESTATIONS OF THE
ONEFOLD-TWOFOLD RELATIONSHIP

If one keeps these aspects in mind, it then becomes evident that whenever the Onefold prevails upon the Twofold or there is a Onefold-Twofold relationship that appears to be confused or indiscriminate, the possibilities that the eclipse might take place are strongly hindered and, as a consequence, the development of the functions of the Twofold are impaired.

This description concerns analysis that has no history, in which the analysand doesn't reach a stage in which he can make a proper use of his own body, since the body doesn't become an actual object.

In the analytic work this difficulty is revealed by an absence of development of constructive processes. Transference objects can't be created with the help of the analyst to arrive at the establishment of an experience of reciprocity in the relationship. Time is experienced as circular and consequently, the analysand continues to produce non-metabolised material, in boring or even exasperating repetition.

When the same kind of difficulties prevail in the Twofold, the eclipse of the COO can't be achieved. Physicality is just ignored. Associations are interminable but they don't produce any development as they are confined to pseudo-abstract areas in which separation anxieties, mourning for modifications and emotional manifestations in general, are absent or almost absent. Also here time is circular, which means that propositions are endlessly repeated and there is no evidence of a state of suffering even in frustrating situations.

These analysands frequently succeed in keeping a very small area free from the consequences of the catastrophe. This area is usually related to the fundamental biological functions and it is used by the mind to establish the Onefold-Twofold process although at a limited degree.

Freud signals this datum in *An Outline of Psychoanalysis*: "Even in a state so far removed from the reality of the external world as one of hallucinatory confusion (amentia), one learns from patients after their recovery that at the time in some corner of their mind (as they put it) there was a normal person hidden, who, like a detached spectator, watched the hubbub of illness go past him"[35].

4.8 THE BY-PASS

When there is a repeated experience of some kind in a relationship with the physical sensations, a kind of paradigm is then established for the basic relation, both in reverie and in analytic relationship. If this doesn't happen, when *it should happen*, in reverie or in individual personal experience, the possibilities of establishing this basic relation are reduced.

These experiences are therefore essential as they determine the development of the mind, if they are frail or lacking, the development of the mind can be greatly hindered.

The COO, at primitive levels, is a body-mind conjunction in which the physical sensations are the point of departure. For the newly born baby touching is part of feeling and, therefore, of "thinking". If this did not happen when it was necessary, any other possibility of touching has to pass through the mind and needs the structuring of what I have called a *by-pass*.

I believe the construction of *by-passes* is one of the main tasks of the analytic relationship, where analyst and analysand create new areas of experience both emotional and cognitive.

The arduous path that goes from physicality to psychic functioning reproduces exactly the biological development of birth in which one body becomes two bodies. The Onefold of the mother that becomes mother-baby can reproduce itself indefinitely in phantasy-life. We all have our body and our thoughts and can reproduce the latter an indefinite amount of times.

In the body-mind relation there is therefore a kind of repetition of the mother-child relation model, from Onefold to Twofold, then again towards Onefold. I name it a relation because it is in the vertical relation and by means of the horizontal relation that the first functioning of the mind is originated.

Sensations are the first conveyance and containment of the different characteristics of physical data. They originate in the function of discriminating internal and external experiences but need external objects to become active and to be felt as belonging. This is why the horizontal relation is necessary. It enables the sensations to gain enough space to become sensory perceptions, emotions and eventually experiences. Sensations appear to be like signs, potentially capable of forming a text in which emerging emotions are the language.

4.9 COO AND MATERNAL FUNCTION

The child is COO and mind, related to each other and to a mother-external object. The mother is mind and physicality, and is both related to the child's physicality and to his developing mind.

My hypothesis about the mother's role is closely related to Bion's masterly and concise definition of the concept of reverie: ". . . the psychological source of supply of the infant's needs for love and understanding"[36]. In the mother this source coincides with the existence of sensory channels emanating signals. Bion writes: "The physical component, milk, discomfort of satiation or the opposite, can be immediately apparent to the sense . . ."[37]

Bion's description seems to allow for the hypothesis that mother's first answer might well be physical when she establishes a very peculiar syntony with the child's physical needs. At this initial stage of the relationship, physical communications seem to gain a kind of prevalence[38] and it is necessary for them to be accepted, integrated and metabolized in the mind of the mother. There is more awareness in the mother's activity than in the child's but the two proceed, so to speak, in parallel.

The prevalence of the physical area is hard to accept for some women while for others it is rather a privileged experience. The latter find it difficult to part from the experience as they seem to suffer the loss of the physicality they had recovered through pregnancy.

Mother's COO after becoming more active in the first stage, has then to gradually fade and make space for mental activity. Similarly the child's mind attenuates its sensations by providing them with meaning and sense.

The horizontal relation is therefore established between the child's COO and the mother's body / between the mother's body and mind, and the child's physicality / between the mother's mind and the active exuberant emotional world of the child.

4.10 MATERNAL REVERIE AND THE PSYCHIC AREA

Mother's availability in creating a space for another person, external to her, is maybe what enables the child to let emotions and feelings emerge and invest the other (the mother in this case) thus establishing the horizontal relationship that supports and allows for the experience of oneself as subject.

In order to be able to regard the baby as another and different person, the mother needs an equilibrium between the physicality and the psychic area, so that she can rely on sufficient confidence in her capacities. The capacities necessary to register the baby's needs and provide for his survival . . .

If she succeeds in tuning in with the signals coming from her baby, a mother is able to observe and wait, without precociously saturating the manifestations of not sufficiently defined needs of her child (the problem of misunderstanding) or being compelled to ignore the existence of such needs (the problem of absence).

Thus mother's capacity for reverie may enable the formation of a *psychic area* that becomes substantial if the child manages to tolerate the frustrations connected to a state of discomfort that one could define as "lack of something".

5.1 THE OTHER

It is just this sense that something is lacking, or that satisfaction is absent that originates the awareness of the dialectic relation with one-self (mind-body) and this perception, in its turn, enables the individual to become a subject in relation to the other. It is therefore in the contrast between a frustrating situation and the presence of a satisfactory object that the child can adapt his mind to an initial communicative process and express the very beginning of an emotional display aiming at communication.

5.2 ONEFOLD AND TWOFOLD: THE SEPARATION BETWEEN THE TWO SYSTEMS

The initial perception of being Twofold and of being two (oneself and the other) is a critical moment since it conveys an amount of primitive anxieties. These anxieties which Klein regarded as coinciding with the depressive position and the perception of the mother as a whole object, in the hypothesis of the COO, become something quite different, as separation (feeling separate) is here referred to the initial relation between Onefold and Twofold, between the COO and the mind.

Whenever there is a situation of intense anxiety, this separation is felt as hazardous or even menacing. These are very conflicting moments and the child experiences them as quite dangerous for his own integration.

5.3 ISOLATION

We can say that there is either an overcoming of the anxieties and consequent psycho-physical integration further increasing the object relation or there is an increase in splitting leading to the sacrifice of one of the two terms of the vertical relation. In this case sometimes, anomalous situations develop such as in acute isolation and in the states named autistic. The isolation may either concern the suppression of the horizontal relation, coinciding with a closure towards the object and the external world or it may concern the suppression, in the vertical relation, of the physicality, in favour of a search for an external object that might be captured and held, in permanent idealization.

5.4 MATERNAL REVERIE AND DEVELOPMENT OF THE MIND

It is obviously not just the presence but rather the quality of maternal reverie that influences the direction and development of the mind of the child. As the COO gives the original imprint to the individual mode of being, so the mother's mind influences the child's mind through the complex and subtle links deriving from their mutual communicative exchanges. These communications may actually be either understood or excluded, emphasized or ignored, by the mother.

Between the COO with its great potentialities, and the mother with her endowment of life (when the mother and the corresponding COO are absent, the child loses himself) there can be either an harmonious or a conflictive relationship. The characteristics of the personality develop consequently and they significantly influence the future life.

When the conflict is intense, the child often silences or strongly controls his emotional life, stifling it in his attempt to maintain the link with his mother. Another possible choice is recurring to omnipotence, a kind of magical-hallucinatory evocation, acting in the absence of or in contrast with a maternal mind that organises experience. The result is a precocious and distorted attempt at an impossible autonomy and, therefore, a pseudo-integration.

Finally, when one of the two terms of the mother-child relation is removed there is also a loss of one of the two terms of the internal relation, either the mind or the body.

One might say, as a conclusion, that the hypothesis of the COO regards physical phenomena and psychic phenomena as a continuum. The possibilities I have had for observation and knowledge have induced me to consider only the transformation of sensory stimuli into sensations, emotions, feelings and thoughts, although I do realise that this is just a segment of the complex course of the Concrete Original Object.

NOTES

25 Freud S. (1905), *Three Essays of the Theory of Sexuality*, SE, London: Hogarth Press, vol. VII.
26 Freud S. (1911), "Formulations on the Two Principles of Mental Functioning", London: Hogarth Press, vol. XII.
27 Freud S. (1915), "Instincts and their Vicissitudes, SE, London: Hogarth Press, vol. XIV, pp. 121–122.
28 Klein M. (1928), "Early Stages of the Oedipus Conflict", in *Love, Guilt and Reparation*, Virago Press, 1988.
29 I am using this term in the meaning given by I. Prigogine. A state of disorder that may, through the interaction of its different elements and forces, reach some amount of order or of unstable balance. I. Prigogine *Entre le temps et l'eternité*, Fayard, Paris 1988.
30 Negentropy or negative entropy is understood by Beavers as: "the utilisation of energy to develop structure and fight the inexorable downhill pull found in any closed system". Beavers W. R. (1976) "A theoretical basis for family evaluation" in Lewis J. M., Beavers W. R., Grosset J. T. & Phillips V. A. (eds.) (1976), *No Single Thread: Psychological Health in Family Systems*, New York, Brunner/Mazel. Beaver's definition of the concept of negentropy seems to be more adequate in this context than A. Kepinski's definition which was referred to in the Italian edition of this text.

31 Tustin F. (1981), *Autistic States in Children*, London: Routledge & Kegan Paul.
32 Winnicott D. W. (1974) "Fear of breakdown" *International Review of Psychoanalysis*, 1:103–107.
33 Ibid., p. 106.
34 Bion W. R. (1962), *Learning from Experience*, Karnac Books, London 1984.
35 Freud S.(1938), *An Outline of Psychoanalysis*, SE, London: Hogarth Press, vol XXIII p. 201–202.
36 Bion W. R. (1962), *Learning from Experience*, Karnac Books, London 1984 p. 36.
37 Bion W. R. (1962), *Learning from Experience*, Karnac Books, London 1984 p. 35.
38 I use the term 'prevalence' because I don't think that the concept of regression is applicable here. During pregnancy or child-bearing or in other unique moments such as adolescence the solicitations that come from the body cause a new outburst of the COO. The latter has peculiar characteristics that are functional to the actual moment and that shouldn't be confused with the characteristics of the infant.

3

EXTENSIONS

A. B. Ferrari – L. Carbone Tirelli[39]

In this chapter we further discuss and illustrate some aspects of the eclipse of the COO which may be observed in the relationship between analysand and analyst and that may, in our opinion, raise some quite significant points about analytic technique. We will hence explore the kinds of phantasies which analysands may produce, focusing upon the specific characteristics of different kinds of ideational activities.

In some cases, as described in Extension 2, the contact with mental phenomena is evocative of the incorporation and expulsion phantasies described by Segal: "phantasies which are, to begin with, of a very concrete somatic nature"[40]. Some analysands seem to hang on to such concrete nuclei as to a kind of protection of the mind from meaning or from thought itself.

Other mental phenomena, described in Extension 1, manifest themselves by an ideational activity apparently varied and mobile but really in little contact with actual stimuli or needs, or with sensory and emotional feelings.

In Extension 3 we delineate some of the functions of the sense organs in the COO's eclipsing process.

In Extension 4 we discuss extensively the concept of *by-pass* referring to the specific phase of analytic elaboration that aims at re-establishing a significant and functional relation between thoughts and sensory data.

EXTENSION n. 1:
ABSTRACT PHANTASIES

The first sensations relate, as we have seen, to the body and emanate from it (Vertical axe) while the first perceptions are only possible in relation to the external world (Horizontal axe). Physicality – this concept has been repeatedly emphasised – is the initial datum in the hypothesis of the COO and also the datum-presence in relation to which the mind begins to function.

The experience of the Eclipse is supposed to enable the mind to receive the datum-presence and register it entirely, though this isn't exactly what actually happens. The essence of physicality in fact can't be fully attained by perception since perception belongs to or is inseparable from physicality.

When a person requires analysis he may do so for many different reasons but what usually determines the decision is, simple as it may appear, a feeling of tension and conflict with oneself and the world. The tension is originated by the limits that the internal and external worlds impose upon the individual's omnipotence.

In the analytic relationship the model of the COO focuses upon the conflict and opens the way to:

a) the relation between the analysand's mind and his body, sensory feelings, emotions and thoughts.

b) the relation that the analysand establishes with the analyst in the analytic relationship

c) any interrelated links between the two mentioned relations

By giving maximum attention to these areas the analyst may then observe, as a session develops, the deep connections between the mode and form in which the analysand deals with himself, his own body and bodily sensations and the mode in which he establishes his relation with external objects, analyst included.

It is often possible to observe that some people have complex relations with their body, their sensory perceptions, emotions and thoughts. Complex and conflicting as one usually sees in interpersonal relationships. Sensory perceptions, emotions, feelings and thoughts may be registered or ignored, or they may be loved, hated, idealised or denigrated.

Since the internal experiences are closely linked to external relationships, the analytic relationship enables comprehension and awareness of modes and forms of the conflict.

For some analysands no experience seems to be possible, including the analytic experience. Some casualty in the progress of the Eclipse of the COO seems to have caused a massive prevailing presence of physical aspects, thus hindering mental functions. On the contrary, an excessive mental activity may sometimes be used to obscure all bodily needs. People who are severely lacking in any of the two terms of the Vertical relation have intense psychic disorders. Those are commonly referred to as psychotic disorders.

The existence of such severely disturbed areas is revealed, in the analytic relationship, by the mode in which the analysand perceives and deals with, or rather *doesn't perceive and deal with*, in the Horizontal relation, with the physical and mental presence of the analyst and by the phantasies produced in the analytic relationship.

In these persons the conflict with the external world becomes almost irrelevant as the internal conflict gradually arises. They appear to be just trying to restrain more than to avoid action. In fact action is felt to be quite dangerous and uncontrollable because of its strong emotional quality. The perception of danger compels such people to invent many stratagems all based upon very elaborate phantasies.

It is necessary to emphasise here that even when the capacity to put in motion the process of thinking is severely hindered or swept away by intense emotions, it is possible to resort to phantasies in an attempt to obtain some form of psychic containment. Clinically such phantasies can be divided into two categories:

a) elaborate mainly abstract phantasies that can't easily be related to physical stimuli

b) phantasies that relate to physical aspects and leave little space for symbolisation

It is thus possible, in our opinion, to question the assumption that in any severe psychic disturbance action prevails upon mental activity. On the contrary, the concreteness of the imaginative activity, impregnated and loaded by sensory quality of experience, is what hinders the elaboration in thought processes. The mind hence tries to make up for the lack of elaboration by a hyperactive ideational activity, obsessional and controlling in nature, poor in content, repetitive in its concreteness and therefore inadequate for the function aimed for.

In other cases instead of the concreteness of the ideational activity impeding thought, one can rather see the opposite – an inclination to produce phantasies of an abstract nature. When links with sensory and emotional experiences have been severed it becomes necessary to refer to situations and behaviours that have nothing to do with experience. Because there is no psychic space to allow for thought, the models of relation are necessarily devoid of metaphorical quality. Mental activity becomes here again a kind of stereotype, although maybe not as evident as in the first case.

In the first case as the phantasies are extremely concrete and don't apply to everyday life, action becomes necessary. In the second case abstractness seems to allow for a shift in models, and occasionally for a scrutiny intended to prevent the interruption of thought, in fact it only enables a pseudo-adaptment to the factual data.

Concrete and abstract phantasies both seem mainly to have the function of protecting the mind. The saturation aims at preserving the mind from the menace that originates mainly from the internal world and from external occurrences perceived as potential vehicles of madness.

An analytic approach that privileges the Horizontal relation (the relationship between analyst and analysand) confronts the analyst working with this kind of patient, with remarkable difficulty, because of the inadequacy of the approach which the analysand may well use as an encouragement for his own persecutory phantasies. On the contrary, by employing the Vertical axe, the analyst can foster the analysand's propensity to observe his own internal conflict, by enabling him to become tolerant of himself and of the analyst's active presence.

> The change from the use of abstract phantasies to the possible initial development of a capacity for sensory perception could be exemplified by the case of a young woman A. aged twenty, who started analysis after some years of isolation. Her minimal mental functioning was characterised by phantasies about establishing relationships with people and the phantasies required very slight or superficial interpersonal contacts. After a year of analysis, during a session, A. must have had some kind of perception of herself as she painfully said: "I feel like I have a new uncovered sensitiveness". When the analyst said that it might be the contact with a sensory perception that originated her anxiety, A. answered using a kind of sensory language: "Coldness frightens me . . . I need other people's warmth". After this communication she withdrew into a sort of distant world of her own.

One can deduce that when the mind is unable to contain an emotion, the sensory datum imposes itself. Such an experience might then provoke further anxiety, as the physical sensations won't be easily or quickly removed. A new construction of phantasies follows, with the aim of creating a distance between the psychic area on the one hand and the physical area with the pain that relates to it, on the other hand. If such passages take place gradually in the analytic process analysands may succeed in gaining experience from them thus acquiring a relationship with their own sensations and emotions, and finally establishing contact with their own self and with others.

EXTENSION n. 2:
CONCRETE PHANTASIES

Analysands who suffer from states of intense emotion and panic usually resort to concrete phantasies. The external relationships are in these cases of an intrusive-adhesive kind and action is both destructive and self-destructive.

Physical sensations that are, in the hypothesis of the COO, the precursors of thought because of their concreteness, are used in these cases of severe disturbance as substitutes for thought. For instance the feeling that one can't contain sensations and emotions may produce a state of anxiety and impotence. The sense of impotence is then transformed into the impulse of being inside the other, of taking the other's shape, in order to be able to use permanently the containment that is offered by the other's presence. The condition of being *with* people is therefore transformed into being *inside* people.

Obviously this kind of intrusive relationship is bound to fail. The separation is just as violent as the intrusion and causes a state of terror due to the menace of losing parts of oneself, either of the body or of the mind, depending on whether anxiety relates to physical or to psychic aspects. These analysands seem to reinstate periodically the initial state of predominance of physicality by reverting to action, a turmoiling activity that overpowers any capacity for thought. This mode can be seen in individuals who act continuously, in an attempt to contain and circumscribe the internal clash of their emotional life and who establish, in phantasy, some extremely rigid behavioural patterns. These individuals regard their behavioural and relational models as adequate anywhere and anyhow, but whenever there is a necessity to actually use them such models become the source of insuperable incongruities.

There are two kinds of attitudes thus deriving. In the first, since the model can't be adapted to reality, the reality-datum is denied so that the model can then be safely "preserved". This procedure doesn't of course really preserve the model but dangerously promotes further rejection of reality. The rejection is just temporary since sensations and emotions are still present and saturate the mind as unthinkable and therefore painfully uncontainable items. In other cases there is an attempt to reduce the menace by an intense fragmentation that strips away any kind of form and recognition, with consequent increase of confusion and anxiety. This is the moment in which analysands usually "act out".

This is the failure of the function of the Eclipse that should have enabled the passage from concrete sensations to the possibility of thinking. Concrete models can't be contained by the mind as if they were objects, as some level of symbolisation is needed to circumscribe anxiety. Symbolisation implies the capacity to transform (translate) sensations and emotions into meanings that might be related to external objects as they are stimulated by and directed to such objects.

One could say that the analyst may only carry on with analysis if the analysand can reach a point in which he considers it important to be able to communicate and name. Communicate to become present, to be there and name to give form to his knowledge. Thus the analysand can establish contact with and single out stable internal points of reference, stable

but not static, and at the same time functional to dealing with the problems of everyday life.

For the act of thought to take place, stability is essential. The mind
should be able to form the necessary instruments for the specific, varying
activities required from it. It is a complex process, thinking is difficult,
arduous, risky and demands painful efforts. The pain has to do with the
necessity of continuously adapting the knowledge to the needs and to the
requests of external surroundings.

The body-mind duality, Onefold – Twofold, is one of the conditions
for the construction of an internal area that may enable self-perception
in both levels, allowing for the passage, through emotions, from the sensations to the capacity for thought.

One of the possible casualties that may take place along this way is
flight from the sensory datum. This kind of occurrence characterises cases
of severe psychic disturbance, where the situation is such that sensory
data seem to volatilize thus hindering the process of symbolisation.

In these severe cases analysands seem to live such situations in a distorted
manner, whenever elaboration of the data of experience is needed, they
avoid it. Whatever the reasons for the refusal, the flight from perception
ends up in a confused retreat in which the mind is the first to be swept
away. The sense of failure then produces omniscience, omnipotence and
hatred towards oneself. Such feelings prevail and are paradoxically used
to try to destroy the proofs of any residual capacity for thought.

In the following example there is an attempt to contain the dread of
madness by using models of phantasy that are regarded as static and
therefore secure.

> An adolescent boy, B. with highly disharmonious mental function-
> ing, managed, after some years of analysis, to perceive and com-
> municate that his fear at the idea of his own madness related to a
> very upsetting experience: a boy who was coming to B.'s aunt for
> lessons had attacked him. B.'s fright was increased by the idea that
> the boy might have been mad, a hypothesis which B.'s parents dis-
> claimed. From then onwards B. tried to deal with that sensory
> datum and the anxiety related to it by keeping a continuous and
> thorough control, as this was the only way – he thought – in which
> mad people could be contained. In a later session a communica-
> tion of the analyst upset his effort to keep his rigid pre-established
> 'text', a text that he needed in order to defend himself from the
> sensations he considered dangerous. The analyst had remarked that
> B. had made an error in calculating analytic fees and B. was sud-
> denly unable to tolerate his own momentary error or inadequacy.
> This exchange enabled B. to describe, on the analyst's suggestion,
> what was upsetting him so much: "I am scared of anything that is

eternal . . . That B. (himself) might be angry forever, that he might remember all his life things that happened a long time ago".

Some technical comments can be made here. We have already said that, from the beginning, the analytic relationship supplies the analyst with information about the mode in which any particular analysand treats himself and his surroundings. It also informs the analyst about the origins of the analysand's knowledge, his capacity to refer to his sensations and emotions, thus obtaining useful information for his knowledge of himself. Finally the analyst comes to know how the analysand uses such data to comprehend his own relationship with the external world.

In the same manner the analyst can take notice of the significance that his imagined presence or absence (physical or mental) has for the analysand and investigate possible modes of communication with the analysand. A complex communication between the two is thus established and the lexicon is based upon verbal exchanges and, even more, upon the passage of sensations and emotions of which the analyst is supposed to have an adequate understanding.

In the analytic relationship it is furthermore possible to ascertain if and how the analysand's mind may pick up and elaborate such sensations and emotions as well as the quality of his archaic experiences. The latter enables the analyst, among other things, to focus upon possible accidents along the way of the analysand's COO Eclipse.

Our hypothesis is that the state of the analytic relationship, the way in which it is modulated in terms of variations of distance, is the principal resource for analyst and analysand, as the horizontal relationship is the principal resource for mother and child, to limit the anxiety of non-sense and enable a disposition towards self-directed attention and listening.

The analysis of the relationship isn't always possible. The analysands we have mentioned in this Extension, appear to be incapable of facing directly the relationship with the analyst, they seem to fear the exchange of experiences and, through the exchange, the establishment of a contact with their own emotions. The analysand can't, as one may see in B's reactions, perceive his own emotions and feel that they belong to him. He experiences instead, at least at the beginning of the analytic relationship, a feeling of foreignness that needs being dealt with for quite a long time.

This fragment of dream-material illustrates our hypothesis. An analysand in a difficult moment of analysis, related the following dream: there was a wild beast in a small cage associated with death, another beast in a bigger cage associated with madness. The cages indicated the continuous but useless attempts at giving form and controlling phantasies. If thoughts couldn't develop and grow, the analysand feared death. If thoughts grew excessively they might overwhelm the mind. The fear of madness!

Presence and attention, together with the customary, accepted elements of the analytic setting, therefore establish the "being in the relationship", the necessary medium. Analysands give every evidence of regarding this medium as a fundamental condition but there is also the possibility that some of them might use the analyst to perpetuate, in this way, the splitting between physicality and thought. Moreover, even when trying to work with severely disturbed analysands, we still refer to the hypothesis that if the analyst offers propositions concerning the analysand's mental functioning, the analysand's curiosity and interest may progressively arise and develop.

This mode of work is different, from the point of view of technique, from the model of investigating the analyst-analysand relationship, but it sometimes appears as the only possible mode, not just with cases of severe psychic disturbance but also with analysands that do have a capacity to approach their own primitive nuclei and to relate to the area of the COO. These are situations in which by considering the relation which the analysand entertains with his own mind or with his own physical essence – the Vertical relation – the analyst accomplishes the same function as the mother who, through reverie, understands by intuition and decodes the sensations and emotions of the child without overpowering them.

This approach may bring positive results, but it is necessary for the analyst to tolerate, possibly for quite a long time, that any analytic proposition might be captured by the analysand and used according to ancient habits. The area for psychic thought is, in these cases, narrow and the model for interpersonal relationship therefore devoid of any metaphorical quality. In this stage the attempt at capturing the thoughts of the analyst and at using them as model-stimuli may produce an unrestrained greed. The mental attitude of the analysand towards the analytic proposition has more to do with stealing than with listening, as the attempt is to persevere in ignoring one's own sensations and emotions and therefore to keep the COO as unthreatening as possible for the mind.

The delineation of such an attitude illustrates further the experience of the patients that have been described in this section. Patients who evaluate correctly their lack of capacities and have no confidence in their own judgement in choosing what is necessary or best for them. Because they still need to give a form to the product of their minds they render them concrete by schematically taking them from people whom, case by case, they think they might trust.

EXTENSION N. 3:
THE FUNCTION OF SENSE ORGANS

During the analytic process, the analysand often communicates to the analyst a sensory perception, a new capacity for contact between body and mind. At this stage the sense organs and the related stimuli are taken into consideration with new interest by the mind. Some precise sensations are then communicated in the session – a bitter taste in the mouth, evoking a feeling of bitterness towards the analyst. The sensation of warmth or of coldness evoking a wish for closeness or for detachment. Emptiness or fullness as a reaction to the other's absence or presence.

Such messages still retain some of their concreteness but they also convey meaning. It is the analyst's task to unveil them, provide them with importance and sense, so that they might be handed back to the analysand somehow more fluid.

Such messages help us to understand further the function of sense organs in the process of the Eclipse of the COO. We stated that the infant has, in our opinion, an autonomous mental functioning since birth. We moreover think that he might have an essential capacity to discriminate his own sensations, a capacity that is expressed through the establishment of initial correlations between different confused physical stimuli. This is the first active function of the mind.

We hypothesise also that such function might take place thanks to a prevailing sensory point of reference, which has the purpose of co-ordinating all the sensations, and is chosen between others and elected to function with this aim. In other words a sense organ that catalyses, each time, the sensory experience itself since sense organs, besides functioning as internal co-ordinators, also signal the infant's needs, responding to solicitations originated by stimuli from the external world.

The capacity of a sense organ to register a sensory experience, capturing it and providing it with meaning by relating it to the object (sense of smell – smell of mother, view – breast, touch – mother's body and so forth) together with the possibility of gathering together other functions of the remaining sense organs, probably is the first step along the path leading to representation, a first step towards the formation of a psychic area and of the activity of symbolisation. Representation is reached when it becomes possible to evoke the object in its absence.

The chosen organ has the function of establishing contacts with the external world through choice and registration of stimuli originating from the latter, its mode of functioning is unique in each individual person. Careful observation brings to evidence that each person privileges one of the sense organs and gives it the function of establishing contact and gaining knowledge of self and of the world.

The predominance that we are describing goes beyond natural maturation processes and stages of development of each sense organ (i.e. allowing the child to recognise through the mouth, the sensations of fullness and emptiness, of sweet and bitter). It expresses, instead, something that is unique for each individual and that makes each person different from all others.

We therefore regard the selected sense organ as an actual psychic co-ordinator, which may be used, in further development, as other sense organs are used. Or it may be set aside as an archaic relic, or again it may be over determined and therefore peculiarly characterise the individual's future activities.

The behaviour of a baby, observed weekly in the first two years of life illustrates the hypothesis of the over determination of a sense organ and may supply further elements of thought.

C. was nine months and two days old when he was found undernourished by the paediatrician who visited him and therefore changed from breast feeding to bottle-feeding. An observation took place when he had been taking the bottle for two days. C. was putting his tongue between his lips as if to suck it and was shaking his hands. His eyes were intense and roaming, in meeting his mother's face he stopped and then continued to move his mouth and lips. Playing with his tongue was something new, when he managed to grasp it within his lips he appeared to be pleased and stopped moving. Mother said she was sorry about the weaning and put the dummy in his mouth. C. excitedly shook hands and feet and moved his eyes around. Letting the dummy out of his mouth he grabbed his sheet, pushed into his mouth, tried to grab it with his lips.

Mother presented the bottle which C. took greedily. He wasn't looking at mother as when he was breast fed, his eyes where now moving restlessly. He sucked rhythmically until his eyes met the light on the ceiling. Then he stopped, raptured, smiling. Mother left him for a bit, then she encouraged him to resume his feed. C. returned to sucking, but stopped again twice when his eyes met the light. Maybe this was how he managed to finish the bottle.

The primary function of C.'s eyes was evident since birth and continued during the first two years of life. Using his vision, searching for points of reference C. struggled to overcome his difficulties, related to hunger and to his relation with the breast.

At the age of four months C. tried hard to master the hazard of attending a crèche. After a few days, he looked around without smiling when meeting the observer in the street, he was astonished and didn't seem to recognise familiar faces. Back at home he became livelier and looked around happily smiling at shining objects such as door handles and at people. A month later he developed a squint in his eye. In this period his main interest changed from people to the working of things.

C.'s eyes which in the first two months of life had supplied a connection and a link between himself and the object, leaving the functions of other organs free to develop, had now exasperated their task. An effort towards autonomy and control of an exceedingly frustrating external reality. The over determined organ now seemed to function instead of other organs, hindering the Eclipse of the COO and the consequent development of mental functioning.

It isn't always possible, to discern the casualties that may have hampered the development of an individual person but in many symptoms one can see examples of over determination of a sense organ. Phobic symptoms often relate to over determination of sight. Over determination of touch, therefore of contact, is visibly related to some obsessional phobias. Over determination of taste and therefore of the mouth, to intense stuttering and to some eating disorders.

In the model of the COO the symptom arises in these and other situations as a sign of a developmental history in which the sense organ had from the beginning a primary function and has been heavily relied upon, because of this function. It is therefore possible to observe both its massive significance when it is present and also to remark its importance when it is absent.

EXTENSION N. 4:
THE CONCEPT OF BY-PASS

In the analytic relationship it isn't difficult to understand through the analysand's modes of communication which is the sense organ that had, or still has, the role of psychic co-ordinator. This doesn't happen with the modes of communication that relate to different kinds of relationship that an individual may have established with his or her mother. The lack of satisfactory exchanges, both psychic and physical, make such modes of communication rather more sensory or the opposite. In more severe cases one might observe a lack of contact with whole areas of experience as described in Extension n. 1. It is also possible that a person may not have had access to some areas of his own internal world because of some physical trauma and that he might therefore have been deprived of some fundamental experiences.

It is in our belief impracticable to retrieve the experiences which internal and external adverse situations have made it impossible to experience since no one can live anew something that was never lived but there still is a practicable solution and that is the construction of a *by-pass*. This is, as we have said, one of the main tasks of the analytic relationship, allowing the establishment, by means of the presence and of the activity of the analyst, of new modes of communication thanks to which the mind of the analysand may tolerate, with decreasing anxiety, the facts, situations and occurrences of his/her actual experience of life.

The analysand may, in this way, construct new modes of communication with himself and with the world. But for this to happen he should be able to establish a contact with his own dearths. This new perception conveys inevitably an intense psychic pain but offers the opportunity to attain capacities that were unknown up to that moment. The *by-pass* can therefore foster the development of *insight*, a new perception that is then transformed into experience.

In order to facilitate the understanding of our assertions we must remind readers that in our hypothesis the production of phantasies is related to the passage from physical sensations to emotions. In the phantasy there is space for the absent sensation. One might hypothesise that when a mode of communication is destroyed only a trace of the phantasy is left, too little for the function to be recovered. When we mention destroyed or suspended modes of communication we refer to the effects that are produced by intense sensations or emotions or both.

If an analysand can transform the analytic proposition into experience, he takes advantage from it and organises his world towards more functional new aims, if he can't the analytic proposition is then just analytic information for him.

When a fact through perception produces experience, growth then follows. When desire, or the absence of experience, replaces facts, facts are easily manipulated and leave no trace; there is absence, emptiness, hunger.

An analysand can feed on the traces of phantasies that come with the physical sensations, he usually ends up in the greed-frustration polarity. Experience is in such cases almost non-existent (or even absent) and the phantasy is let loose and is then manipulated and manipulative. This gives way to a parallel construction that substitutes experience, founded upon non-significant data. There are, as a consequence, no transformations or modifications of the analysand's mental asset as transformations only take place by experience.

Many analysands say, and with reason that "understanding doesn't bring in any change". This statement is what one might call a substitutive opposition, a sterile opposition as it doesn't facilitate or suggest any functional alternatives.

In these cases mental activity seems to exclude both the sensory area and the emotional area, it just simply substitutes the two levels. Concrete data are regarded as "ideas" or often as phantasies, and actively manipulated as such. The Onefold is left out and the Twofold loses its point of reference.

The function of analysis, in other words the task of the *by-pass*, is the re-establishment of a significant and functional relationship between thoughts and sensory data, starting from the presupposition that sensory data are physicality itself.

The analysands that succeed in taking charge of their corporeality soon realise that it implies some responsibility. This enables them to create a space, in their world, for a perception that is represented by their physical qualities and by the physical qualities of the object. The analysands who, on the contrary, are unable to develop this significant functional relationship between thoughts and sensory data die analytically. This relationship develops when analysands realise that it is necessary to give sense and significance to the messages which, through sensations, originate from their own body or from the arousal of emotions in their mind, emotions that cannot otherwise find a proper place and therefore acquire a definite meaning.

> The painful perception of one's own inadequacy enables the introduction of new experiences through the analytic relationship. The *by-pass*, provided by the Analytic Relationship, can be quite clearly discerned in the following example: D. is a young woman aged twenty-two who in her childhood precociously tried to control the anxiety originated by separation and loss – an anxiety that she perceived as uncontainable – by a drastic interruption of communication, on the Vertical axe, between sensations, emotions and thoughts. The anxiety originated by the perception of being left out (by her boy-friend or her analyst, as in her early days by her mother) could only be manifested through abdominal pain, as the digestive system had taken up the containing function, thus replacing the psychic area that was unable to function actively in such situations. The pain couldn't be recognised as anxiety by D.'s mind up to the moment in which the analyst, seizing D.'s bodily language and translating it through his own propositions into psychic and emotional meanings (the function of the by-pass), helped her to establish a more fluid and correct communication along the Vertical axe.

NOTES

39 Luisa Carbone Tirelli is psychotherapist and Chairman of the Italian Association of Child Psychoterapists (AIPPI).
40 Segal H. (1964) "Phantasy and Other Mental Processes", *International Journal of Psychoanalysis*, XLV, 2/3 p.192.

4

HEGEMONY AND SECESSION IN THE BODY-MIND INTERACTION

There is a substantial difference and not only in scientific formulations between science and actual living with its real, difficult experiences. Such a difference is most evident when physical and mental processes are concerned as the latter are characterised by great complexity, uniqueness, unexpectedness.

As I have already mentioned, human beings did regard themselves as superior to nature, including the human body. Furthermore this opinion has influenced significantly the development of dualistic theories, initiated with Plato and then clearly exemplified by Descartes.

C. S. Sherrington, the founder of contemporary neurophysiology, is doubtlessly referring to this dualistic viewpoint when he describes his de cerebrated dogs as mindless conditioned Cartesian puppets. According to W. Penfield[41] when memory and brain are regarded as passive elements, a body-mind dualistic conception automatically ensues. In Penfield's opinion although memory and mental images, sensations and experiences may be contained by the brain, active faculties such as will, judgement etc. are not to be found in the brain as they aren't physiologically represented or in any way reducible to physiology. On the contrary, they are "transcendent". O. Sacks[42] maintains that each person establishes a program for his or her own brain and that decision-making originates from the mind. Neuronal activity, on the contrary, originates in the superior mechanisms of the brain where the mind and the brain meet in a sort of psycho-physical frontier.

This perspective might well enable a more adequate conception of the human being and of the human mind, possibly explaining the growth and

development of human beings in relation to the human physical body.
Spinoza expressed an interesting and surprisingly modern approach, asserting that if one knew more about the body, its complexity, delicacy, potentialities and capacities to interact and develop – which is what I have named corporeality – one wouldn't need so much to evoke a strange or immaterial essence or principle. In "Ethics" Spinoza writes: "For indeed, no one has yet determined what the body can do, that is, experience has not yet taught anyone what the body can do from the laws of nature alone . . . For no one has yet come to know the structure of the body so accurately that he could explain all its functions . . . the body itself, simply from the laws of its own nature, can do many things which its mind wonders at"[43]. Spinoza didn't regard "Mind" and "Body" as two essences in the way that Descartes did, but rather as two Forms ("Thought" and "Extension") in which the body-mind individual person displays him or herself. He maintained that two different manners of description are needed, physical (physiological) and mental (psychological), and that none of the two could ever be substituted by the other. Spinoza's dualism may therefore be identified as a descriptive dualism. It isn't as Descartes' a dualism of essences and substances.

Nearly three centuries later it has become possible to relate, experimentally, to such an intuitive understanding by a theoretical model. The result is an attempt to establish a neurobiological theory of human being, to explain how man perceives, learns and becomes himself.

When facing situations of conflict one is, I believe, entitled to question whether the area of mental activity might have the ultimate aim of taking care of the body or whether it might be urged to accomplish any amount of overbearing actions though possibly appropriate to the cultural context.

One might hypothesise the mind-body relationship as a structural relationship in which the mind is present and intervening just as the physical organs, the liver, the pancreas, the spleen etc. are present. Many pathological aspects may in fact appear when an organ, including the mind, functions excessively or not enough.

In the context of the Twofold relation there are continuous exchanges and one can often see that the mind has an "hegemony" over the body. The body isn't concerned, for instance, with the problem of its own ending, simply because it either lives or stops living. Only by thinking of oneself or by feeling oneself – and this can exclusively happen on a mental plane – one can imagine that one exists beyond one's physical essence, thus achieving self-consciousness.

One might also wonder why cohabitation between body and mind is so difficult. An answerless question as far as I am concerned, for the hypothesis I am suggesting aims at establishing the modes and forms in which the two areas integrate, prevail upon each other or succumb, rather than at establishing the *whys* or reasons for all this. I mentioned in my initial hypothesis that the Onefold and the Twofold develop along widely diverging ways. Physicality could be represented as developing along a kind of normal statistic probability curve, a beginning at level zero, an apical point and an ending, again at level zero. The psychic functioning on the contrary should be represented by a diagram in which the lines develop irregularly and intermittently, progressively tending towards infinite growth.

The re-establishment of a significant functional development between sensory data and thoughts is the substance of the description of the Eclipse of the COO. Whenever an occurrence alters the balance between the physical and psychic systems the sensations and emotions burst out and the COO takes the place of the Eclipse. An event of this kind can be related to intense emotions such as hatred, frustration, desire, fear etc., it shouldn't therefore be regarded as an evolutional progress but rather as a process, constantly unfolding, at different stages, along the entire life of an individual. This doesn't nevertheless mean that the corporeality and the psychic area can't find an integration and harmonise the whole system for this may well happen and the physical area may then be contained by the psychic, while the Eclipse consequently starts.

The Eclipse isn't just a passage from physical to psychic it is the appearance of the mental area. Appearance and development taking place in a space that was formerly occupied mainly by the COO. In the analytic relationship one can nevertheless notice the casualties that might have happened along the development, when there are, for instance, strong defences against obviously irresistible physical stimuli, a person may experience behaviours and actions as alien to his own nature.

> The case of E. is an example of this: E. was a highly qualified professional woman, well educated, sensitive, and with good taste. She lived on her own after a series of personal vicissitudes and satisfied her "desire" by a complex ritual. When the evening of her choice came, she dressed carefully and drank several different alcoholic beverages in order to find the necessary courage, then she went in search of her partner in distant areas, far from where she worked. Her description of the whole process was cool, almost detached, impersonal. Her body didn't seem to belong to her. She talked about the experience in a distant tone – whenever it took place – regarding it with increasing alienation. It was a kind of compulsion – she said – it was her body that was responsible for such behaviour. She herself felt distant from the thing, she refused it.

Many analysands deny or at least put a self-imposed limit to their physical needs. This relates mainly to the two facets of one same problem:

a) the physical essence of the analyst is denied in an attempt to refuse or at least to circumscribe any aspects of physicality, for example the analysand's own physical growth and capacity to generate.

b) the sensuality and sexuality of the analysand's own parents is refused. There is a fear or even a denial of the Oedipal constellation.

This kind of situation may possibly be fostered by the frequent assumption that the analytic relationship is devoid of any physical aspects or that the analyst speaks in the session because his mind is there and present. Many analysands have trouble in the session because they experience the analyst's presence mainly on a sensory level. The analyst is present as long as his voice can be heard by the analysand. The analysand can't keep alive in himself the image of the analyst, including the experience that the image can originate, and the path towards symbolisation is obstructed. Such a difficulty possibly relates to the whole of the analysand's physicality plus the physicality which is attributed to the analyst. On the other hand, many mechanisms that might appear, at first sight, as successful symbolisations – because they do mentally create anew the absent object – reveal themselves to be mental activities that aim at making reality itself unreal. They have the appearance of symbolic processes as in the passage between emotion and thought this kind of analysand annuls the emotion and creates a thought that isn't therefore a symbolisation. In the sequence emotion-thought the emotion isn't metabolised but just excluded.

A model that might help us to understand, as an analogy, this elaborate mental construction could be seen in surrealistic painting, where the actual absence of any emotion is just what provokes emotion.

Analogously, emotion is excluded by those people who have great capacity to relate, photographically one could say, all the details of their daily experiences. They are in fact trying to compensate their incapacity of bringing their emotional experiences to the sessions.

Since all these situations are quite common, it is therefore necessary to keep in mind the Onefold-Twofold relationship so that one can then pay attention to phenomena that speak, so to say, a different language from the one usually spoken by the analyst, when he is communicating with the analysand's mind.

The model of the COO allows for the appearance, in the analytic relationship, of significant correlations between physical events such as anorexia, bulimia, aerophagia etc. and analysands' modes of thinking and of being. The task of the analyst is to focus attention, and to point out to the analysand, the signals that come from his mind about his body, so that the analysand becomes progressively able to structure a sort of outline of his body. Something more than just a sketchy mentalisation, rather a notion founded on the actual presence of the body.

My hypothesis may find useful applications when dealing with the behaviours that are usually defined as hypochondriac. Some of the states commonly defined as persecutory anxieties, may be regarded as the communication of intense difficulties of the mind when it has to deal seriously with the body. The body conceived not as a strange hostile object, contrasting in aims and objectives but as a presence, entitled to its own necessities. The hypochondriac doesn't seem to be able to accomplish a proper Eclipse as the Twofold continues to be in conflictive terms with the Onefold. I believe that this favours the passage to physicality of all the aspects that the mind is unable to transform into thinkable thoughts. The hypochondriac with great accuracy seems to choose organs and functions of his own body in which to confine all the psychic aspects that would be otherwise difficult to metabolise.

The conflict may increase to a point in which a person experiences physicality as persecutory. Each organ becomes a kind of menacing detritus that the hypochondriac calls, in turn, stomach-ache, liver-ache, heart-ache etc. In very severe cases there are also ritual gestures. The mind seems to be obliged to perform a series of acts that have the aim of preventing the relation with the body from becoming a proper phobic violent confrontation, as this is considered, with reason, highly dangerous for the mind since, when such an occurrence takes place, it becomes impossible to mentalise the physicality.

> The case of F. is an example of this. F. was an educated young woman who went through a dramatic experience. A very close member of her family had a devastating surgical operation. This event seemed to be at the origin of F.'s request for analysis. She was obsessionally frightened at the idea that she might swallow poison, or lethal doses of medication. She feared that food might be poisoned as well and therefore she made herself vomit. She constantly feared that she might contract organic incurable diseases and underwent frequent extenuating medical checks. Eventually a fragment of a dream seemed to throw some light on her mental state and sufferings: "there was a dark menacing sea but the water wasn't deep and I could therefore walk on some kind of slabs . . . walking I saw many relics around, ancient Roman and Greek relics; marble torsos and heads, blocks that could be recognised as parts of bodies of statues fragmented by time".

One can often observe, in these cases, that the aspects of physicality occupy the mind in the form of pieces or residues, things in the concrete sense. In clinical practice one can frequently find that some patients behave as if they had a remarkable uneasiness in the area of the Onefold – Twofold function and a kind of rigidity hinders the dual functioning. It is then important to discern which of the two aspects predominates in the psychic activity. If the area of physicality prevails the analysand deals with himself and with the object in a kind of mental atmosphere in which sensations, impressions and emotions win over, and strongly condition, the activity of thinking. If the Twofold prevails, the analysand may then recognise his needs but will tend to register them rather than trying to satisfy them. These analysands often say that they get very little satisfaction from life. Their perception is correct but they do not realise that it is their body that is missing the dialogue.

Occasionally when this attitude is expanded to its extreme consequences all experiences are transformed into rational data. Later, in the long distance, life is perceived as defective: "I woke up late" they say, referring to life. This means that they hadn't realised, up to that moment, that it is necessary to include emotions in one's life, in order to have an experience of wholeness.

It is interesting, for the analytic research, to distinguish the cases in which physicality seems to be just ignored, from the cases in which it is pushed away either because it is felt to be or to have been painful, or because it is felt to be humiliating, or even explosive and therefore uncontainable.

It is actually possible to experience physicality without excessive conflict, maybe not a proper functional wholesome balance between Onefold and Twofold but a kind of reciprocal adaptation that eventually privileges one of the two areas. The mental area tends to prevail in most people, not in actual opposition, but rather in a kind of non-apparent conflict.

One might ask – what is it that one tends to ignore? Probably some elements related to the perception of issues connected with space and time, to one's existence in life as a body, as a mind. Some people have, for instance, significant modes of dealing with their own rhythms in relation to the environment.

I am thinking in particular of modes of dealing with such difficulties as we all seem to have in looking after our practical needs as sleep, food, work, effort, pleasure, rest etc.

There are people who seem, for instance to experience their physical essence in a way that is similar to the manner in which the child experiences himself when he acquires the capacity to move and to orient himself in space. These acquisitions originate a sense of triumph and of power, going further than the actual physical capacities and resources. Such people behave in a way that indicates that their mind has learned to deal functionally with the body but that it can't or doesn't want to contain "the enthusiasm" provoked by sensations of pleasure and power originated by physical exercise. They consequently, tend to put up a challenge, by practising for instance high speeds with a scarce capacity to recognise danger.

One can see that these situations have to do with the functional dynamic equilibrium in the relation between corporeality and psychic activity as well as with the passages that originate from physical sensations, emotions, feelings and that enable the mind to reach symbolisation. This development takes place when it isn't hindered by such difficulties as we have called "casualties", in the process of growth.

An actual incapacity for symbolisation doesn't, in our opinion, exist in itself except in people with extreme damage of the brain. In people with severe psychic disorders this capacity is present, although temporarily obscured by a concrete thought, that sometimes creates an almost insurmountable obstacle for the re-creation of an adequate capacity to think. Sometimes some concrete aspects are functional to the psychic sphere. Someone might invest an object with so many intense concrete meanings that the loss of such an object might never be elaborated, even when the capacity for abstraction is satisfactory. The non-elaborated mourning may then be encapsulated in a circumscribed area of the mind, without creating a significant obstacle to the mind's whole functioning.

This doesn't happen when the emotion is really intense and extensive. In such cases it can't be transformed into a feeling so as to enable further steps toward symbolisation. Thus the concreteness is originated by the emotional intensity, not by a thought, and it is the emotional intensity that saturates every possible capacity for elaboration.

When a person is about to undergo a surgical operation his mind has to acknowledge that the body will suffer a lessening and that the lessening will have consequences on the mind's image of the body. When this happens the mind clings to its knowledge of the physical body and of its functions and resists strongly any modifications that might alter the body's *gestalt*. One might think, for instance, of the case of the shadow limb. On the other hand, when the body has to undergo a challenge and to make, physically speaking, the best possible job, the mind may accompany it but it has to be in the shade.

Different subsystems suffer from different ailments but the whole body doesn't seem to suffer. Similarly the mind doesn't suffer in itself but because it uses, applies and modifies feelings, emotions or thoughts in order to accomplish its psychic operative activities.

In some cases one of the two areas prevails upon the other. In some other severe situations the physical needs are ignored by the psyche or vice versa, in others the mind over or underdetermines some parts of the body. At the extreme limit there are cases of self-mutilation taking place during psychotic fits. Such disturbances compel some people to use a mirror or to confabulate within themselves. They have the necessity of recovering their physical or psychic essences, which have been temporarily lost, and cannot picture their missing essence except by sensorily seeing their own reflected image or listening to the sound of their own voice. These manifestations are usually displayed in moments of great personal crisis.

When, on the contrary, the sense of one's own existence is threatened, the physical area becomes the point of reference for the mind. Apparently, in these situations, the perception of one's own identity may be recovered through the corporeality or by what one might call, almost as in a paradox, "the mind of the body".

The body-mind interaction is a field of interest and comparison also in neurophysiological and psychological sciences both with human beings and with animals. G. Croiset[44] for instance, has done some interesting research showing that there is a complex correlation between emotional stress and immune responses in rats. What actually happens is that when the emotional stress produced in the tests appears to be surmountable the immune response increases, when it isn't surmountable the response is unchanged and when the stimuli of the test require responses that are in reciprocal conflict the immune response diminishes.

M. Fleshner[45] found a reduction in serum antibodies in rats exposed to social defeat. The stressful event has in this case just a social quality with no painful physical stimuli, and it still reduces the immune function.

The conclusion is that when there is an external aggression, the immune function tends to augment, enhancing the capacity for survival. When there is a prolonged conflict or a social defeat the original immune response comes to an end and a different function is activated; a more "mental" function which deals with the environment and with stimuli originating from it.

This second or "mental" section contrasts the original physical positive response to stress and originates a weakening of the bodily responses. But the decision whether the stress may be surmounted is highly variable or even casual. The disturbances of the relation between body and mind are extremely subjective on the whole. This can be easily seen even in laboratory tests with animals, and that is why a great number of experiments is required for any statistic significance to be achieved.

One should furthermore keep in mind that as biologic evolution proceeds, the areas of functioning that deal with the external environment become more and more important, and naturally develop, as their endowment, a symbolic system of internal signification. It becomes therefore possible for an individual to turn against himself or even against his own biological life-saving reaction.

In these situations one would expect the mind to lose the function of filtering and transforming the endogenous stimuli and the capacity to mediate with the external world. One would expect it to become an autonomous self-reverberating system that couldn't be used to potentiate any vital drives but would rather tend to hinder or antagonise the spontaneous defensive organisation which the body enacts against pathogenic aggressions.

Where, one could ask, do such specific characterising individual differences come from?

I think that it is possible to assert that they are mainly originated by experience, as the latter powerfully conditions every single mind. Only a few biochemical internal modifications are actually known at present to researchers but, of those few, some may be regarded as already characteristic of a mental state or even of mental alterations. In other words these biochemical modifications are not the cause but rather the consequence of an altered state.

When someone suffers from hallucinations he is obviously using the cerebral structures capable of originating the hallucination. Such structures activate all the neurones, or all the substances that have an influence upon the neurone and that relate to that particular physiologic situation. The altered mind is actually using the body to develop its own pathologic identity and any biochemical alterations are, in such cases, the result of a specific particular mental state.

Inversely, the body may initiate a mental disturbance, as one might observe in some cases when there is a severe alteration of a body organic function. If for instance someone is about to develop a diabetic coma, the mind can't be expected to function normally. Its anchorage to the nervous cells, or neurones cannot take place satisfactorily when the whole system and its possibility of survival are threatened by the dramatic lack of insulin.

Although there may be a constant reciprocal relationship between body and mind, it isn't nevertheless possible to establish a concrete connotation for any mental state, just by identifying a substance that may be responsible for it. When an unforeseen casualty takes place in the area of physicality, the system responds with an amount of mental answers but it also produces the substances that might help to tolerate the painful event.

There is a continual interplay between any act that might be regarded as an almost "utterly mental event" and the somatic consequences of the latter. Similarly a primarily physical event may be of enormous consequence for the mind. In the relation between mental situations and immune processes one can see the connection quite precisely. The immune responses are phenomena of complex organisation and can therefore be influenced even by slight mental events, as the complexity is easily disturbed by the alteration even of one element. For instance, the emotional stress caused by a loss could be insurmountable and the global organisation of the responses could be modified and lead to an abatement of the defensive system. If, on the contrary, the emotional stress were to be surmountable, a series of biochemical responses might facilitate the immune processes.

Chemical substances sometimes also tend to intensify the pre-existing orientation and general disposition of the subject. An exciting substance may have a sedative effect on a calm, peaceful person but it may increase the aggressiveness in someone prone to criminal activities.

It has been demonstrated that any emotional, psycho-social, or even just anxiety provoking stimulus, acts upon the hypothalamus and, through the hypofisis, determines an increase of the adrenogenic hormones and of other not yet totally defined substances[46]. When the hormones increase in quantity the immune responses vary, i.e. the thymus is inhibited in its lymphocytic production, with consequent loss of defences against neoplasms and related pathologies. The oncogenic factors may be present but inactive in healthy individuals and that might remain inoffensive when the immune system is intact, tend therefore to develop.

The cellular activity called Natural Killer seems to be of essential importance in defending the body against cancer. The interferon is believed to be the main regulator of the N.K. and to be released by the cells under the direct influence of the Central Nervous System[47]. Furthermore, M. Irwin found low amounts of Natural Killer in women who had undergone extensive changes in life and feeble immune responses in depressed patients[48].

It is well known that the body continually develops cancerous cells and that the immune system destroys them, an inhibitory interference of the immune system can increase the possibility of survival of the cancerous cells and these might multiply and originate neoplasms. It is nowadays proved that emotional stress can contribute to the development of cancer by interfering with the normal reparative processes of the damaged DNA[49]. Harassing occurrences, even of a common nature, may furthermore significantly modify natural physical defences.

Returning to the main vertex of this discussion I believe that it is possible to hypothesise that a state of emotional stress might require a great amount of energies apt to confront the environment. This situation might consequently cause a diminution of the mental cathexis that should be devoted to the organisation and the unconscious co-ordination of the different physical sub-systems. These have the capacity to preserve homeostasis when in presence of external stimuli, such as spoken words for instance, or a change in temperature etc.

Trying to establish, for example, whether the function of self-thermoregulation should be regarded as belonging to the body or to the mind would be useless. Likewise in case of an excess of heat or of cold originated by metabolic or endocrine irregularities. The sub-system, in fact, only functions in and for itself, it has no access to global perceptions or to what one might call the intent of the system.

Experiencing psychic pain might therefore be considered as a safety device to avoid becoming irreparably mentally ill. The same might apply to physical pain in relation to the body.

The enormous amount of information deriving from sensory functions can, at any given moment, wholly transform the body-mind relationship. The violent untamed emotions still persist deep down but the interaction between body and mind may rely on the activation and reorganisation of the functional areas related to sensory experience.

This doesn't of course imply that the reorganisation happens by the defeat either of the psychic or of the physical area. Some people, for instance, experience a state of depression after a surgical operation and need to reorganise their physical sensitivity via "unconscious" tests of their own reflexes. They are actually structuring anew their contact with physical sensory reality. This kind of reorganisation is a general phenomenon and can happen on many different occasions – after childbirth, after surgery with or without a mutilation etc. It is a necessary state for children who need to incessantly reorganise their own world.

Although the process leading to the Eclipse of the COO is always the same, one can see that it can be quite complex and that it may need any number of adjustments. Such capacity for adjustment has previously been extensively attributed to the mind. Clinically the process may be understood by observing the modes of communication between the Onefold and Twofold of the analysand and by underlining his or her degree of perception and of experience. This procedure progressively supports growth.

When an analysand's focal points are touched and mobilised in analysis, deep emotions are unleashed and furthermore provided with a clear physical quality. This implies that when the analyst operates at the psychic level he also necessarily modifies some aspects that belong to the physical domain. Furthermore, whenever there is a physical reconstruction, the pre-eminence of a sense organ may cease in favour of another. The physical changes that some analysands undergo during their experience of analysis are quite well known. Often there seems to be an increased capacity to look after their own body more, widely speaking their looks, accompanied by an improved capacity to express their needs. Sometimes the needs aren't expressed, yet there is evidence of a kind of visible, concrete or even tangible message. It isn't here a question of attributing a psychological significance to the organs or a symbolic value to objects. The theory of symbolic over-determination of organs isn't very satisfactory, maybe because it originates from the oversimplified equation between organs and functions.

In mentioning the body and its functions I am referring to a full and complete state of activity in which all sub-systems relate to the so called "physical system". The latter is presided by a kind of "black box", called "psychic system" that has no casual origin but came into existence for the specific *ad hoc* aim to allow the best possible survival of the physical system. The Twofold therefore receives and organises informations that are both internal and external to the system and progressively occupies the area that is left free by the Eclipse of the COO.

One can thus understand how the relationship between the COO and the mind, or between the two levels of functioning that can be observed from the initial phases of existence, is of vital importance all along the individual life span. Although the slow Eclipse of the COO might progressively make space for aspects belonging more and more to the mental area, therefore capable of absorbing the ethological drive, it seems highly unlikely that the Eclipse of the COO might reach a full and complete expansion. Emotions never really lose their violent, intense, unpredictable quality and are, all through life, arduous to contain and transform. As it is, the mind probably represents a valid protecting screen for the body, and the body, in its turn, for the mind, except in the frequent disharmonious states in which one of the two prevails upon the other.

In these pages I have very often used the word "body" to designate the full and complete activity of all the sub-systems relating to what I have arbitrarily called a physical system but I have also often stated that there is very little information about the body in itself. The information we all have about our body derive from phantasies produced by the mind in relation to the body and to anything that is mobilised, in the body, by such phantasies. By the term body I do not mean, it might be useful to repeat, the object of medical practice or of medical sciences but rather the body that is perceived, lives, the actual individual corporeality, a body that since the beginning of neonatal life experienced maternal reverie, that was fully taken care of by a mother so that mental experiences could be experimented (baby talk etc.), or again so that mother could minister the mental states and the body could therefore experience itself (muscular or cutaneous pleasure etc.). Such a condition enables the child to experiment that the body "communicates" through different levels of functioning and reaction, and that it actually becomes present with an amount of different features, through its sub-systems, in the global mind-body system.

Contemporary research work in paediatrics, H. Als' of the Boston Children Hospital about premature babies among others[50], seem to highlight the intense and specific relationship between Onefold and Twofold. The brain of the premature baby seems, in fact, to be capable of registering environmental information but not of regulating the input. This is due to the lack of maturation of some neural circuits related to the cortical associative areas, responsible for the selection of inputs and therefore for the inhibition of some of them. These circuits are formed, according to L. S. Siegel[51] between the 26th and the 40th week of gestation.

The preterm child[52], even in the very basic functions of life, shows evidence of an instability of homeostasis that may persist some time after birth so that environmental modifications (auditive, visual, tactile stimuli etc.) may determine a loss of stability of the cardiac, pulmonary or thermoregulating functions among others[53].

Severely premature babies usually appear to have very few postures, their movements are limited and their sleep is prolonged. These aspects can be seen, according to Als as part of a "time-out signal", a request to be allowed to re-organise their rhythm and autonomous control (breathing, cardiac pulse, temperature, digestive and excretory functions) as otherwise a state of turmoiling disorganisation might ensue. Als developed a model for the assessment of the development of premature babies which he called "Synactive Theory of Development"[54]. He regarded the different aspects of the premature baby's behaviour as the result of the interaction of several sub-systems. The development of the sub-systems takes place according to an established sequence and it is only when each system reaches some kind of stability that following system can begin to function properly. The sequence could be outlined as follows:

a) the autonomic organisation
b) the beginning of organised behavioural responses
c) the reciprocity with the social environment

Very premature babies are characterised by a lack of stability. Environmental stimuli can therefore provoke a loss of equilibrium of the whole system. Such babies are unfortunately unable to signal, codify and hence express their state of internal disturbance in order to limit the upsetting stimuli. It has therefore become necessary to find methods of observation of the babies' spontaneous behaviour, and to avoid methods implying any manipulation. It is also necessary to use special care in any kind of medical therapeutic intervention. In 1982 Bottos started using a *swinging heated incubator* trying to recreate the intrauterine situation of stability and flexibility, in order to promote both the autonomic development and the control of vital rhythms. Als introduced *marsupial care* to adequately solve problems related to the baby's posture. By concentrating all hygienic care in periods in which the babies are awake or just sleeping lightly, avoiding all intrusive not strictly necessary therapeutic manoeuvres, reducing unnecessary strong sounds and lights, it has been possible to improve the level of autonomic control and to attenuate states of apnoea and consequent need for oxygenation.

Obviously when there is no efficient psychic containment, physicality fully reveals its immaturity. P.A. Gorski[55] remarked that when premature babies went home to their families they often had paradoxical responses – such as refusal, vomiting, hyperextension of the head, breathing difficulties etc. – in answer to any exaggerated or excessively intrusive stimulation from their parents. Clearly physical immaturity hinders normal psychic development and any condition of physical turmoil tends to expand in absence of boundaries when there is no adequate psychic container around. The use of the *marsupial care* (introduced by Als) relates significantly to both the physical and the psychic areas, it seems to have a kind of double function, connected to the Onefold and Twofold relationships.

It has been a difficult task, in this whole section, to find adequate names for physical sensations. Medical terms, for instance, refer to a knowledge of the body that is quite distant from any kind of self-perception and therefore of personal experience. It is generally well known that in sleep and in dreams, on the contrary, there is a rich source of information about the complex and intense body-mind relationship. In sleep the body gets rid of its waste and proceeds to self-reparation while the mind is supposed to rest by detaching its sensors, so to speak, from the external world. In sleep the sub-systems may well prevail, for the psychic super-structures, oriented towards the external world, greatly reduce their functions. The activity of the physical sub-systems is both basic and unintentional, but it still might enable some kind of mental transformation in the form of dreams. M. Klein believed that all physical situations are met by some kind of mental activity. Some dreams provide examples of this hypothesis, for instance the dreams that relate to bodily needs.

In sleep and consequently in dreams, the distance, correlation or inter-relation between body and mind is reduced, if compared to the distance in wake. States of sleep in adults can be compared to states of wake and sleep in new-born babies. In the states of wake of adult life, on the contrary, both systems – that is, the body and the mind – have much more extensive global needs. Finally in sleep the physical and psychic systems are in the best condition for a possible development of functional exchanges and integration.

I have spoken elsewhere[56] of the function of dreams. In my theory the dream is a mode of facing new events by producing hypotheses that the mind can then integrate and develop. This might explain why the day's residues may be thought of, and regarded in analysis, as either useful or sometimes even ineffectual communications.

I have stated earlier that the physical system has different times of development from the psychic system. I am now again stressing this notion while discussing the privileged function of dreams in integrating the two systems. States of severe mental disturbance create, on the contrary, the maximum distance, yet, even in these cases, the physical sub-systems seem to be able to preserve their biological vital functioning and there often isn't any apparent negative physical consequence. On the contrary when the actual vital capacity is reduced there seems to be a global problem, it becomes a question of life and death. Some people have scarce vital capacities and these seem to favour death, as death is seen, in some extreme cases, as the only and perfect response to life.

NOTES

41 W. Penfield (1974) *The Mystery of the Mind. A Critical Study of Consciousness and the Human Brain*, Princeton University Press.
42 Sacks O. (1990) "Neurology and the Soul", *The New York Review of Books*, Vol. XXXVII, N. 18, Nov. 22.
43 Spinoza B. (1677), *Ethics*, translated and edited by E. Curley, Penguin Books, London 1996 p. 71–72.
44 Croiset G. et al.(1987), "Modulation of the immune response by emotional stress" in *Life Science*, 40, 775–782.

45 Fleshner M. et al. (1989), "Reduced serum antibodies with social defeat in rats" in *Physiology & Behaviour*" 45, 1183–1187.

46 Riley V. (1981) "Psychoneuroendocrine Influences on Immunocompetence and Neoplasia" *Science*, 212, 1100–1109.

47 Heberman R. B. (1982), "Possible Effects of Central Nervous System on Natural Killer Cell Activity" in Levy (ed.) *Biological mediator of Health and Disease: Neoplasia*, pp. 235–248.

48 Irvin M. et al.(1987), "Life Events, Depressive Symptoms and Immune Function" in *American Journal of Psychiatry*, 144,4.

49 Setlow R. B. (1978), "Repair of Deficient Human Disorders and Human Cancer", *Nature*, 271, 713–717.

50 Als H. (1986), "The Neuro-Behavioral Development of the Premature Infant and the Environment of the Neonatal Intensive Care Unit" in J.P. Cloherty, A.R. Stark ed. *Manual of Neonatal Care*, Boston: Little Brown.

51 Siegel L. S. (1982), "Reproductive Perinatal Environmental Factors as Predictors of the Cognitive and Language Development of Preterm and Full Term Infants" *Child Development*, 53; 963–973.

52 Bottos M. et al (1987), "La funzionalità come chiave di lettura per la diagnosi precoce delle lesioni neuromotorie del bambino" in Bottos M. et al. (eds.) *Neurological Lesions in Infancy: early diagnosis and intervention*, Padova: Liviana.

53 I wish to thank dr. Bottos for providing me with a bibliography on the subject.

54 Als H. (1982), "Toward a Synactive Theory of Development: Promise for the Assessment and Support of Infant Individuality" *Infant Mental Health Journal*, Vol. 3, n. 4, 1982.

55 Brazelton T. B., Davidson M. , Gorski P. A. (1979), "Stages of Behavioral Organization in the High-Risk Neonate. Theoretical and clinical considerations" *Seminars in Perinatology*, 3: 61–72

56 Ferrari A. B., (1983) "Relazione analitica: sistema o processo?" in *Rivista di Psicoanalisi* 29,4, 476–496.

SECTION II

The Dawn of Thought

5

THE OEDIPAL CONSTELLATION

HISTORICAL FOUNDATIONS

The Oedipus Complex is a concept of fundamental importance for the development of psychoanalytic theory. Psychoanalysts have relied upon it for their technique during several decades both to measure their patients' psychic development and to forecast potential therapeutic results.

Freud[57] gave the name of *Oedipus Complex* to a functional compound of different aspects of the personality which he had discovered while observing affectionate relationships and orientations of desire connected with the phantasies about, and/or the loving attitude towards, the parent of the opposite sex. Together with a wish for death of the rival parent such a configuration expressed the Positive Oedipus, while hatred for the parent of different sex and love for the parent of the same sex expressed the Negative Oedipus.

Freud mainly focused upon the choice of the object, although he also delineated the importance of the Oedipus complex in structuring the personality as well as in giving shape to interpersonal relationships. He situated the Oedipus complex in the phallic stage of children's psycho-sexual development, between three and five years of age. He described furthermore a pre oedipal phase, characterised by a dual relationship, and a triangular Oedipal phase leading to the conclusion of the Oedipus complex, before the beginning of latency which is when super-Ego and Ego-Ideal take shape. This is – according to Freud – the development of the Oedipus complex in such situations as one might call normal.

Freud also mentioned that there are infinite possibilities for adjustment in this process, and that in extreme cases actual barriers could appear, capable of originating extremely severe psychic disturbances. Freud's description of the disturbances which relate to the Oedipus complex is still in use, to this date.

In the Oedipus Complex one can see that there is maximum involvement both of physicality and of the psychic area. On the one hand it brings to the surface the conflictive inter-twining of the child's feelings and phantasies in relation to the parents, on the other it coincides with the phallic stage of the libidinal drive which closely relates (as all stages do) to the corresponding organs or bodily apparatuses.

Freud universalised such phantasies by referring to myth and ascribed a fundamental importance, for sexual identity and for the choice of the object, to the corporeal physical datum. He laid the foundations of his theoretical construction upon instincts and upon mental representation (as exemplified in all his hypotheses: libidinal development, request for erogenous satisfaction, points of fixation etc.).

The multiple feelings, the choice of the object, the innumerable possibilities of identification, the models of the psycho-biological functioning influenced by evolutionary and cultural features, lead to a geometrical growth of the elements involved in the conflict as well as to a variety of possible solutions.

It is an articulate and complex process, bearing incessant developments. Focusing on the dynamic aspects I am therefore suggesting the term "Oedipal constellation" instead of "Oedipus complex" as the astronomic designation seems to better express the diverse multifaceted aspects that form, specifically structure and organise a common area of the psyche.

The term constellation implies the meaning of a great vastness and variety properly representing the psychic time and space and their infinite capacity to expand. Even Freud felt doubtful about the use of the word *complex* as inadequate for a pertinent and exhaustive definition of the concept, though it did express the multitudinous elements involved.

M. Klein investigated the Oedipus complex further, deepening her understanding of the concept from a relational perspective and widening the field of observation to include the first years of life. By throwing light upon the rich world of phantasies of the infant, she created the foundations for the comprehension of the origins of mental life and opened the way to the investigation of primitive disharmonies.

M. Klein[58] anticipated also the appearance of the Oedipus complex to the second half of the first year of life by drawing attention to the traces present in the first depressive elaborations of the baby. In the paranoid-schizoid position, Klein stated, the primary anxiety of the child is dominated by the urgency of his need which drives him to accept external reality. As the gratifying experience is repeated, the urgency orients towards the appearance of the external object relating to the actual need. The passage to the depressive position changes the characteristics of anxiety and coincides with the change from partial objects to whole objects, when

102

the child has to face the fact that mother couples with father. The passage is a hard task for the child, Klein described it as an intensification of the rich production of phantasies and as an expansion due to new emotions and feelings that establish the dawn of the Oedipal situation. Klein therefore mainly focused on the psychic features of the Oedipus process and described its hyper-stimulation by phantasy life.

Bion[59] renewed the concept of Oedipus complex and developed a totally different perspective by considering separately its different elements and hypothesising that they might well be a kind of metaphorical sample of the structure of human individual behaviour. The new outlook is thus expressed: "... I shall rehearse the Oedipus myth from a point of view which makes the sexual crime a peripheral element of a story in which the central crime is the arrogance of Oedipus in vowing to lay bare the truth no matter what cost"[60]. Bion focused upon several different points: the Sphinx that creates the riddle and then proceeds to destroy herself when the riddle is answered, Teiresias the blind man who has knowledge and tries to dissuade the King from his tempting action, the oracle who encourages the action which Teiresias laments and finally the King who answers the riddle and then suffers the blindness and the exile.

There is a scattered collection of ruins: curiosity, arrogance, stupidity are part of the human condition and have an important role in it as they express the individual capacities and the limits in using personal mental resources. Bion's outlook is concerned both with the activity of thinking and with the physicality as it appears in incest, blindness, exile and death. Furthermore it expands the theoretical model of M. Klein by stressing the importance of the Ego's capacities for self-observation and for taking responsibility of one's own perception and for the whole experience. In Bion's opinion myth involves both the psychic and the physical areas. His view isn't distant from Freud's view since the latter regarded the myth as closely related to physical and instinctual drives.

THE OEDIPAL CONSTELLATION

From the moment of birth human beings belonging to most historical cultures, are involved in a triangular relationship with the male/female couple to whom they owe their life. Individual development is thus characterised by two opposing forces: the need for one's parents, who are indispensable for the preservation and development of life, and the need to become detached from them in order to be able to trace the boundaries of one's own individuality. The link between the child's mental function and the registration of the sensory perceptions belongs to an area of activity which is internal to the child – though it takes place with mother's indispensable participation and help – and introduces the child's own individual functional development.

103

The history of the child's individual detachment from the mother is a painful and complicated history. When detachment begins to take place things become even more complicated for the child is bound to register, though he may like it or not, a perception of the father, perception which was anticipated in a pre-conception. When this happens harmoniously the triangular relationship is established and it then begins to function developmentally, bearing its advantageous but sometimes also onerous consequences.

The following case is an example of the consequences that may derive from a difficult and incomplete organisation of the perception of the mother and father figures in the Oedipal constellation.

> G. is an adult woman who appeared to have, initially, a very archaic Oedipal scenery dominated by the character of a hostile, dangerous, judgmental, non accepting mother and by a little girl who felt competitive and aggressive towards her. G. felt that her mother was powerful and overbearing and was also quite envious of her mother's "power". "Today – she said – I find myself saying that I cannot bear a comparison with my mother. Why is that? I wonder, it is a kind of weakness that I have. I am thinking that in those days I was really envious of her! Everything my mother has seems to become of some kind of vital importance. I was terrified as I thought that I couldn't survive without the things she had, the things she could give me! I still feel panicky and it then becomes true that I can't survive without her. I am also thinking that because I think she is so powerful this makes her really overbearing, really over- powerful. She is tyrannical but I know how to deal with that. The fact is that I attribute even more power to her, actual power, more than tyranny. I always thought that it was a very negative aspect but it isn't true, I have actually envied her tremendously for it!". Because G. didn't take responsibility for her desires and for her potential capacities, but rather projected them on her mother, nor did she take responsibility for her own feeling of hatred she then became entrapped in a very archaic passive and almost completely impotent condition from which she could only envy the person upon which she had projected her own potential and her feelings of hatred. As analysis proceeded G. began to acknowledge and to own her own hatred, envy, aggressiveness. The Oedipal constellation was nevertheless still quite static, blocked at a very archaic stage, and lacked the dynamicity that was necessary for the evolutionary development of identity. Furthermore it was crowded and hampered by the exasperating fight/confrontation with mother which endlessly postponed the inclusion of father.

This enables, in my opinion, the definition of the mode in which phantasy-life influences the characteristics of the Oedipal constellation:

1) The Oedipal constellation is a dynamic configuration that constantly tends to reach an equilibrium. The equilibrium is reached when the images of *Ego, Mother, Father* reach a level of representation that is functional to the individual state of psychic maturation.

2) The Oedipal constellation originates the imprint for the development of the psychic individual sphere and acquires different modes and forms of expression according to the different individual developmental phases.

3) The Oedipal constellation is *the ground upon which the research and the organisation of individual identity is based*, including gender identity. It is an unceasing research and a continuous challenge for sexuality since the latter is re-examined again and again, during the whole individual life, at the light of each new experience. The organisation of the Oedipal constellation occupies and somehow delineates the entire human existence.

> During her analysis H., a young woman, realised that she was unable to "give birth", through publication of an essay, to a long research work which she has carried out for years. She suffered greatly from this and linked her suffering to an anxiety connected to the inability to bear children. The difficulty was exasperated by a belief she had about her own femininity. In this area she suffered very deep resistances in letting her gender identity develop freely, as she presumed a very close link to exist between femininity and maternity. She did elaborate and contain in part her anxiety by becoming a mother, but continued to be paralysed by the possibility of "giving birth" to a work which was, in her mind, almost finished. She in fact started to ruminate about it and in so doing greatly augmented her anxiety. At some point of her "labour" she told about a dream: "I am in a restaurant and am sitting at a table with a man, a woman and my father. The woman is an expert in my own field. I talk to her but without mentioning my own complete research. My father says I should tell her about it, as an exchange of ideas might be useful and I suddenly turn to him angrily, because I feel he is intruding into my own affairs and say – How can you know what it is that I want to do? – I then woke up in the utmost anxiety and thought of something which I felt was certainly originated by the dream, although I wouldn't know how. The reason I am not making my work public is because I fear that, in so doing, I may trouble my father and mother!". H. then continued: "In the same morning as I was walking into the library I had this thought – I am going to ask to be allowed to give a paper about the subject – and I did! I understand now that, as in child-bearing, if the baby can be born everything is fine, but if there are

problems then some help should be provided". In her dream and in the consequent thoughts H. visualised the scenery which was saturating her mind: "By holding my work back I stay on as a young daughter, close to an adult father and mother. They act and are the main characters, I look at them, I am their public and post-pone the moment in which I will become the main character of my own life, with a real job, real earnings, a real autonomy. In the past I didn't want to disturb them so that I wouldn't be disturbing my own position as a spectator. All this seems absurd now".

4) The Oedipal constellation might be said to belong, in its archaic form, to a phylogenetic inheritance.

5) I define the Oedipal constellation the point of equilibrium between the vertical and horizontal dimensions, and consider it *the founding structure of interpersonal relationships*.

6) Excessive projective and/or introjective identification may easily cause the rupture of this delicate equilibrium.

7) The rupture of the dynamic balance which characterises the Oedipal constellation originates a loss in the sense of identity.

8) The Ego's form and temporary dispositions depend from the equilibrium of a complex psychic configuration on the foundation of each individual person's Oedipal theatre. The latter comes into being and is organised by the compound of a person's experiences and relationships.

9) However one may observe it, the Oedipal constellation can be defined as similarly functional in both sexes

10) The appearance of problems and of inhibitions in the development of children may be regarded as a sign of disturbance in the elaboration of the basic triangular relationship that engages the Oedipal constellation since the beginning of life.

J. aged 34, was a woman who often said that she had "no inter-est in becoming a mother". Eventually she had a relationship with a man and discovered with him some aspects of her own feminine sensuality and sexuality and she also thought at some moment that she might like to have a baby after all. She actually became preg-nant twice but was then unable to tolerate the explosive conflict between anxiety, pleasure and violent hatred and therefore had vol-untary abortions on both occasions. A kind of internal scenery eventually took form in the analytic sessions. At the beginning of adolescence whenever J. felt that she was alive and that she was a woman (in her body, mind, emotions etc.) she also felt violently destructive. The facts were that J.'s father and mother quarrelled violently and came apart when she was still in the cradle, and her father told her mother that their daughter would love him much more than she, the mother, ever had. The mother told this to J. when she was 12 and insinuated that the father might have had incestuous desires towards her. After fighting and being unfaithful to each other for years her parents eventually divorced when she was 17. J. seemed to develop a kind of theory: "nothing can be born in me and from me as my existence was the source of destruction of man and woman, of masculinity and femininity and of the possibility of a relationship between the two". With such a theory J. established that she could only exist as the daughter of a mother who needed someone for whom she could suffer. J. could only feel guilty for the world's pains and for her mother's suffering. Her intense, violent hatred was explained by her feeling that she was after all a victim of other people's insensitiveness and aggressiveness. Whenever she experienced pleasure or felt that her life was rich and complete, the anxiety related to her destructiveness came forward and she felt driven towards violent self-punishing behaviour. Thus she was unable to hang on to her pregnancies. She tried to get rid of her anxiety by getting rid of the babies and, at the same time, punished herself for she "dared to exist" or, for a moment, "dared to have the power of giving life to another being". Her punishment really consisted of a kind of self-castration.

I have already mentioned that, at the beginning of life, phylogenetic inheritance strongly influences the manifestations of the Oedipal constellation. The archaic infantile Oedipus is characterised, mainly, or even solely, by a predominant *exclusive desire to possess*. The desire to possess – a mainly phylogenetic feature – is then transferred into the ontogenetic area where it becomes a compound of organised affective relations. The child seeks, by trying to possess, a "reasonable" kind of reassurance from the uncertainty that is consequent to the loss provoked by birth. Deprived children living in institutions may survive only if they manage to structure or refer to internal parental figures or to substitutes, not just transitional objects but actual substitutive objects, real fetishes.

When the wish to possess is missing or frustrated, autistic situations may derive. Initially the child experiences the parental figures with ambivalent feelings through projections and introjections that facilitate the phantasies of possessing the parents and condition the quality and roles of internal relationships. Later playful relationships with other children facilitate the process of personal individuation and the distinction between self and others. It is another important step on the way of identity formation.

My hypothesis is in agreement with Klein's idea that the Oedipus complex should be regarded as contemporary to the very first appearance of aspects of the depressive position but it is divergent in placing the conclusion of the Oedipus at the end of life. It is also quite distant from

Freud's notion that the Oedipus should be regarded as belonging to the time of life which comes before latency. My belief is that *in latency there is a strong reinforcement of the quest for identity*, progressively approaching the ontogenetic area and increasing the risks of frustration by interpersonal relationships and experiences.

> K. had recently suffered anorexia. She hated her physical aspect for it didn't correspond to her ideal and said that she loathed being a woman and that she thought of her body as of a "traitor". "When I was five I was lovely – she said – nice and plump, my hair long and thick, a proportionate nose. I used to love wearing short skirts so that my legs would show. My mother wouldn't let me dress as I liked and insisted that I should be 'good friends' with the boys and nothing else. At the age of seven I wanted to learn to dance but my father wouldn't let me. I so much wanted my father to love me and understood that there was just one way for that. I had to become as rational as he was, so I became the best student in my class, but it was just because I learned everything by heart".

Thanks to play and phantasies children gradually amplify their contact with external reality. Reality overcomes children's interest for the Oedipal relationships and tends to drive it into the shade. Children then begin to form new identifications which in their turn contribute to enriching the structure of the Oedipal constellation. Thus the ontogenetic area swallows the archaic phylogenetic drive. The experiences of children in latency aren't connected with an open wish for self-investigation or understanding but do relate to a process of discrimination and differentiation of the capacities for introjection so that they may become more adequate and functional to individual needs. Children may, in doing so, come to perceive some sense in their existence, though they may not, as yet, grasp its meaning.

If a mental function typical of childhood – when the process of individuation/differentiation hasn't as yet fully developed – is employed in adulthood, it originates an ever increasing hiatus between the psychic and physical areas.

> A woman in analysis said she couldn't remember the years of her life between the time she was four and the time she was seven. "It seems as if when I was seven you came along and took me by the hand, but when I was four . . . I see myself as a fat little girl in a muddy pool. I was unaware, poor little thing." The analyst said that the muddy pool might well represent a sort of undifferentiated wholeness. "Undifferentiated . . . Masculine and Feminine . . . I still find it useful to be like that . . . Why am I thinking of a little girl who has been raped? It is as if I didn't want to see . . . As if daddy had done

something which I don't want to remember . . . but I have always known . . . It frightens me as I don't know whether it is a wish or a memory". If the child accepts that she has now become a woman she has to transform her relationship with her father and mother, she has to take responsibility for her femininity and her "being". The sense of time and the perception of the limit of each finite experience allow for the organisation of the Oedipal constellation.

The phallocentric theory of psychoanalysis with its exclusion of the feminine components and emphasis upon the sexual aspects is mainly responsible for the somewhat distorted vision of masculinity and femininity. In Freud's view, the choice of the object, influenced also by the phylogenetic drive determined by the genetic inheritance, establishes the gender identity that is fundamental also for the solution of the Oedipus complex. In my hypothesis, on the contrary, because I recognise the function of the ontogenetic area I do not foresee a conclusion for the Oedipal situation but I believe that it develops progressively in adolescence and in adult age. The responsibility for the never ending research of one's own identity is one of the adolescent's main tasks.

"Then I had a strange dream: in a very tall building, offices mainly I believe . . . at least . . . it was full of windows I took the elevator with another girl, it started at a terrible speed, we didn't even know where we were going, I became dizzy then I felt so terrified that I pressed the alarm button. Then the fear was that the elevator would stop between two floors and we couldn't get out". The dream seems to be about a blocking situation in the evolutionary progress of identity. One might imagine that L. when she was about to become an adolescent felt terrified by the incomprehensible transformations in her own body, by the unknown area of experience that was in front of her, by the deep fracture and dazzling transformation towards an unknown world (the uncontrollable elevator climbing at terrible speed) marking the change from child to adult, that is, the beginning of adolescence. One might also hypothesise that, because she was unable to contain the anxiety provoked by change, she may have nurtured the illusion of gaining control by putting a stop to her growth. This kind of answer generated more anxiety, claustrophobic this time, being blocked halfway, imprisoned between the two floors, unable to go forwards, or backwards! The dream continued: "Then I had a very strong sexual impulse, because there was only that girl and the impulse had to be satisfied anyhow, . . . while I kissed her she took from her mouth something like a mouthful of tobacco and some blades, it was a dangerous and unpleasant situation . . . One couldn't tell where the desire came from! Then I came out of the building, I couldn't tell the floor ... I can't say I was actually terrified, more confused I think!". Here the desire was mixed with guilt, it was intense and unrestrainable as a pure emotion, characterised by a state of turmoil. Femininity and adult sexuality were confused with an infantile sexuality in which the wish to possess, typical of the phylogenetic period, prevailed.

The path leading to the definition of oneself through the selection of identification opens the way to an ampler freedom in the choice of the object. The sexual election therefore takes place while the identity is developing and, in its turn, helps it to develop further.

My hypothesis diverges from the Freudian position in two substantial points:

a) I believe that specific phylognetic competencies are included and contained in ontognetic competencies and that both concur in the structuring of identity

b) I essentially object to Freud's idea that there is a kind of deterministic influence in the individual choice of the object and rather believe that the choice of the object is made freely in most cases.

BASIC FEMININITY, BASIC MASCULINITY

The idea that the object may be chosen freely enables me to introduce another hypothesis which I think has always been present both in myth and in individual experience: *the coexistence, enclosed in the framework of the specific genetic sex of every individual person, of feminine and of masculine modes of being.* Such dynamic forces, which press from inside the entropic area, I name *basic femininity and basic masculinity.* They are of extreme importance for the dynamic structuring of identity.

Basic femininity and masculinity may well be regarded as a phylogenetic preconception about the differences between sexes, provided with and conveying information about the functioning of the two systems – the man and the woman. Such information possibly relates both to the specific (respected) aims of each sex and to the tasks of both genders, including potentialities, peculiarities, realisations (it may be regarded as a kind of implicit regulation, following the law of minimum effort as in any phylogenetic information). What actually happens in harmonious situations is that the basic femininity and masculinity either function according to the genetic inheritance and therefore reinforce gender identity, or tend to favour the identifications with the other sex therefore establishing a process that enriches the personality.

The biological genders then meet and intersect with the specific psychic organisations originating in three principal factors:

a) intrapsychic experiences belonging to the vertical and horizontal areas, to the Onefold and to the Twofold, to the internal and external worlds

b) the production of phantasies related to such worlds

c) the movements on the scenery of the Oedipal theatre

The feminine and masculine modes of being can thus be imagined, represented and experienced by each person according to his or her individual possibilities. On these grounds each person somehow creates a kind of personal solution, according to the personal history and peculiarities, to deal with the specific chromosomal sex.

The following example illustrates a disharmonious conjunction of the three above mentioned factors. The quality of the conjunction in fact hindered M. in dealing with her femininity: "There was this dream, I was walking and mother said – "Look you are all crooked!" – Indeed I was walking with my back crooked and my feet turned inwards, so I told her – "You never realised that I had these malformations! You never took care of me! I was just an intercourse for you!" I don't really remember if I did tell her the last sentence in the dream. I wanted to tell her, maybe I was ashamed, but then, in conclusion I did tell her! I wanted to tell her that she never took responsibility, she never noticed!" There seemed to be a kind of overlap between the analysand and the mother. It was evident in the analytic material that she was a severe judge of herself, that she didn't take responsibility for herself and that she therefore projected upon her mother her own intense self-criticism: "I feel great anxiety if I become aware of myself – she said – it is as if I were looking at myself from outside, but I am not afraid of being ugly anymore, of not being pretty. I am kind of not important. Maybe it has always been like this. The awareness that someone might find me attractive was of no relief to me. A young man once told me – after I had said that I had only one son – that he would give me many! I felt almost hurt, how dare he? He had spoken lightly but I felt afraid that everybody would see me under that light, that people might say to me: "You have so many boy friends!" People might have thought that I had a sexuality, the idea made me so terribly anxious, it seemed as if I was bound to find excuses. Other girls had two or three boy-friends at the same time, I had to say that I hadn't, that mine were just virtual! They thought I was 'fast' and I felt sorry about that. But, after all, what that young man had said could have well been a compliment, as if he had recognised I was somehow valuable! 'Fast' on the contrary means that one doesn't behave properly". One can see here that the developmental blockage of the Oedipal constellation is related to a hindrance in the assumption of the identity, gender identity first of all. The desire for sexuality isn't recognised, it is only somehow expressed through feelings of guilt and through a deep devaluation of femininity. This is in a way connected with her accusing words to her mother: "I was only an intercourse for you".

Needless to say, in the analytic relationship, the sexual features that dominate the Oedipal constellation should be regarded just as phenomenological expressions, like all other harmonious or disharmonious manifestations. The Oedipal constellation functions as a kind of centre of gravity or, more precisely, as a fundamental point of reference for the development of individual personality. It is, furthermore, influenced in the horizontal dimension, by projections and introjections and by basic femininity and masculinity. Finally individuals tend to discover in their experiences a fundamental preconception[61] of the existence of father and mother figures. Psychoanalytic practice shows that all the above mentioned elements are the factors which supply the Oedipal constellation with its specific individual character thus originating a variety of efficiently functional or of disharmonious answers.

This is the case of a young woman, N., who expresses alarm and an intense anxiety related to the research of her own identity, connected with the problem of choosing and defining her gender identity. When saying that she would like to re-establish a relationship with a young man which she once was in love with she said: "Maybe I don't know what the truth is or don't say it . . . I want to keep myself away from a deep relationship with a man". Her anxiety about the question of identity appeared to be related to her own specific model of the Oedipal constellation. She had an intimate, worrying closeness with her father and a conflictive and exceedingly envious relationship with her mother. Her emotions were so strong that she was unable to elaborate them. When she approached the area of emotions she immediately developed an allergic rash on her body, mainly blisters on the palms of her hands. Her hands were regarded, in the Oedipal scene, as an inadequate (for they are too small) mode for an exclusive contact with the paternal figure: "I, as a child, was the only one who washed him when he had his bath, the only one who waited for him when he came back". The possibility of establishing a relationship with others (especially with young men) was originated thus, but it was a relationship that had to do with looking after them, taking care of their problems. Sometimes she even felt the need to attack them, "make them suffer" so that she could them proceed to console and support them.

O. was a young woman aged 25, she had been in analysis for about a year when this session took place.

O.: "Yesterday I dreamt that my mother died. I can't remember exactly, after that someone touched my body frontwards but I placed that hand behind . . . I thought that my mum's death is that when she left I kind of cancelled her . . . better being touched behind than in front."

Analyst: "When your mum died your femininity also died, but femininity is internal so there is hatred for your mother but also for yourself. Why don't you try and think why she dies? What is it that unclenches the hatred?

O.: "I do understand that some of the things I do really hurt me . . . this thing that I can't manage, it is as if I ate too much . . . I don't know how to say it, I feel 'normal', I go out with my friends I even went to a party. A girl-friend asked what it felt like to drag the boys so much. I don't feel like talking to people, I don't care, if I were different they wouldn't behave like that, mine is just an attitude."

A.: "Seducing everybody and then saying no? What does it mean? You say you feel ill at ease but I think you feel quite ambivalent."

O.: "I am thinking of when I put the hand behind, I always try to be on my back. Oh! Last night I had a dream. I was making love and then at the crucial moment in comes my sister saying that I should go and speak to N. on the phone. N. is vomiting and is very sick!"

A.: "What do you think?"

O.: "That I halted something."

A.: We have a model of you as a child walking into your mother's room and finding your mother and V. making love. They do not stop.

O.: "It was my first experience, I had never seen my father and my mother together . . . My sister ran away, I was alone, the three of us alone . . . (she cries)

A.: "It is difficult to accept one's femininity after such an experience, if there is a confusion between what one felt at that moment and what one may feel in a loving relationship today".

In order to become a woman, to assume her own femininity O. had to accept her own experiences and feelings and to feel and discern them from one another. She needed to be able to discern joy from pain and love from hatred and to recognise them as her own. It was the price she had to pay in order to grow up and to succeed in establishing an adequate relation with the world.

When the conflict can be dealt with, the identity develops and achieves a kind of dynamic equilibrium that enables continuous re-examinations and re-organisations of each emotionally significant situation, leading either to further developments or to a delay, depending on the case. The possible variations will then continue to function all through life and only become extinguished with death. When, on the contrary, the conflict is, for some reason, arduous to deal with, the development of the Ego may then be hindered and the structuring of the Oedipal constellation may be arrested.

"When I go to bed and say my prayers – I am almost ashamed to mention it – something comes to my mind. It is about when I used to stay awake pretending that I had a tooth-ache. I felt that I had been bad, that I had spoiled their party. I felt responsible for every-thing, though I couldn't deal with anything. I couldn't fall asleep because if I didn't listen I couldn't control. I was there to save my family! My father! If I ask myself now what I was like as a child it is as if there had been some violence, a kind of rape, or some-thing dirty, but it was my fault! I always feel that I must justify myself, whenever I have a sexual desire, it is as if I didn't deserve it! The other thing is that I see everybody as if they were small, though we are all adults by now. I see us small for it feels safer. Even in the past, being "small" meant "no sexual maturity".

The analysand appeared to be caught in a primitive kind of Oedipal constellation related to an idea of herself as 'capable of spoiling someone else's party' (her parents' party) if she dared, harbouring feelings of curiosity, or desire. Everything had to be still, she had to catch her breath or she might break everything around her. She attributed a potential of destructiveness to any feminine pleasure or desire that she felt emerging.

"I am thinking – she said – that the problem is in looking, in the way in which I show myself. As soon as someone looks at me I feel that I am someone who behaves badly. Then I think that in all my relationship with my mother, I always denied myself the pos-sibility to look. I remember there was a mirror, it was impossible not to see, but I never saw anything, as if the mirror were opaque. There was a boy, he was kissing me, I looked at myself from out-side, saw the whole situation and thought "you are ridiculous", then the craving was gone. When I left the session, the last time, after we had spoken of this, I thought you must have been angry. When I said that boys were looking at me I believed that you were thinking something like "How can you expose yourself like that!"

When I dream I can't look at myself, if I look I can't fix the image.
I feel dirty for looking, or that the thing I look at is dirty, and
makes me dirty. Looking means being involved in or even taking
part in the guilty action".

Looking was for this analysand equivalent to being involved or
even taking part in the guilt, in other words 'participating' in the
parent's erotic games. But looking was also the analysand's privileged sensory channel (the psychic co-ordinator that provides the
means for the perception of sensations, emotions such as hatred,
envy, desire etc.) and it compelled her to confront herself with her
real life, with the fact that she was now a woman, and to abandon the undifferentiated condition in which she had obstinately
sought refuge. She could thus begin to notice some 'proportions'.
Time passed, she couldn't really control it, her father and mother
were growing old, she was bound to change in her relationship
towards them. She herself became older. She had to face her own
'growth' in its historical reality, the space/time co-ordinates which
were blurred when she was a child. She now needed to 'grow up',
assuming a definite, differentiated position and facing the conflict
with the 'other woman' – her mother.

Because I consider the Oedipal constellation from a new perspective, regarding the choice of the object as an ontogenetic achievement, I have come to
believe that the concept of perversion, a concept that has been employed by
psychoanalytic thought in a rather reductive and simplistic manner, should
also be revised. It seems in fact to have become less and less adequate to
contain the complex and dynamical elements of identity and, even more, of
gender identity. In the new perspective it seems more and more difficult to
discern desires, behaviours and acts that might be defined as perverse.

In Freud's view, because the Oedipus complex has phylogenetic origin,
it has an unique character closely linked to the area of instinct and very
limited possibilities for further development. It only allows for the enclo-
sure of the sexual sphere in a kind of polarity of alternatives, perversion
and its opposite – that is the non-perversion – somehow implying normality.

Thus limited in its horizon, the concept of Oedipus complex develops
in clinical practice, some aspects which partly betray Freud's point of view.
In 1905 Freud wrote: "Thus the extraordinarily wide dissemination of
the perversions forces us to suppose that the disposition to perversions is
itself of no great rarity but must form part of what passes as the normal
constitution."[62] Perversion, he apparently suggested, might well be part
of normality.

In our scientific discipline the concept of perversion tends to have quite
a restricted meaning for it is connected only to the area of sexuality. The

introduction of the ontogenetic origin to include and absorb, as it were, the phylogenetic response seems nevertheless to be more adequate and respectful of the metamorphoses in gender identity. The gender identity thus acquires a kind of dynamic quality that enables it to respond flexibly to all kinds of individual needs and vicissitudes. Finally, by giving attention, in clinical practice to the aspects that I have named as basic femininity and masculinity, psychoanalysts may discern, in the complex of stimuli and reactions that characterise the area of gender identity, the presence of attitudes and choices that are pre-eminently defined in psychoanalytic literature as *perverse* but that are actually quite necessary to the specific individual configuration.

My hypothesis seems, in other words, to allow for the overcoming of a static understanding of sexual behaviours, the kind of pseudo-moralistic attitude that discredits scientific research as it transforms it into a kind of stiff set of preconditioned rules in which the aim of reaching a harmonious psychic development is forgotten.

In the new different horizon which the hypothesis discloses, we might possibly agree to call perverse, really and truly perverse, the static maintenance of behaviours which are alien to the functional development of any given individual, emphasising that the term 'perverse' may really acquire meaning only if it is referred to the vicissitudes of a single specific individual in a specific situation.

The following case illustrates some perverse features hindering the realisation of the processes necessary to the pursuit of identity. This analysand provides us with an example of static repetition of behaviours which definitely does not respond to his own functional needs, as he repeatedly relies on a mode of mental functioning which keeps him distant from the perception of his own vital necessities. Is this to be considered perverse behaviour? Again in this case the term appears to be dense with burdensome meanings, ponderously related, once again, to the sexual sphere. I would definitely prefer the denomination "altered behaviours" as this might better illustrate the great amount of variables which intervene in the pursuit and formation of identity.

P. is a 35 year old man who asked for help as he suffered from an invasive anxiety about being, on the whole, inadequate or, even worse, a failure. He spoke about the strong inclination he had felt since the age of sixteen to use feminine underwear. Since sexual maturity until he was 25, he had sexual intercourse with men, then he became interested in women, mainly in prostitutes. He stated that he felt that he now very much wanted to seduce women. He was capable of understanding that these behaviours and feelings were related to his search for identity, gender identity in particular. He mentioned that his homosexual intercourses had the aim of enabling him to learn how to use his own penis: "to be penetrated in order to learn how to penetrate!". Though there had been, up to that moment, little information about the analysand's Oedipal constellation and therefore about the specific mode in which the masculine and feminine characters were organised in his mind as well as about the relationship which he established with them, one could still think that his was a rather peculiar mode of facing the lack of experience about his own masculinity and that, lacking for some reason, the consciousness of his masculinity, he was trying to dig it out by using the basic femininity of which he seemed, on the contrary, more aware and confident. He did think that his phantasies were strange but he felt that it was somehow natural to think of himself wearing feminine underwear.

My hypothesis is that the relationship/confrontation with the other sex might appear to him as an extremely anxiety-provoking mode of learning about his masculinity. Adolescents often complain that they don't know "how to do it technically" though they might have received information from peers, read books about it etc., before facing the unknown lot of their first sexual experience, over-whelmed by the turmoil of unfamiliar sensations and emotions. Their experience is unique and unrepeatable and may therefore originate a deep anxiety which makes the feeling of solitude of the actual experience impossible to tolerate. One might hypothesise that the analysand might have turned to his similar instead of facing the difference and "covering the gap" towards the other sex. "To be penetrated in order to learn how to penetrate" is almost like saying: "Teach me practically how I might use my penis". At the same time the gap is covered by "dressing with femininity" his unknown and unexplored masculinity. All this seems to lead to a sort of arrest rather than to a choice of identity. The analysand hadn't chosen heterosexuality nor – could we say he had definitely selected homosexuality. He said he had no interest in men, didn't want to touch them, he thought their body was useless to him and that he could do without it, he was only interested in their penis. He mentioned that he had transgressive phantasies in which he was the main character and a great seducer, he also had the habit of dressing like a woman and of having sexual games with men and women. Sometimes this took place in a group but only with unknown partners and in occasional meetings. By so doing he would become very excited and had an erection that enabled him to have his homosexual intercourse. In the group he also needed the presence of a woman, acting as a kind of tranquilliser for him.

One felt that, though he was an adult man, married, with children, his psychic scenery was still quite archaic and that there was a predominance of the phylogenetic aspects in which the feminine figure, well-known and ever accepting, made him feel reassured and encouraged while he was showing off as a great seducer. He seemed to be a kind of child, not yet an adolescent, unaware of his being a male, using a stratagem that he thought would avoid the obstacle but he was actually just slowing the process of knowledge and acquisition of a gender identity. He described a dream in which two penises were facing each other while an electric discharge went from one to the other until eventually they appeared to be almost one on top of the other. The analysis was now requiring to investigate whether he regarded the emergence of his masculinity as a violent competitive element of conflict with his own father, therefore impossible to be thought about or dealt with, and whether he had decided that his only possible choice was to avoid the obstacle and take refuge in an amplification of the basic femininity. In any case by continuing in this undifferentiated situation in which masculine and feminine modes confusedly coexisted, possibly kept him protected from the feared anxieties and from aggressive conflictive inclinations that didn't allow him to investigate and discover his own specific mode of being.

One might therefore regard as perverse the static continuance of behaviours that are totally distant from his need for investigation and self-knowledge, rather than the sexual phantasies or the dream material he had brought.

IDENTITY AND THE EGO

All human beings who are born on this earth are born either man or woman. A look at the physical aspect is sufficient to establish at birth the difference in sex, but the physical nature doesn't alone establish the definition of the gender. It is not just a question of being born man or woman but rather a question of being *that one little boy or girl,* with that one physical apparatus and instinctual cathexis.

All human beings have to face, in their life, the problem of their own identity, something that goes well beyond the question of gender identity. Identity has to do with recognising oneself as an entity among other entities, and this process requires different elements as well as peculiar biological and psychic characteristics accompanying each individual during the whole life. The specie each individual belongs to, the social status,

118

the culture of the group, the capacity to create myths, the religious choices, the ethic, poetic, and aesthetic sense are some of the elements which form the essential endowment of each individual.

Psychoanalysis has endeavoured for a long time to deal with the problem of defining the question of identity by using the term Ego, first employed by Descartes, though it is a term that carries the burden of metaphysical implications.

In 1920[63] Freud moved on from the initial delineation of Ego (a direct and intimate derivation of the Id, as a result of the impact of external reality and of identifications) to a partially new definition of an Ego as a person (system) and an Ego as an agency, both pertaining to a compound of psychic aspects of which the Ego is just a part.

The concept of Ego as person relates more closely to the essence of Freudian topography than the Ego as agency for the latter implies dynamical aspects which don't, by definition, belong to the former. This might well be one of the essential problems with Freud's notion of Ego. It is an Ego that constantly oscillates between primary and/or secondary processes.

I wish to investigate the nature of the Ego using the concepts of vertical and horizontal axes in order to circumscribe, on the one hand, the essence of the Freudian Ego, and on the other to delineate a hypothesis on the basis of my own experience.

In the vertical dimension the primary psychic processes prevail. The language of the Ego is therefore easily overwhelmed by states of alteration originating in the arousal of intense conflicts. Thus the field is easily opened to states, often temporary, of depersonalisation, hallucination and de-realisation.

The horizontal dimension may foster the manifestation of the primary psychic processes in two ways. It may support or even nourish such processes by supplying an even temporary stability or it may perform its complementary function imposing reality, mitigating distortions, and thus offering more adequate and functioning instruments. Such features belong by definition to the area of secondary psychic processes.

Some of the difficulties which Freud found in mapping and circumscribing the different aspects of the Ego might have been due to his not considering the Ego as the combined entirety of all founding aspects in the psychic system in other words as the combination of body and mind or the continued blend of versatile and very dynamic adjustments going well beyond the narrow limited conception, for instance, of the Cartesian Ego.

My hypothesis doesn't allow for the relations in the system to be considered symmetrical. For example when the reality principle imposes itself in the vertical dimension connected with the body, the process takes place in modes and forms that are very different from the modes and forms that could appear in the horizontal dimension. The modes in which a reality which originates in the external world (horizontal dimension) appears to the individual have a different meaning, a meaning with different functions, from the modes that are elaborated by the vertical dimension. Everyone knows about the psychic conflicts that are generated by this kind of asymmetry, originating in the different modes in which the internal reality gathers and faces external reality, and vice-versa.

This may well have been one of the reasons why Freud attributed to the Ego so many different and somewhat irreconcilable functions such as the control of movement and of perception, the reality test, anticipation and temporal organisation of mental processes, the functions of rational thinking and their opposite, misjudgement, rationalisation, compulsive defences against instinctual needs, opposition to or acceptance of the latter, objective knowledge and its systematic deformation and, finally everything that means, justifies or opposes reason and passion.

I do realise that in dealing with this subject, I am in danger of getting caught in all sorts of possible misunderstandings as the concept of Ego isn't at all defined, it isn't even linguistically determined. The meaning of the Latin word Ego or of the English "I" cannot even be properly described. The French linguist Benveniste[64] asserts, for instance, that the word "I" only acquires its meaning in relation to the specific sentence in which it is used and to the specific nature and conditions of such a sentence[65]. Even in this very reduced context it may appear as a somewhat excessively dense or even rigid notion.

The nucleus of identity is, nevertheless, above all what each human being feels that he or she is and that doesn't ever change, not even in the most dramatic situations. One may well change, one may adapt to the most incredible situations but one still continues being oneself. Human beings have a kind of resistance, a profound continuity, even when experiencing extreme conflict between opposite or antagonist drives, when they are compelled to chose something that is the opposite of their actual desire.

During life one is constantly driven by one's wishes, choices, expectations to which one endeavours to respond with attitudes that do no always reach their aim and satisfaction. Furthermore one often has impossible objectives and life anyway continuously brings forward new and further situations. One changes, consciously and unconsciously, acquiring and losing parts of the world, interests, motivations, choices and preferences, up to a moment in which one feels different, sometimes even indifferent or extraneous to oneself. Yet one still is oneself for one still is Onefold and Twofold.

> Q. was an adult woman who, after three years of analysis, had taken better responsibility for her own life, activating a harmonious mental functioning, creating links, learning from her own experience. Nevertheless, at some point, a different response became quite evident. Again she reacted to the perception of significant internal and external changes by hindering her own research for new meanings and endeavouring in every way to re-establish her old "theo-

120

ries". During a session the analysand said: "I do perceive the emotion but, instead of following it and experiencing, I drop it because it doesn't correspond to the idea that I have of myself. I just consider my idea, the idea of myself, of my Ego. So there is nobody in my mind to receive my emotions. It is as if I had put a fake puppet there to avoid the anxiety of that empty chair where there is nobody to receive my emotions. I should be there instead".

Analyst: "Which "I"? You are changing all the time, do you realise that?"

Q.: "It is true. I am not anymore the person who came into this room about three years ago, what is it then that gives me the sense of continuity?"

How can we possibly demarcate an identity that is so deep that the term "I" isn't sufficiently significant for it? In order to come out from such a difficulty we may dismiss the rigid concept of Ego and rather think of a dynamic entity, capable of expansion or contraction which we could name *ego configuration*[66]. The term seems to indicate adequately the concept of identity, of its variations and fractures, and to qualify its intense versatility and plasticity, as well as the different degrees in structuring.

Again I find myself in agreement with Freud's crucial contribution when he seemingly tried to establish a closer significant relationship between the biological representation and the psychic transposition: "The ego is first and foremost a bodily ego . . ."[67] The idea here seems to be that the Ego may be regarded as a psychic system originating from the specialisation of corporeal functions.

I do find myself in agreement with such a formulation if one limits it to the definition of the concept of Onefold, though the existence of the latter may only be conceived in the relation Onefold – Twofold.

The essence of what I am suggesting by the concept of ego configuration is precisely the possibility of discerning the two components, Onefold and Twofold, and of identifying the contributions which each of them can bring to the structuring of individual identity. For the structuring to take place the relation between Onefold and Twofold shouldn't become a fused relation, a kind of overpowering or domination of one upon the other. It should on the contrary respect the separateness and distinction between the two and permanently allow a functional opposition, relating to different contexts and necessities in the area that has been defined as ego configuration.

R. was a twenty year old bulimic young woman who said that she had discovered that she was terrified by the full perception of pleasure, especially when it was linked with situations that had to do with femininity. Her Twofold was totally predominant and had a defensive function. The equilibrium was altered between the

Twofold and the aspects of physicality, related to the intensity and the satisfaction of desire. During a session the analysand eventually introduced a difference between saying "to be a woman" and saying "to be a female". The second sentence conveyed, according to her, a kind of blind, mindless, animal-like quality which highly devaluated the concept of femininity. The first on the contrary conveyed features that weren't necessarily feminine (the capacity to develop one's projects, the intelligence etc.). She said she felt intense annoyance or even repulsion if a young man, whom she liked very much, showed interest towards her such as, for example, taking her hand. In these situations she used to draw back, almost in disgust, then she would tell him that other girls were prettier and more desirable than herself, up to the moment in which the boy left her and went to the girl which she had indicated. Then her 'foresight', as she put it, was confirmed. Eventually she became able to abandon her theory that she had an unfavourable or unlucky destiny, and realised that, if a boy she liked became interested in her, she found herself perceiving, very clearly and intensely, that she actually "existed" and was "taking a shape" – the shape of a "female", that she was becoming defined, she was growing up, occupying space, and that the feeling that she had desired, for her femininity, was qualifying her specific existence. This perception, nevertheless, immediately originated an intense anxiety that she might get lost in her own mental space, which she felt to be limitless. The process of gaining distance from the perception of existing was then increased by means of a massive hindering of her sense organs. She said she couldn't distinguish sweet from salty food, warmth from coldness and so on. This might have been an extreme attempt to defend from the anxiety unclenched in her by the emotional flood related to gender identity which was becoming progressively more precise, thanks to her analysis and her process of growth.

The different points which I have been discussing lead me to reconsider the concept of splitting inasmuch as it is regarded as a defence mechanism. I do not intend to revise the function of splitting in protecting and regulating mental life as it is an activity of selection, a decisional function that facilitates individual psychic growth and shouldn't be confused with negation or disavowal. In this meaning one might rather define this process a "selective function" rather than a splitting, as it provides the possibility of doing away with useless or unimportant elements that are devoid of meaning or of function, a mental activity that is quite similar to the discriminating activity of memory. Something that is done all the time while acting or, more generally, while living.

It isn't therefore the role of splitting but rather the context in which it takes place that I am going to discuss as I believe it would be advisable to exclusively use the term splitting to indicate the defence mechanism that takes place in openly disharmonious situations. In the other cases I believe that the dynamic concept which I indicate by ego configuration is somehow in contrast with the notion of splitting of the Ego or even hinders the use of the latter. I am inclined to use terms that have a lesser drastic meaning and that seem to be more coherent and in line with my notion of ego configuration, such as limited cohesion or fragile structuring etc.

If one, on the other hand, were to follow strictly Klein's definition of splitting, the single phantasies or the phantasy life, which any individual believes to be excessively dangerous to be retained in the circuit of mental activity, should then be regarded as definitely and irremediably excluded from the ego configuration. One should be reminded that this process originates an extremely severe and irreparable loss, leading to great impoverishment of the individual's psychic resources.

One shouldn't nevertheless exclude that, in some specific situations with many constructive features present, some of the elements, excluded through splitting a long time before, may be eventually recuperated.

> This is the case of a young woman who chose splitting as her mode of mental functioning thus causing a total impoverishment of her own psychic resources. In analysis a re-emergence of rich but threatening psychic material took place initially in the form of dream material and then, some months after a crucial dream, in the form of "inexplicable visions" during the sessions. In the dream there was a newly born baby, lying close to a mother who didn't look at him, she rather ignored him. The baby risked being suffocated by an overflowing excess of milk flooding his face. In the dream the analysand watched the scene without intervening. Months later, in the "vision" she saw her own mother breast-feeding her brother who was six years younger than herself. She was upset in seeing that her brother seemed to be about three years old. She then felt that she had to ask her mother about this and discovered that her brother had been breast-fed to the age of three. When such events took place the analysand's mental apparatus couldn't contain them, maybe because it was still immature or maybe because the events had an extremely intense emotional effect on her. Some time before the dreams and the visions, she said something about herself, that could now be better understood thanks to emergence of the split material: "My mother told me – she said – that when I was about nine or ten years old, I was in hospital quite a long time because I had stopped eating. I have no memory of that and I can't understand why I did it. But I do know that I began eating again because I couldn't avoid it". The

123

analysand then associated feelings of disgust and suffocation to the scene of the vision ("too much milk for too long") mixed with unconfessed feelings of hatred and of hatred and envy. Milk is both an element of richness and vitality and a suffocating murderous inundation. The contradiction in the datum is so profound and radical that it becomes "unthinkable" and has to be excluded as the mind cannot contain it. Thus the symptom is produced and it is just as dramatic and contradictory. She stopped eating as if she needed to die, in order to be able to live.

Klein focused very significantly on the use of splitting as an extremely functional defence mechanism. She also described the essential importance of splitting for the survival and growth of the infant in her hypothesis about the paranoid-schizoid position. I believe that this kind of splitting may be regarded as positively functional even when it takes place beyond the first months of life and up to the end of latency years. From there onwards, if the mechanism continues to exist it acquires a mainly disharmonious character.

Splitting presumably happens when a highly persecutory experience takes place. Its ultimate result is, nevertheless, that the splitting becomes an insoluble problem in itself. This aspect is often clinically significant. When the splitting is taking place, the split material is interesting as it is exactly the material that is regarded as impossible to face, the actual object of terror. When, on the other hand, the splitting has already taken place, something quite different, almost opposite may happen. The mechanism of splitting may become in itself the main mode of mental functioning, whenever an even minor threat of possible frustrations is present. Hence a permanent dangerous impoverishment of the psychic resources is determined, permanent because no one can in fact remember what one doesn't in fact know has been forgotten. This extreme situation only refers, of course, to very severe cases.

S. is a 40 year old woman who revealed since the beginning of her analysis an almost insurmountable difficulty in establishing a contact with her emotional states. She expressed them through her visual, auditory, olfactory and synaesthetic sensations. When she said therefore: "I see . . . I listen" she exclusively meant that she saw through her eyes and listened through her ears. She said that if there was silence at night she felt compelled to make noise: "Listening to the noises I know that I am there, otherwise silence invades and crushes me out, or I suddenly think I am deaf . . . I can't be in total darkness as it makes me anxious that I am blind". She said that she had no memories of her past though some traces appeared in analysis, "visions" or olfactory sensations that she couldn't explain. Such phenomena appeared to be coherent and syntonic with the questions that were discussed in the sessions. At the beginning of each session she seemed to have nothing to say, but then, with the help of the analyst, she ended up discussing significant subjects. Experiences seemed to leave no trace in her, even when she came to daily sessions. Every session would begin with her saying: "Do say something, I can't just be silent". One could see the results of continuous splitting. A splitting so continuous and massive that the analysand's mind became as bare as a lifeless, desert, lunar landscape. Every vital issue, every perception and emotion induced a sudden, intense, unspeakable, uncontained anxiety to which the analysand responded by an impulsive compulsion to eliminate. She immediately "cut off" all possible connections between sensations and emotions on the one hand and their potential meanings on the other.

In the section of "Clinical Applications", where the case is presented in more detail, the function of the analytic relationship will be explored in relation to the prevailing influence of splitting upon the mental functioning.

The situation of the individual who cannot forget what he remembers though he may oppose a "temporary" refusal to perception (disavowal) or artificially endeavour to disown it (negation) is quite different. Disavowal and negation as defence mechanisms, needless to remind, have been discovered and described by Freud who admirably discussed their functions with his usual astonishing capacity for intuition and accuracy.

In the following example one might hypothesise the presence of a disharmonious use of disavowal as a defence and observe its implications in the analytic dialogue. T., in the course of analysis, managed to structure an image of herself composed of contrasting aspects. In the past she used to simplify the picture of herself and made herself blind to some of her own characteristics which she then projected onto someone else, with whom she then established a dependent relationship based upon envy.

T.:."I don't know what to do."
Analyst.: "Your system is structured to forget the experience which you have of yourself while living so you don't realise that you are already *doing*."
T.: "I don't have myself anymore. I don't even have my suffering. I just perform my destructiveness and thus get evidence of my system and of my monstrosity. It is perverse, I do realise that."
A.: "Can you see better what you call perverse now? Your forget-

125

ting doesn't mean that your mind doesn't register the experience, it is just that you ignore it or refuse it and then interpret it using your own preconceived theories. This means perverting the order and functioning of your own mind."

T.: "I wonder if I can tolerate suffering since I have created this whole system to take distance from it."

A.: "If you can bear all this, that is the consequence of your inadequate attempts at self-protection, why shouldn't you be able to bear the painful aspects of life? You do have a measure of your capacity to tolerate pain."

T.: "I can't understand that."

A.: "This is because you try to forget or refuse your experience. Your friend's death! Don't you believe?"

T.: "Yes. It's true. I suffered. I suffered and was able to recognise the pain for her absence."

A.: "It seems to be an acute and intense pain."

T.: (Crying softly) "Just that."

A.: "Can you feel that this pain is very different from the pain which you cause yourself with your distorted manner of treating yourself?"

T.: "Yes. Totally different. This is a precise limited pain, the other, the one I cause to myself is unlimited and can't be dealt with."

I believe that, in dealing with technique and clinical work, the term splitting could better be regarded as referring to a violent final act towards the analysand's ego configuration, while the terms negation and disavowal could apply to acts which, though interrupting perception, still enable it to continue to exist inside the ego configuration. The denied features, the features which a person refuses to perceive and the possibly recuperated features, all continue to belong to the ego configuration which continuously tends to be discomposed and recomposed in new kaleidoscopic assets.

This intense degree of dynamicity is the essential feature and deserves to be highlighted together with the discomposures and recompositions of the different harmonious and disharmonious levels of the psycho-physical system of an individual.

The concept of ego configuration also opens to, and harmonises with, the hypothesis about the co-existence in every individual of both masculine and feminine modes of being in the frame of any one specific genetic code. The asset of the ego configuration is in fact what enables a person to deal with basic femininity and masculinity, for the latter are projected, according to individual possibilities, upon the maternal or paternal figures and thus confirm the specific equilibrium of the Oedipal constellation that is functional to individual needs.

I have stated earlier that the Oedipal constellation determines the ego configuration, yet it is the ego configuration that enables the renewal of the Oedipal constellation thanks to different and new experiences.

In the child's Oedipal constellation there is first the mother[68] and then the father. Father and mother function as prototypes for an inexhaustible series of other characters, to which infinite roles are attributed, ontogenically chosen roles, functional to the research of personal identity. Characters and roles that, as I have already stated, always refer to the initial Oedipal games and to their phylogenetic origin.

In the Oedipal theatre many and varied scenes may be put on. When the ego configuration has little cohesion and a limited amount of structure the scene may be populated by live objects, sometimes whole, sometimes in their emphasised or deformed parts. The scene may also be inhabited by inanimate objects provided with anthropomorphic or zoomorphic characteristics. Mountains that become terrific Cyclopes, shadows that become invincible animals, dark nights that take the aspect of implacable murderers, embroideries or stains that give life to deadly and repelling insects in a terrifically persecutory atmosphere. All this happens because a highly destructured ego configuration is easily and deeply influenced by all elements present in real life.

In their actor's role the objects may represent emotions and feelings of different kinds and aspects, delusion with sounds, voices, ghosts, shadows etc. depending on the emotional intensity present when the ego configuration loses its structure.

The complexity of the ego configuration is revealed by the thick population of characters that creatively and sensitively characterise the images they originate.

Each individual constructs his own warp, in other words a kind of personal compromise between the vertical and horizontal relations, the warp then binds and determines the action of the characters of the Oedipal scene, leading either to harmonious or to disharmonious equilibria, depending on the possibility of supplying the components of the ego configuration with coherence and consonance, or the opposite.

SOME THOUGHTS ON ANALYTIC WORK

The application of my hypotheses may open the way to significant modifications in analytic work. First of all it may contribute to cultivate further the analytic capacities to listen and to investigate with obvious advantage of the relational situation in the *here and now* of the session. It may enable the understanding of the patient's actual feelings of the moment and the comprehension of the complex of emotions, feelings, mental states which take shape in the innumerable characters of the Oedipal scenery, evoking and representing the past and present vicissitudes and needs of the analysand, expressed in their more or less archaic forms.

In order to evaluate the patient's degree of structuring, it is very useful for the analyst to observe the emotional movement and the internal and external relationships, both affected by feminine and/or masculine modes of being.

The analytic relationship creates an unconditioned space for the patient's internal world, thus enabling the dynamic world to be revealed. One might see for instance that a patient with severe symptoms related to the absence of mobility of the ego configuration also reveals in analysis a kind of numbness in the Oedipal constellation.

U., a young woman, associated the event of becoming an adult with states of aggressiveness and violence endeavouring, for instance, to exclude her father from the Oedipal scenery in order to delay temporally the perception of her becoming, and being, a woman. While this question was being dealt with in her analysis, she had a dream that might well be regarded as an initial admission of her difficulty in perceiving her own "growth" as well as the emotions related to it. In the dream two hamsters were torn to pieces by a group of cats which she tried to stop, an uncle of hers said that he would do "an operation on the brain" to one of the two animals and precisely cut its scruff. Some kind of force, unrestrainable at least in her perception, was threatening something that was "small and fragile" and which U. didn't want to lose. "I couldn't preserve the two hamsters and cried desperately and helplessly. A terrible pain . . . I had this dream just after the session in which we spoke of my fear of growing, I don't know if it has to do with the development, with what is happening in the sessions. I feel as paralysed as if I were in a marsh, things are confused. The most frightening thing is that I am motionless and don't know what direction I should take. It is as if I were small and confused. I am afraid that I am giving so much power to my mother just to keep my situation unchanged". The analysand appeared to have a deeply conflictive relationship with her own mother. She was influenced and "overwhelmed" by her mother's judgement but also felt a deep silent hatred hidden behind a kind of submission which she called "hiding behind the vestment". "It is as if I had always lived with a vestment on – she says – subdued to my mother's influence, it was sacred for me, and when she judges or bosses me around I feel paralysed as when I was small". A manner of keeping the situation stuck by distancing the perception of one's own sensations (in the dream the uncle cuts the scruff of the hamster wounded by the cat), the ones that are connected with pleasure and sexuality more than all the others. When the analyst asked her if she was afraid of perceiving tenderness, pleasure, desire U. answered: "I believe the mistake is in denying that a man may give me such sensations! So afterwards I have a grudge and actually say that I had no pleasure . . . It is all quite strange, relationships are difficult . . . it is either just about feelings, like here in the therapy . . . one has to deal with the fear of loss, or of death . . . it is hidden, it is as if tenderness might evoke loss. If one experiences it, one then can't bear the loss if someone dies. I always think I am afraid that if I become part of a couple then, if the man dies, I will feel such pain, now I also feel it but . . . then I realise that the really fierce pain is about mother and father, they are the eldest in age so if one feels the tenderness, the loss is immediately there".

One can hypothesise here the presence of an intense anxiety related to the notion that time is limited and unarrestable, a notion that the analysand hasn't metabolised, a death anxiety in other words. The ego configuration is blocked in a childish mode of functioning, timelessly bound to a subdued mode of relationship with static authoritarian parental figures who exercise an overwhelming power upon her. If she decides to live they will die and, furthermore the analysand doesn't want to perceive that they are becoming old and approaching death as this would mean perceiving that time is passing for her as well and that she is bound to live and eventually die as well. Every possible movement is perceived as a threat to this state of affairs, but this state of affairs originates another kind of anxiety connected with the sensation of being "imprisoned in a kind of marsh" and of not finding her way out.

Some traumatic experiences destroy the structure of the ego configuration and originate disharmonious features. Such experiences are in some cases added to, or grafted upon, the vicissitudes of the Oedipal situation and thus tend to recompose it. In other cases these destructive experiences may require a revision of the whole structure of the Oedipal constellation.

The analyst of course aims at facilitating the development of the new revised structure. It is therefore necessary, in clinical work with patients with any kind of symptoms or difficulties, to explore both the Oedipal constellation and the ego configuration, at first separately and later in their reciprocal interrelations. When a revision of the Oedipal situation is necessary, this means that there has been a more or less partial loss of identity, and that the nature and intensity of the loss is related to the severity of the actual disharmonious state. The analyst has to rely on his sensitiveness and experience in order to firmly but delicately accompany the patient, at the moment in which he is more vulnerable, without invading the area of the patient's most personal choices.

The elaboration of states of mourning may in some cases give us an example of the research of new equilibria and new modes of functioning aiming at contrasting the de-stabilisation which has taken place in the Oedipal situation.

> V. was a young woman in analysis whose ego configuration severely lacked cohesion. The dramatic and traumatic event of her mother's suicide caused a sudden breakdown and she therefore repeatedly needed psychiatric residential care. Between one admission and the other V. attempted suicide by taking drugs. When V. was eight her parents had divorced and she stepped into taking father's place in looking after her mother, in satisfying her mother's need for love and in taking a paternal role with her younger brothers. Omnipotently she regarded herself as essential to and worshipped by her mother. When she thought of her own marriage (her mother died when she was eighteen) she had phantasies about a relationship between herself and her mother, and her future husband was expected to be a kind of guardian for that. Work with this analysand showed that, because she hadn't been able to elaborate her mourning for the loss of her mother, her Oedipal situation was de-stabilised and pushed out of balance for a long and painful period of time. Her Oedipal scenery was persistently anchored to phylogenetic requests. She was imprisoned in a childish mode of thinking, a possessive mode and was therefore compelled to dangerously postpone her search for identity, gender identity above all. Thus the analysand maintained that her sexual relations had the aim of turning people into slaves and keeping them close to her (her sexual activity was indiscriminate and promiscuous). "I bait the hook with vague hints. The ones who understand know what I want, if they want it as well – all for the better". She also went out with homosexual groups and tried to join a homosexual association that had some kind of political flavour. She felt transgressive but also uneasy and only became aware of her uneasiness with the help of analysis. V. apparently found it very difficult to structure her gender identity and couldn't grasp the notion of a mode of being alone that really meant "being alone with herself", as this caused her an exceedingly intense anxiety. In order to avoid the anxiety she had continuous erotic contacts, feeding the omnipotent illusion that she was thus controlling the other's movements, her own distance from the other, and in some ways her own emotions and involvement. Possibly an intense hatred, maybe towards life that had deprived her (by the separation between her parents and the death of her mother), of the protection and warmth of a family, originated the process of self-

distancing just at the moment in which she was about to begin to know herself and structure her own specific mode of "being".

When the Oedipal equilibrium becomes rigid it may lose its stability in several ways. It seems important to highlight that:

a) In some cases the sudden loss of stability activates emotions and feelings which then bring out aspects and behaviours that are felt as terrifying and dangerous. In such dramatic moments the mind of the patient may give shape to some unforeseen omnipotent and tyrannical character which then imposes itself as a kind of director upon the ruins of the Oedipal equilibrium relating to the ego configuration itself. The director is created and nourished by a paralysing paranoid panic and commands all egoic functions, overwhelming all the other characters – which may be representing needs, emotions, fears, parental images, masculine or feminine points of reference – and distributing forced roles. One can observe how day after day the director-character can easily tyrannise the personality, sadistically, masochistically or self-destructively, through behaviour that recalls the activity of Klein's archaic cruel Super-Ego, originated by the use of rigid operational structures scarcely connected with reality and incompatible with the introduction of any new models. It may be useful to specify that such behaviour does not relate to an experience of regression but rather to a pathological organising principle of the personality, specifically structured for the aim. In other words a substitute of the constructive functions of the ego configuration.

b) It sometimes happens that the de-stabilisation of the Oedipal equilibrium originates a state that may transform the basic femininity and masculinity into persecutory figures, either seductive or destructive. In severely disharmonious situations for instance, the gender identity is easily questioned or even upset. When such a disturbance takes place, analysands express their sense of loss in analysis, as well as the terror that they may have lost the characteristics of their gender identity.

c) The de-stabilisation of the Oedipal equilibrium may damage the internal points of reference and establish a potentially self-damaging behaviour which in less severe cases may be facilitated by repeated failures, phobia about one's emotions or refusal of physicality. The same disharmonious state may be caused, at an intrapsychic level, by an excess of destructive envy, lethal competition or of the narcissistic excesses that concur in determining, in extreme cases, the elimination of all the characters belonging to the scene of the theatre. The ruins of such theatre will be then dominated by a lone dictator.

The examples that follow illustrate the relation existing between the Oedipal constellation and gender identity in the frame of the ego configuration.

In the first case, though the Oedipal equilibrium which W. has established is an attempt at composing the elements relating to basic femininity and masculinity in the vertical dimension, it is also so fragile and rigid that it becomes severely de-stabilised in the presence of new, unforeseen and unknown emotions, originated by significant modifications on the plan of the horizontal dimension.

In the second case X., the analysand appears to have a highly disharmonious ego configuration dominated by a single character with whom she totally identifies. She does acknowledge the persecutory aspects of the character but she cannot abandon it as it contains some of the founding facets of her own mind. It is therefore a question of diminishing its expansion and of harmoniously making space for the voices of all the other psychic components.

The definition "false self" is in my opinion of little help to describe this phenomenon which I believe to be much more complex. It is not a question of regarding anything as false or to be disposed of from the psychic scenery of the analysand, but rather of harmonising the analysand's ego configuration, making space and giving prominence to each component, including the one that is considered "false".

W. was the youngest son of an alcoholic prostitute mother. He never saw his father but had phantasies about him. "Surely a man from the south, very much of a man". As a child he used to play girlish games and often had girlish attitudes. Apparently he was his mother's favourite, a cuddled, gentle, sensitive child (his two sisters were drug addicts while his brother was violently masculine and behaved delinquently). When he was six years old his mother died. In adolescence he seemed to solve the problem of gender identity by becoming a homosexual. He felt compulsively attracted by "very virile men" (just as his father was virile in his phantasies) and had violent sado-masochistic sexual intercourse with them. He identified with Kim Basinger, the actress, and dressed just like the Italian singer Patty Pravo. He wished he were a female, hid his penis, had phantasies of undergoing surgery in order to become a woman.

It is possible to hypothesise, from these initial data, that the search for complete identification with feminine figures may be seen as W.'s extreme attempt to save himself from the loss and destruction of the feminine figure by an underlying persecutory figure. W. "enters a woman's skin" and saves his mother (by becoming the lovely actress, or singer) but loses himself as a son. He needs confrontation with his father figure but this is an impossible operation as there are no father figures around (except for the violent delinquent brother)and the need is compensated by an anxiety-provoking phantasy of a threatening, omnipotent and terrifying father (all the more terrifying since he is unknown) that has to be kept at bay by seduction. Here are the characters of W.'s Oedipal scenery indicating the main, basic woof of the constellation.

The structuring of gender identity takes place through an exasperation of the elements of basic femininity deriving from the horizontal dimension in an attempt to protect a basic masculinity that doesn't get enough physical foundation (the body is slender and frail if compared to the brother's body) or enough psychic support (no strong male figures for masculine identification) so that it can't be expressed, strengthened and enriched in the act of existing and of being experienced. Because he has taken the femininity upon himself (mother) at the cost of damaging his masculinity, W.'s Oedipal scenery now hosts two characters: analysand/mother and father. The necessary movement between the three figures that composed the Oedipal constellation is thus blocked. The unity between masculine and feminine features is regarded as violent and can't therefore promote creativity or growth. The process of differentiation-individuation is arrested. The resulting homosexuality cannot be considered a choice but rather an imposition, as it is an answer to anxiety. It is a disharmonious element for it is based upon a stiffening of the modes of identification in the Oedipal constellation. Psychically it is a situation of such extreme conflict that an identification with the other sex prevails. There is therefore no enrichment of the personality and the way to a modulated acquisition of gender identity is barred.

W. started analysis when this defence proved inadequate for the elaboration of the affective urges awakened by social pressures which made his passage from adolescence to adulthood undeferrable, as well as by the beginning of a homosexual relationship that was significant in terms of affects. Homosexuality was a disharmonious response but it enabled him to postpone the question of the choice of his own gender identity and to reach some minimum degree of aggregation in his ego configuration, extremely fragile but reassuring for him. In beginning a loving relationship, though with a partner of his own sex, he felt exposed to a bursting uncontainable emotionality that he dramatically expressed through a rupture of the same ego configuration which he had "gathered" with difficulty up to that moment. He presented himself in this way to the analyst at the beginning of analytic experience. A homosexual who said that he couldn't recognise himself when he saw himself in the mirror, who couldn't find his way out in the street being in the grip of states of depersonalisation, and

who had lost his sense of time. W. was also pray of states of terror. He could see himself from inside, and could see his internal
organs, he was also extremely anxious about dying. He had tried
to get rid of his fear and anxiety through an incessant homosexual activity, but he had now started to think, and though his was
a kind of delusional thinking, it did originate a kind of restricted
space suitable for the beginning of his analytic work. From this
moment onwards the analytic relationship enabled him to reconsider the characters of his Oedipal constellation and to start a
process of reconstruction of a rich ego configuration and of its
articulated components. He could, in other words, begin to trace
and differentiate the elements of his basic femininity and masculinity which he had previously "condensed" in a unique character, in order to cling to the illusion that he was actually controlling
his aggressiveness and violence. As a conclusion of this process he
seemed inclined to take upon himself his masculinity (different
from the masculinity of the father figure which he had once idealised) softened and enriched by the creative, loving, sensitive features which belonged to the area of basic femininity.

An analysand once expressed her gratitude to the analyst as she
could now see the anxieties and the pain she had been in when she
had put up her rigid dysfunctional defensive barriers. Her thickest
and more frequent barrier was her capacity to interrupt her perceptions (attack on sense organs and on their function of psychic
co-ordinators) so that she didn't have to take in the emotion that
was reaching her mind through her sense organs.

X.: "You grasped my human essence and didn't let yourself be led
astray by me, by my tricks; you understood my human essence and
my suffering behind my devilish self-blocking. This has been of fundamental importance for me as I tend to forget my own suffering,
I tend to forget myself and I am simply pray of "my monster" once
I have put him in motion. X. defines "monster" the compound of
preconceived ideas about herself and her relationship with the
world and with life; her theories mixed with her hatred, competitiveness, blind violence, envy. "My monster – she says – becomes
my second ego, my identity".

X.: "I am thinking that I must approach my monster and restore
the dignity of my perceptions and feelings, even to the monster so
that it will become less horrible, or even funny or at least it will
be reduced. I can't and must not destroy it for it contains something of me . . . My problem is that I am scared of myself, of what

134

I can do. I need a dam to limit me, something good and human, that might help me to acknowledge myself. I live amidst monsters, but you are offering me a flower. Thanks to that I can move about in the room. Why can't I find this flower by myself? I think this is quite the key of my state of dependency and anxiety about dependency. If someone else becomes so frightfully important for me, things can't possibly work".

Analyst: "Your gratitude is a critical affair then. The question is that you tend to keep your monsters to yourself and attribute your flowers to others. Then you love and hate the other but above all you are envious, that is, you envy something that actually belongs to you though you don't recognise it does".

X.:" I cut myself in two and keep the hatred to myself, leaving the love to the other. There are aspects of myself which I have frozen in challenging my father and mother – my hatred, my perseverance, my stubbornness, my rationality. I feel guilty and disgusted by all this, yet those might be important features of myself. Maybe they contain my strength which I should retrieve and use.

Analytic interventions should, at all times, highlight the mode in which the analysand is making his characters act on the Oedipal scene. The latter will thus throw light upon the analysand's own mode of development. On the whole, analytic work (including both the vertical and horizontal dimensions) should obviously relate to the analysand's actual possibilities of elaboration. Dreams, associations, memories, desires, expectations and needs should be seen as instruments that may foster the definition and the strengthening of new internal projects. All this may enable the analyst and the analysand to visualise the psychic movements, following the phases of growth and the related new capacities to tolerate anxiety and to deal with conflicts.

In this way, the analysand's proposals, more than any paradigmatic model, enable the analyst to perceive, in interaction with the analysand, the complexity of the situation and the mutual commitment to a shared experience. This doesn't mean that the transference[69] should be regarded as a concept whose importance is diminished but that it should be precociously taken into consideration and employed as a kind of guidance for analytic propositions, depending on the specific emotional urge that is experienced by the analysand when he requests the analyst to participate to any particular internal situation.

The analysand's models of development can be observed in his mental functioning which generously provides evidence of the degree of cohesion of his identity in the modes and forms of his relating to himself and to his emotional world. Modes and forms indicate the degree of structuring of his ego configuration both in the vertical and in the horizontal dimensions. Progressively enlarging his awareness and knowledge of his internal world and acquiring confidence in himself, the analysand can make more space for the horizontal relation and for external reality. His new capacity to make space for the other in his internal relationship can be perceived, in the analytic relationship, as an increase of suitable material for the elaboration of the transference.

The theory of the Oedipus complex used to provide most valuable information and revealed the deep multifaceted human essence together with its dynamics. A scenery in which love and hatred, father and mother, son and daughter lived and acted in a dramatic atmosphere, allowing in the analysand's paradigmatic essential aspects, capable of originating development and acquisition.

The hypothesis of the Oedipal constellation may be regarded as a more complex and functional instrument, as it links with every day life and with an unceasing experience of different equilibria both for analysand and analyst. A powerful experience that may produce vast modification in the analysand, connected with his choices in life, his behaviour with emotionally significant figures, his active existence.

NOTES

57 Freud S. , (1905) *Three Essays on the Theory of Sexuality*, SE, London: Hogarth Press, vol. VII.
58 Klein M., (1952) "Some Theoretical Conclusions regarding the Emotional Life of the Infant", in *Developments in Psycho-Analysis*, Hogarth Press, London
59 Bion W. R., (1958) "On Arrogance" in *Second Thoughts*, London, Heinemann 1967 reprinted by London, Karnac Books 1984 p.86.
60 Ibid. p.46.
61 I am using the word preconception as it has been used by W. R. Bion and am extending it to the Oedipal area since in archaic stages phylogenesis dominates and conditions the Oedipal scene.
62 Freud S. (1905) *Three Essays on Sexuality*, SE, London: Hogarth Press, vol.VII p.171.
63 Freud S. (1920) *Beyond the pleasure principle* SE, London: Hogarth Press, vol. XVIII.
64 Benveniste E. (1996), "La nature des pronoms" in *Problèmes de linguistique générale*, Gallimard, Paris.
65 Benveniste also states that the form "I" only exists, linguistically, as the word that actually pronounces it. (Ibid.)
66 In Italian the term configurazione egoica emphasizes the dynamic and temporary quality of the configuration rather than the static essence of the Ego (T.N.).
67 Freud S. (1923), *The Ego and the Id*, SE, London: Hogarth Press, vol.XIX p.26
68 A reminder might be necessary that the mother is, in my hypothesis, the third in addition to the Twofold, in the Concrete Original Object: thus a triadic situation is formed, different from the Oedipal triangle that will follow.
69 I am employing the term "transference" in its more extended meaning, that is as a model for object relations. Cf. the section "Analytic Applications".

6

EXPANSION OF THE CONCEPTS OF VERTICALITY AND HORIZONTALITY

THE CONTACT NET: A HYPOTHESIS

My hypothesis about the Eclipse of the Concrete Original Object (COO) implies that the sensations (Onefold) have in themselves a kind of tension that drives them towards the harbour of the mind (Twofold). Sensations may therefore be expressed through emotions and feelings and may be qualified as potential sources of thought.

With the denomination COO I am emphasising the existence of a unity composed of a physical body, the sparse sensations that come from this body and a mental apparatus characterised by the functions of perception and notation. For this reason we may conceive, developing from the Onefold to the Twofold, a line that connects physicality to the progressive structuring of the mental area. Along this line of development, the COO begins its Eclipse and consequently reduces its original turmoil.

The COO is the datum, the mind begins to function by relating to this datum-presence. The history of the development of any mind and of its functioning, including the disharmonious aspects, may therefore be regarded as a continuous attempt at understanding the corresponding individual physical essence.

Sensations and emotions therefore *require* being "thought", it is a process that necessitates a specific focusing on such sensations and emotions in an area that could well be defined as *mental*[70] (an area, in other words, liberated every specific time by the Eclipse of the COO) and that makes abstraction and thought possible.

How can such a process take place with a datum-presence? The body, by its continuous stimuli, obviously interferes with, contrasts and disturbs

the processes of thought. The human mind incessantly experiences turbulences of this kind and these are then often transformed into conflicts.

The emotional world may establish a contact with the area of thought
by promoting or rather by stimulating an opening towards the rational
and abstract aspects that will then be able to represent it, inasmuch as
there is, at each moment, the minimal required condition which has been
defined here as "mental area". By mental area I mean the distance that
is required for the sensory stimuli to be focused upon and "enabled" to
originate the foundation of thought.

I think that this notion of a mental domain may allow for an expansion of the concepts of verticality and horizontality. The dynamic relation
between the two complementary dimensions implies the co-existence of
two areas, one entropic and the other negentropic. As I have stated, the
hypothesis of the COO presupposes two kinds of primary relationship,
the first, child / external world / mother, enables the *primary horizontal
relation*, while the second, mind / COO is the *primary vertical relation*.

It seems important to remember that in the vertical relation the COO
isn't just the body, commonly understood as the objective datum but rather
a body that emanates sensations, a living body, an active presence. An
object for the mind that registers it but a subject in respect of the external
world.

The COO is at the same time object and subject. The mind is therefore bound to regard this entity as intimately belonging to its own
individual identity; an integrated feature of the latter but, at the same
time, a diametrically opposing presence, almost an other, distinct from
itself. The diversity is sometimes dramatically experienced. One might
think of cases of severe illness, or the death threat that might originate
from the COO.

These two primary relations are established at the beginning of life and
continue all through life, though not linearly but rather through continuous restorations and mutual referrals. It is therefore possible to isolate
and discern, amidst the different aspects of a personality, the symptoms,
attitudes and actions that prevailingly link with the primary vertical relation and the ones that link with the horizontal relation, not so much as far
as their genesis is concerned but rather for their present dynamical essence.

One might usefully describe the two relations as axes or co-ordinates.
The single elements of a person's life, the different features of personality
can be then regarded as points of encounter of the segments originating
from the two co-ordinates, representing in fact the individual's actual experiences, starting from the sensations, emotions and feelings and
progressively reaching a more unitary mode of expression, or manifestation, in thought. The foundations of such a process I postulate as a *contact
net*, originating in the intersection of the continuously emerging sensations-emotions with the *versatile possibilities of thought* (with the latter

138

stimulated by the former).

The points of intersection I will call *knots*.

The contact net is therefore the result of the vertical and horizontal dimensions but, at the same time, allows for the articulation of the two dimensions[71]. It is the place in which representations belonging to the horizontal area are invested with a significance relating to the vertical area. One should keep in mind that the horizontal dimension enables the representation of anything belonging to the vertical dimension but doesn't provide meaning (emotional content) as providing meaning is the task of the vertical dimension.

It may prove useful, before discussing the functioning of the contact net, to clarify the relation existing between the vertical and horizontal dimensions on the one hand, and the classical Freudian systems – unconscious, preconscious, conscious – on the other. When I mention the Freudian notion of unconscious, I refer to the hypothesis which Freud formulated around 1920 in which the distinction between unconscious and preconscious was based upon a differentiation inside the system (from this perspective, my notion of an ego configuration could well be regarded as the notion of a partly preconscious and partly unconscious entity). Freud's main interest was, at this point, in the dynamic rather than in the topic quality. A change in perspective which unquestionably imposes itself in the clinical experience. The mechanisms involved, distinctive of a primary process, were mainly condensation and displacement. The contents, indicated in Freud's 1915 paper "The Unconscious" were the "instinctual representatives". The instinct nevertheless, avoiding the direct opposition between unconscious and preconscious, was instead placed on the border between the area of the somatic events and the area of the psychic, together with – I would like to underline – the archaic matrices of sensations and desires, the phantasies, the dreams, nocturnal and diurnal, Oedipal sceneries, infantile experiences, parapraxes etc.

The preconscious system is usually regarded as separate from the unconscious system inasmuch as it is affected by the influence of secondary processes. This is nevertheless a rather indefinite differentiation as, on the one hand, some unconscious contents, like phantasies, are modified by secondary processes and on the other some preconscious elements like the dream's day residues are altered by the action of primary processes. Freud's main differentiation between unconscious and preconscious is based upon the fact that the preconscious is entrusted with the function of word representation and therefore with verbal language.

In my hypothesis I focus predominantly on the importance of the vertical dimension. The horizontal dimension couldn't provide the individual person with the particular qualities of a specific object. Yet if a person were to rely just on the vertical relation he couldn't know a thing about himself. The two dimensions are complementary, we can only consider the vertical dimension in relation to the horizontal and vice-versa. There is no person, even a newly born baby, who doesn't have some sort of capacity to somehow elaborate external stimuli. In referring to the notions of consciousness, preconscious and unconscious one is anyhow referring to abstractions useful as they may be. In other words, on the one hand the unconscious may only be grasped if one temporarily sets aside consciousness, but on the other hand the unconscious is unconscious only in relation to consciousness. Because the unconscious doesn't exist on its own, one could even say that the unconscious and the vertical dimension are one and the same. They may be the same thing if the unconscious is uniquely seen in its dynamic functional aspects. Verticality, which is also a construction, is likewise formed of the unconscious aspects which are produced and used at every moment by the needs of the individual and which in turn determine, unknown to himself and often ignored as far as their modes and forms go, the actual actions of the individual.

This is the essence of verticality in its dynamic manifestations. The active manifestation of such unconscious aspects. The verticality should therefore be regarded as extending from the depth of the entropic area, including the turmoiling states, to the conscious and relatively balanced situations.

I will describe later the connection between consciousness and the contact net. It seems rather evident that the notion of a conscious system closely relates to the notion of horizontal dimension as the latter includes the external world reaching all possible cultural boundaries.

I would like to add another observation relevant to the matter in question. I am once more referring to Freud who, making use of his analytic experience, employed the concept of Preconscious to describe anything that is implicitly present in mental activity but not necessarily present in the area of consciousness. One could say, in other words, that the Preconscious is unconscious "descriptively" but that in order to highlight its meaning we need to include consciousness. This introduces a kind of catch. The dynamical aspect contained in the notion of preconscious is so developed that it is really difficult to reach a definition. As it is, it actually belongs both to the unconscious and to the conscious systems.

This position of Freud's has been often, though delicately, criticised by most researchers. I believe, on the contrary, that it has been one of Freud's fortunate findings, not just for the reasons that have been mentioned before, but because it is undeniable that in clinical work there may exist an unconscious presence, potentially apt to become preconscious and finally conscious, in the interaction of the actual analytic dialogue.

The vertical and horizontal dimensions, articulating in the contact net, enable the development of all the processes required for this "function".

My hypotheses don't intend to diminish the importance of the notion of libido but rather to highlight the structuring of personality from an initial undifferentiated state. The latter gradually differentiates and distinguishes itself and, thanks to the simultaneous presence of an initially small mental area, allows for the transformation of sensations into emotions and representations originally, into visual representations later, into thoughts eventually and therefore into language.

The contact net which should allow for the dissipation of the emotional surplus into its meshes, enables its knots to have the potential function of *significant correspondences*, encouraged by the mind's constant capacity for registration.

The meshes' actual intersection isn't due and doesn't grant the appearance of the knots. There may be turbulences and disharmonies in this dynamic, and there may also be conflicts both when the knots are not sufficient and when it is impossible to produce more.

> Y. a young man aged 25 began analysis as he wished to overcome his frequent panic attacks which prevented him from moving about freely. He came to the conclusion that it was his task to "tidy up his mind from the untidiness provoked by the mode in which he experienced sensations, emotions and thoughts". The area of physicality confronted him continuously with the limits created by his feeling through perception, something of which his omnipotent phantasies had always deprived him of before.
> Y.: "I realise now that I have no capacity to interpret the signs coming from my body. Or rather I always attribute a catastrophic meaning to everything".
> The analysand couldn't as yet activate any significant correspondences which, starting from his sensations and emotions, could enable him to give his thoughts a form. This was why he distorted the sensory stimuli by adding a catastrophic meaning. Nevertheless the fact that he was beginning to realise the mode in which he was disposing himself towards himself indicated the possible formation of a contact net. He knew he was frightened of any experience about himself as living and continuously perceiving broke the order which he tried to establish in every situation. This caused an instability and he tried, on the contrary, to create and preserve static equilibria. The analysand realised that living and perceiving continuously brought him back to the awareness of having a body, a physicality with which it was necessary for him to become involved as it was his only source of meanings for any of the sensory and emotional experiences which he perceived.

Because of its dynamic essence, the contact net may undergo continuous transformations. This polymorphism characterises the whole individual life though it restricts its boundaries as time goes by. The essence and the transformations of the net cause the identity to assume a composed, multifaceted and ever changing nature. The meanings are multiple and there are many internal contradictions, nothing is ever static or absolute.

The significant correspondences one might describe as processes of thought articulate from the gathering and the functional expression of emotions (I am afraid, I can't sort myself out, I feel lost; or on the other hand, you are lovely, I love you, I hate you etc.). As it is, the process of thought grasps and synthesises the *emotion* regarded as dominant, providing it with meaning, but the contact net, amidst its emotional turbulence, suggests and somehow propounds the emotion that has the hegemony at that moment.

The notion of a net could erroneously evoke the notion of a bi-dimensional quality, whereas the function which I am attributing to it is fully multi-dimensional.

The model of the net seems to represent the system in which, in each individual, the sensations and the emotions tend to flow towards thought. Thought gives a name and a meaning to what is activated in the sensations-emotions of the moment and, for this reason, I believe that this is the area in which the dawn of thought is hosted and assisted.

An example of this function could be found in someone who, looking at a starry sky might imagine that, by uniting with an ideal line a few stars, he could assign a shape and a meaning to the whole indistinct mass of stars.

These versatile possibilities of thought are the result of constant psychophysical processes whose value is due to the unceasing registration of experiences.

The appealing aspect of this hypothesis has to do with the fact that all such operations do not originate in universal formative and informative principles as with the laws of any scientific discipline. They are not automatic in practice or action, they aren't actively and constantly directed by consciousness or by any specific principle or finality. They just preserve Freud's penetrating proposition about the unconscious tending to become conscious.

The role of the net thus provides a functional answer to the continuous requirements of the thinking system – an answer that can sometimes be characterised by disharmonious results.

The extension and depth of the contact net are in every moment functional to the capacities and to the integrity of the thinking system and can be referred univocally to the latter. The signs coming from the sensations and from the emotions shouldn't therefore ever be regarded as disharmonious. The genesis of situations of tension and conflict is in the modes in which sensations and emotions are dealt with, since the thinking system isn't always in a position to elaborate significant correspondences.

Z. was an eighteen year old girl. The first representation of a developing identity took place during the second year of analysis when her experiences were still chaotic but there was an initial capacity for thought. One could have said that a mental area was being established in her, formed by the knots of the contact net, and that it enabled her to give form and meaning to her still confusedly gathered sensations and emotions. Here is the appearance of the first thread to form the first knot or significant correspondence. After a session in which she had expressed herself in a very confused manner but where occasionally intense and violent emotions had appeared, she managed to describe her state of mind through the image of a string extended above the surface of the sea, dangerously shaken by the turbulent motion. The string was thin and she therefore felt she was being pushed up by the strength, the thickness, the volume of the waves and then dragged downwards. The string permanently oscillated, the analysand felt her head was heavy and her body, like a bow, tense and painful. The weight that pushed her under the wave was the weight of the turbulence which hadn't yet become emotion, awareness, thought. Her affects were in a "flood" and therefore tended to put aside many beginnings of thought, she didn't develop them as she couldn't provide them with meaning and a name. She experienced them as painful whirls or tangles which she could only overcome by trying to destroy them, destroying things, destroying herself. This difficulty in staying with herself made her feel even more fragile and weak, a thin thread violently dragged downwards. She remarked that if the thread had been stronger it wouldn't have oscillated so much in the incessant waves and maybe even the waves could have become smaller and less turbulent. Her protection, her defence was that of becoming rigid and aggressive but this attitude made things even worse as it was a kind of defence that made her feel guilty, anxious and desperate. In synthesis, it seemed that the image of the thread extended above the water had to do with an initial perception of the potentialities of her own mind, just a filament of a mind for the moment, but light and flexible, and therefore capable of resisting without breaking amidst the turbulences of the waves-sensations; not yet capable of containment but of keeping and accompanying the sensations and emotions, and therefore, through analysis, of joining with other threads and of forming knots and eventually the contact net. The latter could then take the place of the unyielding barrier which she had up to that moment opposed to the chaotic downpour of her own emotions.

The contact net can't always establish significant correspondences. The lack of correspondences may relate to the intense quality of emotions but also to the incapacity of the thinking system to harbour them. This difficulty may be due to an excessive distance imposed by the mind between itself and the emotions or to an obvious fragility that makes the progress towards thought impossible.

A newly born baby was crying in the arms of his father. Mother was in another room. The grandmother hopped around father and baby singing loudly. This behaviour seemed to express the grand-mother's incapacity to tolerate the anxiety which the baby's crying was causing her since she didn't know how to respond to it. She was therefore using her voice, uselessly trying to make him stop crying, but actually adding her anxiety to the baby's anxiety, sat-urating all available spaces with her need for self-reassurance. The mother then realised that, in the past, she used to have the same attitude towards herself, for she used for instance to cause herself a physical pain whenever "unnamed" emotions such as an intense anxiety or even an intense pleasure appeared. Now she could understand that it was essentially a question of tolerating "the anx-iety of not knowing" so that one could then find a meaning for the sensation or emotion, instead of saturating the space with answers that had the aim of silencing rather than of "co-responding".

In the case of AA. the main difficulty was in his having constructed a rigid thick barrier against his emotions which he regarded as primitive and unmanageable. He regarded hatred as destructive-ness, with no possible mediation, love as possession. As a result of such an internal attitude there was an inability to register mentally while emotions that couldn't be recognised or named manifested themselves in the body. In one of the first analysed dreams emo-tionality was represented as a neonate who was kept in such cold weather that it risked being frozen to death. " I feel unaware" he expressed himself thus "of what happens inside me and of some of my reactions. I feel that I can't put myself in contact with my emotions, that I can't understand them". Actually he often aggressed sadistically both himself and the other – and was quite unaware of it – when faced with emotional manifestations which he couldn't recognise or take up in his mind. The arrest in the estab-lishment of a contact net, capable of enabling the metabolism of emotions, coincided with the beginning of adolescence, possibly because of an intense hatred towards his younger sister and of intense death anxieties related to the sudden and intense percep-tion of solitude and change. In the section of Analytic Applications this case is further illustrated showing how a dramatic event coin-ciding with the beginning of adolescence was used by AA. as a kind of first brick of the barrier which took the place of the contact net, with consequences also on the constellation of his Oedipal scenery and severe arrest of the process of discovery of gender identity.

Whenever significant correspondences do not succeed and fail their function this probably happens as the consequence of their incorrect position in the mental area of the individual. The perceptions are in such cases necessarily deformed.

The lack of significant correspondences in relation to the Onefold and Twofold systems, or the lack of adequate relationships between sensations and emotions on the one hand and the thinking apparatus which enables the emergence of thoughts on the other, modifies the contact net creating an obstacle that can be compared to an actual *barrier*. The barrier can emerge as an extreme defence against the blind automatic response that develops when there is a strong pressure from an intense and continuous stream of sensations and emotions that cannot find a form or an harbour in the contact net. The latter then tends to become more and more rigid and insurmountable to the point in which it eventually becomes saturated. At this point the communication between the two systems becomes confused and the conflict immediately arises.

A female analysand mentioned that she had experienced an intense pleasure in perceiving the scent of the newly mowed grass and that she had thought that someone who couldn't perceive such a fragrant smell must suffer from some deprivation of vitality. Then she immediately remembered that her mother couldn't perceive smells at all and that she couldn't ever be able to perceive such a fragrance and to experience such a pleasure. A few hours later she realised that she couldn't perceive any smell either. When talking about all this she mentioned that she could still hear her mother's voice saying to the family: "When you become adults I will be free to die, as I will be useless at that point". She added that she felt guilty whenever she felt alive and happy for being alive, whenever she felt she was enjoying some pleasure. She felt in such moments that she was destroying her mother whom she saw as unhappy, sacrificing herself, always concerned with giving, unable to experience pleasure. One may suppose that the perception of the scent of the grass reached her mind filtered by the contact net and that she was thus able to recognise its meaning. But it was just that meaning that unclenched the terrible certainty that her own vitality would produce her mother's death. A long established system was aroused. The vital and intensely pleasurable perception was immediately linked with the terror of provoking the mother's death. The message that came from the net was therefore refused, the net closed and was transformed into a barrier. Because the net had become a barrier, the experiences and thoughts that used to provoke anxiety in the past were transformed into theories, or into universal general assertions which hindered the analysand's possibility of learning from experience. One might also hypothesise that the sense of smell was, for this analysand, the sense organ chosen to become the "psychic co-ordinator". The analysand herself stated that, in the past, she used to perceive the smell of her mother's milk just as she now perceives the scent of grass. She perceived the smell and recognised it as a source of pleasure and intense vitality, she sucked the milk greedily but then realised that, by living, she was progressively destroying her mother – "the carrier of the fragrant aroma of milk and of such vitality". At that point she would vomit all the milk she had taken in. Her mother – she said – didn't understand the reason for such a "refusal of her own milk" and took her for useless medical examinations, thinking that something might be wrong with her digestive apparatus. This situation has to do with the fundamental question of death and with the fundamental responsibility one has towards the person who has granted one's life. By living one is in some way killing one's mother. This state of affairs is in conflict with the deep universal desire – omnipotence.

The conflict between Onefold and Twofold may originate many different sceneries. Two of those seem to indicate the vertices of extreme oscillation: 1. Emotions overwhelm thought (causing reversion to situations of the turmoiling kind). 2. Thought closes upon itself (saturates itself) in an extreme defence therefore denying the existence of the emotional world. Neverthless this doesn't mean that the person doesn't experience any turbulence. The latter is in fact experienced as a state of intense anxiety.

A woman came to analysis in the condition described in point 2. She was an adult woman and seemed to have succeeded, since the beginning of adolescence, in annulling the perception of her own emotional life. By living as a "robot", by transforming each choice into a duty and by relying on her capacity to imitate, she has managed to reach the present day apparently unscathed. An intense anxiety had started to appear. When she went near her mother she felt intense and painful shivers in her arms, almost like an "electric shock". She avoided, for this reason, meeting her mother but then felt extremely guilty. Her anxiety was the reason for her request for analysis. During the first few months of analysis it was obvious that this analysand was unable to give name to any of her emerging emotions, but she gradually began to express them through sensory perceptions – vision, smell etc. The only emotion which she could recognise was anxiety that appeared as a "cramp in her stomach". Except for that, she believed that she had nothing to say and that she didn't experience emotions or any feeling whatsoever. In one session she stated that her arm shivering in the presence of her mother had disappeared while her anxiety had increased in frequency and intensity, and she was then able to recognise the link between the two phenomena. When she progressively managed to recognise anxiety as an emotional state in itself and to allow it to take part in her mental area she didn't need to express anxiety as "shivering" anymore. The analyst could then stress that the only emotion which she recognised was anxiety and hypothesised that anxiety might have been a kind of container for any other emotion. The hypothesis was expressed as a metaphor. The analysand was using anxiety as a kind of huge cupboard in which one could hide any odd object in the house. As a consequence of this mechanism, the "house" always seemed to be empty and poor (in the sessions she used to say that she had nothing to say, that she didn't think or feel, that she had no memories or, in other words, no experience of the past, neither remote nor close) and the "cupboard" was about to burst as she incessantly thrust new experiences in it. The analysand liked this metaphor very much and immediately entered the subject of opening the cupboard and tidying things up. She asked herself how she could open the cupboard without being overwhelmed by its contents. Continuing with the metaphor and working further upon the question she managed to understand that, up to now, she had only considered two ways, shutting the cupboard or trying to open it but then hurriedly running away. Now for the first time she saw a third possibility. She could open and stand on one side, so that she may look at what came out without being overwhelmed. She allowed for the possibility of accessing her own mental space and recognised, took responsibility for, and gave meaning to each sensation and emotion emerging from her mental space. She didn't fly anymore but stood "on one side". One might regard the perception, obtained through the metaphor suggested by the analyst, as a first significant correspondence of the contact net which, from now on, will be able to activate correspondent sensations-emotions and meanings and to overcome the rigidity that had formerly transformed it into a barrier.

These thoughts originate in clinical experience – by the contact net. I am not suggesting a structural concept, I am only investigating the processes occurring just at the moment in which they may be observed in the framework of the analytic relationship.

The confused stream of sensations flowing towards the contact net undoubtedly achieves, eventually, its own possible "period"[72] or, in other words, its rhythm, in a way that enables this initial model to become fixed and impressed. The shape and mode of this first model then facilitates the following passages towards more elaborate and complex perceptions. The latter then create the foundations for potential and further development of the quality of thought.

Apparently, the individual learns about being an individual not just through self-consciousness but rather, initially, through self-observation. Self observation actually incessantly produces and modifies "theories" (or, one might say, *empirical perceptions*) in the vertical dimension, internal to the body-mind relationship. Subsequently it expresses other distinctions, from the meaning and role ascribed to different persons to the differentiation between animate and inanimate objects. This process starts (initially) from what Bion described as a preconception, it then becomes knowledge *but just in the sense of the condition of knowing.*

I am aware of the danger of becoming enmeshed in a tautological discourse. I am trying in fact to discern and make known, or in other words to throw light upon, specific mechanisms with the help of some tested instruments. In clinical practice the importance of the vertical relationship may be appraised by considering both its internal dynamics and the modes in which it is configured when it appears in the horizontal relationship. "Analytically" speaking, the research is useful if it promotes self-observation both on the vertical and on the horizontal levels.

The analytic relationship is the support of this double observation which is at the same time a presence and an attendance[73]. The co-ordinates that enable discernment of the development of the Ego necessarily derive from the understanding of this double origin – vertical (from Onefold to Twofold) and horizontal (from the system Onefold-Twofold to the world).

The vertical dimension (related to the moment in which contents acquire their meaning) is complementary to the horizontal dimension. If one leaves aside the horizontal dimension one may then gain access to the Ego configuration, that is to the abstract entity that only exists as a function; but by leaving out the horizontal dimension, there are no images or representations left. The contact net and the two dimensions together, can now be better and more precisely defined as they offer the possibility of using representations to give form to a world of meanings and, furthermore which, unconscious material representations. Thus the vertical and horizontal dimensions may, through the contact net, enable the representation of the internal world of an individual.

Knowledge of reality originates a vision of the world. The latter, functioning on the vertical dimension, fosters the creation of relational contexts, in which the horizontal dimension has its fundamental impact. Internal and/or external vicissitudes may tend to hinder and even impede such a vision and its specific characteristic of intense dynamicity, thus giving origin to non functional situations on the intrapsychic level, as well as in the field of affective and social relationships. An excess of emotion hinders the capacity to think. The emotion is thus furthermore increased and the sensory aspects therefore tend to reach a state of indiscriminate saturation.

One could imagine that the same experience might determine the definition of different and specific visions of the world depending on the different emotional tone in which the mind perceives it. I have already said that emotions may be thought about in two different perspectives, their intensity and their quality. From the vertex of intensity one could say that an emotion may be metabolised when there is a capacity to contain it. From the vertex of quality that its significant and harmonious aspects appear both in the Ego configuration and in its functioning.

I would also like to emphasise that, when disharmonious aspects are present, experiences may then be elaborated in modes that bear either depressive or manic characteristics. I am using such terms just to indicate abstract categories or general trends in the mental functioning of each individual.

In states of depression what actually seems to happen is that disharmonious aspects seem to mainly draw the source of their conflict from the area of the horizontal dimension (the Oedipal constellation, the Ego configuration and the world). In manic states, on the other hand, the individual elaborates experiences in the Onefold-Twofold system, therefore in his or her own vertical dimension external reality doesn't have as much influence as in states of depression and there are many more possibilities for free and extended manipulations.

Aspects of Freudian[74] and even more of Kleinian theory have suggested and established the idea that the internal world relates to introjected external objects. The hypothesis of the COO modifies such a vision thus enabling a more definite and circumscribed understanding of the relationship between the mind and the body, between the mind and its own object. It is the area of the vertical relation, then further illuminated by the relation with the external world contributing to the establishment of the horizontal relation. The COO defines the human being in the original aspects rather than in the relation with the world, it isn't therefore related to the processes of introjection, it isn't formed by any external contributions.

In my hypothesis the Onefold-Twofold system functionally enables access to any kind of experience. There is always some knowledge that is, or at least can be referred to, the system itself. Any kind of experience relates therefore to the vertical relation and to the first significant perception of one's corporeal experience.

Sense organs have an important function in this process. It is possible to chose any of the sense organs to function as the principal mediator of the comprehension of self and of the world during and beyond the original turmoiling condition. With this choice it becomes possible to establish the first correlations between the different and sparse physical sensations. The first sensory point of reference acquires the function of a co-ordinator of sensations (other senses may also have the same function). I have named it "psychic co-ordinator". If hearing and touch are the first sensory organs that develop such a function (for it is well known that they are active since intra-uterine life) one might imagine that taste and smell possibly become active when a life separated from mother begins. Smell could well become active with the first pulmonary breathing and taste with the first sucking and swallowing of milk into the digestive apparatus. The two senses could thus well be the first two sensory mediators of the infant's discriminating function, necessary for survival. They might just shortly precede the establishment of the function of "seeing".

The first comprehensions of the corporeal experience therefore originate the initial psychic structure. The latter then becomes extended inasmuch as the experiences of life unceasingly and dynamically originate a modifying drive.

In clinical work it is often possible to observe that if one of the sense organs is pre-eminently used or, on the other hand, neutralised so that it can't be employed as the psychic co-ordinator anymore, the phenomenon often reveals precisely the disharmonious area or the point of maximum urgency that is originating the analysand's anxiety.

Previous clinical examples indicated that the use of smell or of hearing as psychic co-ordinators is to be regarded as quite frequent.

> An analysand emitted a sound very much like a little cough in the first period of analysis. He actually said that he could only feel he existed when he managed to "hear his own voice", he actually meant "hearing with his ears" for he had managed to neutralise frequently his own propriocettive capacities.

The term "seeing" is used both for "seeing with the eyes" when the mind is blinded or saturated and therefore unable to seek the meanings of thought, and for "seeing with the mind's eyes" when the mental area is available for thought, through a harmonious functioning of the contact net.

The use of taste as psychic co-ordinator is rare, in my opinion. For this reason I would like to quote the case of a female analysand who was anorexic at the beginning of analysis but then changed to a stable bulimic condition[75].

> AB. was exasperated by her own compulsive mode of eating and consequent increase in weight. When the analyst encouraged her to ask herself what the function of such behaviour might be AB. was silent for a moment and then answered: "I don't know, it feels as if I can't stop introducing food into my mouth. I seem to be search-

ing for a taste that I cannot find". The taste AB. was actually trying to find, might have been equivalent to some specific original aspect which had been lost. A kind of psychic point of reference without which she felt she was obliged to continue to: "follow obsessionally the outlines and profiles of any object she was looking at". This latter was in fact the ritual which, in her expectation, was bound to protect her from the anxiety of being lost in the absence of space which seemed to characterise her mind at this point. In this situation the bulimic behaviour seemed to aim at two functions: on the one hand the need to placate the anxiety of "emptiness" and of solitude, on the other hand the more sophisticated function of seeking something quite specific and necessary to the individuation of the analysand's own "being". One can therefore hypothesise that the bulimic behaviour might have a life oriented function when it comes after an anorexic phase that was characterised by an attack on life, contrasting death anxieties. When the analyst spoke of the possible function of the "search for taste", the analysand associated to this the terrifying experience of having to discriminate and to express her own choice. Later she mentioned she had seen a few months old baby-girl refuse orange juice from the hands of her mother and accepted it later from the hands of someone else. One can see, here and in other cases, that the vertical relation meets with the horizontal relation and that a powerful interrelation is established between the two. The psycho-physical material of the mental functioning of the individual is thus established.

The passage from Onefold to Twofold is the first specific aspect of the vertical dimension, the mode and form in which the latter – complementary as it is to the horizontal dimension – not only gives meaning to the first differentiation between object and subject, but establishes the initial important discrimination between *living* and *perceiving*. When such distinctions don't take place disharmonious consequences ensue.

An example of such disharmonious conditions could be found in particular states, defined as psychotic, which some women experience after childbearing. Such states are determined by the mind's difficulty to contain the COO's violent irruption: difficulty caused by the newly born baby's presence and even more by the wreckage of the limits of the body under the pressure of sensations that are perceived as menacing for the balance of the vertical dimension. In fact, the hard, troubled developmental path, leading from the physical to the psychic experiences, actually reproduces the biological event of birth, when one body becomes two bodies.

In the body-mind relation one can see a model of relation, similar to the model of the mother – child relationship, going from Onefold to Twofold and then again tending towards the Onefold. I say it is a relation as the principal function of the mind is in the vertical relation and in the relationship with the other (originating the horizontal axe). Sensations, the first physical data that are contained and known through their differentiated characteristics, originally have a discriminating function, in respect of internal and external experience, but also need external objects so that they can be activated and owned. This is one of the many functions in which the horizontal relation expresses itself and becomes vital for the sensation to gain its necessary space so that it can then become a sensory perception, an emotion and eventually an experience. Sensations are like signs and are potentially capable of forming a text, the initial arising emotions draw up the first draft of this text.

The child, COO and mind, establishes a relationship with the external object – mother. The mother is, in her turn, mind and physicality and relates to the child's physicality and developing mind.

The mother is the one who establishes significant correspondences and gives functional expression and meaning to the emotion which the child is experiencing in any given moment. The mother anticipates and catalyses the functioning which the child eventually needs to form and develop his own personal contact net.

The mother's role, as I am hypothesising it, has been masterfully synthesised by Bion in the concept of reverie "as the psychological source of supply of the infant's needs for love and understanding."[76] In the mother the source is nourished by the signals originating from the existing physical channels. Thus, in Bion's words, "The physical component, milk, discomfort of satiation or the opposite, can be immediately apparent to the sense."[77]

Bion's description emphasises the extreme significance of physicality in mother's first response to, and specific attuning with, the baby's particular physical needs. In the initial stage of the relationship the physical responses prevail[78]. They should be accepted, integrated and metabolised by the mind of the mother. The latter should in fact function with some level of awareness, different from the child's developing awareness but somehow parallel to it.

Thus the horizontal dimension is activated by the relationship between the baby and the body of the mother, between the mother's body and mind and the child's corporeality, between the mother's mind and the active, exuberant world of the child's sensations and emotions. The mother's willingness to make space for someone who is not herself is possibly what enables the child to put out his sensations, emotions and feelings. This allows the child to begin to feel that he is the subject of an experience.

If the mother is attuned to her child's signals she is then capable of observing and of waiting for the expression of her child's not yet defined needs. Thus she may avoid saturating them prematurely (the problem of misunderstanding) or ignoring their existence (the problem of absence).

In this kind of situation the mother's capacity for reverie may enable the formation of a *mental area* that can then develop further and reach its full functioning if the baby can tolerate the frustrations deriving from a state of discomfort that I define as privation. I actually believe that the state of privation, or of lack of satisfaction, stimulates the child's awareness of a dialectic relation with himself (body-mind), and that this perception enables him to become a subject in relation to what is not himself.

The contrast between the frustrating situation and the presence of a gratifying object causes, in its turn, the child to dispose the mind towards an initial process of communication. There is, in other words, in the comparison a kind of emotional tone or colour that actually aims at communication. In this very delicate moment, when there is an initial perception of being Twofold and of there being two individuals (the me and the other) very intense primitive anxieties appear. Such anxieties are considered by M. Klein as coinciding with the Depressive Position (perception of the mother as a whole object): in the hypothesis of the COO, they are regarded in a different perspective, here the "feeling of being separate" is seen as related to the dawn of the relation between Onefold and Twofold, between the COO and the mind.

Whenever there is a situation of intense anxiety the threat of a fracture between Onefold and Twofold is experienced by the child as dangerous for the process of integration. The state of anxiety may then either lead to a condition of increased psycho-physical integration fostering the link between body and mind (harmonious relation), or to phenomena of intensified conflict, ending in the sacrifice of one of the two parties of the vertical relation (disharmonious relation).

If the child denies his physical dimension, the mind then begins to search for an idealised object that it can capture and keep permanently idealised. If, on the contrary, the vertical area is separated from the horizontal area, it turns towards states of isolation and causes disharmonious states usually described as autistic.

Obviously each of the disharmonious aspects connected with the vertical and horizontal relationships has serious consequences both upon the ego configuration and the Oedipal constellation which may both either express phobic manifestations against the individual's emotionality, or conditions of unrealisable autonomy deriving from false integrations.

It is thus possible to identify turbulences prevalently pertaining to the vertical area. Specific situations in which psychic reality is denied under the pressure of intense internal conflict originating in threats (real or presumed) against the ego configuration or in the deforming roles which have been attributed on the stage of the Oedipal constellation.

One of the possible consequences of these situations is the loss of discriminating capacities and the confusion between *needs* and *functions* including among other phenomena an attempt to deny external reality.

When this happens the field is then left free for a hypertrophy of the ego configuration in all the possible varieties and expressions of mania.

All such processes are of course conditioned by the presence or absence of a fundamental element, that is the horizontal dimension. The latter in fact charges in with extreme powerfulness when the relationship with the world, and therefore with data deriving from external reality, has to be included.

In the horizontal dimension all the elements and the dynamics that correspond to the expansion of the vertical dimension are present and active and there is also the wholly absorbing presence of the other. This double presence makes the terminations of the contact net extremely complex as it involves two systems, the Ego and the Other in the process of transmission. The latter doesn't only take place in the intrapsychic area but extends to all the variables of the other's presence and, consequently, to the communicative process.

The Other's existence and appearance cause a peculiar situation of instability. A condition which favours communication and can take place at any stage of development, though it doesn't actually depend on development. It is active in childhood, in adolescence and, most of all, in adulthood.

Instability relates to turbulence and to conflict but is necessary to life. It is the result of the presence – confrontation of the contact net, whose function is to evaluate the mode and form in which the presence of the Other might be included in a constructive exchange.

Attentive examination of the above questions enables me to formulate a hypothesis – still needing further detailed definition – about the vertical area being immanent in the individual while the horizontal area is mediated by mother or mother substitute. Thus, the maternal figure would introduce the child to the horizontal dimension completing, in this way, the child's existence. The integration of vertical and horizontal in one system then encloses and maybe also somehow defines the whole destiny of an individual's life.

THE PRESENCE OF THE CONTACT NET IN THE ACTIVITY OF DREAMING

Lengthy clinical experience has convinced me that dreaming may offer an interesting model to clarify the presence and role of the contact net. I believe the latter has a significant role not only in the functions which I have described up to now but also in determining the necessary conditions for dreaming to take place.

The case of AC. provides an example of the importance of dreaming, as an initial activation of the contact net, in states of deep and intense anxiety related to the acquisition of gender identity. A sequence of dreams develops in the space of a fortnight from the moment in which artificial insemination has taken place to the moment in which miscarriage puts an end to the project. The material of dreams is seen by the analysand as a kind of monitoring of what is happening inside her own uterus. Still, many of the elements in the dreams (herself appearing as a man "as beautiful as her own father", a famous singer with an androgynous aspect carried in triumph by masses of people, a little girl with a mongrel, alone and lost, searching for her mother etc.) appear to be forms and outlines of a deeper problem, related to the establishment of gender identity as well as of anxieties connected with the progress leading to differentiation and individuation.

In order to formulate my ideas I need to refer to Freud's latent contents, that is the complex of meanings, all extremely active and eloquent in the language of dreams, produced by the Unconscious system manifesting itself through images.

Language, one might wonder if the term is appropriate to dreams, in other words if dreams should be regarded as a kind of language or if they should not. Technically they shouldn't, as they shouldn't be placed on the same plane as verbal language. Dreams are characterised by a level of concreteness which doesn't belong to language. It is difficult in dreams to discern the formal or expressive element from the meaning even during the secondary elaboration or at least in some of its phases. What happens is that by describing the dream in words one is somehow both introducing the dream itself and the distinction between the signifier and that which is signified. For this reason I think it is preferable to be cautious when using the term "language" in an undifferentiated mode while discussing dreams.

Language itself has unknown origins. We know that it doesn't originate from an autonomous development and that it doesn't' evolve in the mind of any single person, as it is formed on a symbolic plane, in effusive and diffusive forms etc., through a "distancing"[79] or, even better, through the creation of a mental space. If the area of language becomes eventually more active and specialised and if the area of exchanges becomes more complex, a culture is then created. This implies very close relations between saying, thinking, doing etc.

Maybe dreams enclose language in themselves. No dreamer can, in fact, do without language. The product of dream-work, that is the dream, could well be considered as a mode of expression, one of the possible *language registers*.

Freud regarded the activity of dreaming as the result of two specific operations. The production of dream-thoughts (latent contents) and their transformation into manifest contents. Dream work transforms the former into the latter. In discussing the transformation Freud stated that the manifest content is never "creative" as dream work doesn't derive from an activity of the intellect.

In a 1914 note to *The Interpretation of Dreams* Freud stated: "It has long been the habit to regard dreams as identical with their manifest content, but we must now beware equally of the mistake of confusing dreams with latent dream-thoughts"[80]. I think that these two perspectives are located at the two extreme ends of a wide range of possibilities. Inside the range we may locate dreams in which what is hidden and what is revealed coincide, and where latent and manifest contents are conjoined, rather than being separate. I believe furthermore that creativity is to be regarded as a vast phenomenon travelling further than an intellectual operation. If one were to deny the creative essence of dream production, the dream would still be an interpretation and therefore – as far as I understand it[81] – a creative act. An interpretation of the elements that, at the moment in which the dream takes place, make up the specific equilibrium of the internal world of the individual, as well as the potentialities for development, in time, of new desirable and expected adjustments. Each individual has different peculiar modes of dream-working.

It is obviously still necessary to clarify the particular meaning that should be attributed to the concept of creativity. If by creativity one understands the capacity to produce (by means of an elaboration that must necessarily belong to the secondary processes) objects, works of art, thoughts, scientific ideas etc., dream work can't be regarded as creative. Nevertheless, because secondary elaboration can't in any way be separated from the dream, there is, in the latter, obviously a kind of internal plasticity, a capacity for, or disposition towards creativity, understood in its usual sense.

Since no dream that has been dreamt can be caught in its original appearance, nor can it be told or spoken about at that level, one should acknowledge, in my opinion, that dreams have the essence of transformations, or at least of translations, like all manifestations of thinking processes expressed at any possible level. This is, furthermore, a characteristic that dreams seem to share with many other forms of communication.

Finally, the communicative dynamic of dreams expresses itself, in my hypothesis, through and by means of the horizontal and vertical relations. The former is concerned with representations (daily residues etc.) and the latter with the actual elaboration of signs concerning harmonious or disharmonious states of psychic activity, that is of signals about the situation of the mind and the needs of the subject.

AD. a female analysand who was moving from a state of anorexia (agoraphobia – claustrophilia) to a state of bulimia (claustrophobia – agoraphilia) told the analyst about three dreams. The language of such dreams expressed the modification that was taking place in her mental area. In the first dream she experienced intense anxiety and a feeling of alarm. She was on a ship sailing in deep waters but the ship had a leak on one of its sides. In her dream the analysand was both in the area where the water flooded in and outside that place watching water "drip out" from the leaks – like blood from a wound – she said. As in one of Escher's pictures, she was both inside and outside, she was inside and outside her own mental area, which felt flooded and emptied at the same time. In her second dream the analysand was trying to escape from a thief who was chasing her in the narrow, dark, unknown, back-streets of a town. The chase was due to a misunderstanding, as the thief wanted to steal the fur coat which she held on her arm, but which didn't belong to her. In the third dream the situation was completely different. The analysand was in a consulting room, which appeared to be wider than the real one, sitting by the analyst, watching her mother come in together with her (the mother's) husband. The presence of the analyst made her feel strong and calm, so that she could observe aspects of her vertical dimension, such as her relation with her own basic internal masculinity and femininity. Eventually she walked out of the room and found herself in an even wider room, such as a hotel's main entrance-hall, with plenty of people moving about, as in a party. Wide spaces appeared in this dream, well defined and limited, and the position of the analysand was also well defined. Internal and external sceneries were at last kept separate and the analysand's position in their respect was clear. There was plenty of air, there was movement and a kind of vital richness which the analysand could now recognise, thanks to the re-establishment of the vertical relation. The three dreams expressed the analysand's change. She didn't have to resume her anorexic condition as the area of mental functioning wasn't perceived as a menace by her anymore.

It may be necessary here to specify that I am not at all aiming at describing the dream's essence or nature, its origin, functions and intents but rather at analysing, in the light of the hypothesis of the contact net, the possible relations intercurring between the specific activity of dreaming as well as its production – the dream – and the models of the vertical and horizontal dimensions. I am using the term model in the sense in which Bion uses it: "The model may be regarded as an abstraction from an emotional experience or as a concretisation of an abstraction. The latter has affinities with the transformation of a hypothesis into terms of empirically verifiable data"[82].

One might suggest that the use of the model of the horizontal dimension is exceedingly obvious. The manifest content of a dream consists in fact essentially of the narrative of the person involved who uses images, situations, states of mind, facts etc. all inherent to everyday life and originating in the surroundings and culture to which the individual belongs. The dream elaboration is similar to the processes of imagination, to creative impulses or even to the work of art in its fictional essence.

Freud eventually came to consider the manifest content of the dream as a narrative. Then he designated it as a transformation or translation of the latent content.

Day-dreaming also belongs to the same category, except that there is greater cohesion or "coherence" between day-dreaming and latent contents than between the latter and dreams. In fact in day-dreaming latent and manifest contents almost coincide, something which doesn't happen with dreams.

Freud seemed to believe that it is verbal language that introduces the element of coherence not belonging to the pre-verbal stage in the area of primary processes. He also remarked that language continuously produces contradictory statements which carry some meaning with them. I believe that every internal experience must own some level of "coherence" though it may have its discrepancies, at least in the sense that it must bear some meaning. The coherence carries sense with itself, not logical sense, but a sense that can be regarded as analogous to the tensions, discrepancies, condensations, displacements, symbolisms etc., carried by any verbal formulation.

I wish to introduce here a few very brief clinical notes in order to illustrate and clarify my conceptualisation. The examples originate in work with patients whose primitive sensations-emotions, never recognised as such, or provided with specific meaning before, could actively emerge only as the analytic dialogue developed. They were patients who had formerly chosen as their mode of defence a deep massive negation of anxieties and terrors, which they had therefore been unable to acknowledge and nominate up to that moment. These analysands were incapable of producing any significant correspondences by referring to their emotional flow but could produce, during the sessions, some visual images which they usually called "visions". Such visions were related to specific emotional contents but, without the help of their analyst, these patients couldn't provide them with any meaning or function.

> During a session about gender identity and hatred towards her own basic femininity, a young woman said she was seeing a mimosa bush completely covered with flowers and so intensely and sweetly perfumed that she felt quite nauseated. On another occasion, when her hatred for the central part of her body was beginning to configure (she hated watching in the mirror her abdomen and breasts)

she had, for few days, a vision in which she saw herself as a monster with a huge head over two very thin legs. The head was provided with eyes and nose but had no mouth and it was round and smooth like the heads of extra-terrestrial characters in fiction. The vision induced intense anxiety.

Another example, a woman who had been travelling alone by car said: "I suddenly realised that I was going from one place to the other and that time had passed while I was crossing space". The perception of time was so acute and sudden that this person was obliged to displace herself again out of time but the perception did nevertheless cause a devastating state of panic. The person looked at her hands (which were as smooth and white as the rest of her complexion) and said she saw them covered in stains and wrinkled. "At that moment – she added – I was seventy"

Another situation: A man said he felt a pain in his stomach, like a cramp or a twinge, imprisoning something. When the analyst asked if the twinge was imprisoning an emotion and if he could recognise the emotion, the man, after some difficulties said he was having a sort of vision. A hand was coming out of his stomach and was reaching up, wanting to steal his breath and carry it down into his stomach.

One feels that these patients manage, through the production of visions or actual day-dreams, to bring to the light zones and aspects belonging to the entropic area that have been long since shut off. And even more they may, through negation, have hindered the activation of their own capacity to think and to develop the most important function of elaboration

Going back to the "coherence" of day-dreaming, one should say that it is mainly due to the essential presence of the horizontal dimension. The latter is strongly connected with external reality and therefore establishes a sort of compromise that is absent or almost absent in nocturnal dreams. One can imagine that, in dreams, the contact net is available to facilitate the functions which I have described as "versatile possibilities of thought": the vertical dimension is thus enabled to operate "freely" and to express modes and forms that provide a meaning for the psychic activity, continuously relating, nevertheless, to the horizontal dimension for all such elements as are necessary for its representation.

An analysand (female) succeeded in replacing reality with a "dream reality" by inventing and impersonating, since adolescence, an ethereal character until she eventually became a mother without ever taking into her psychic dimension the real meaning of her femininity and maternity. Eventually, after some analytic work had taken place, she discovered the pleasure of sensuality and of sexuality, establishing a new intimate relationship. Almost immediately after she had let herself be carried by her own pleasure, she had a dream in which a "luxurious and coarse" woman told her that she was totally incapable and covered her own face with a kind of white thick substance which she extracted from the analysand's body. When she woke up the analysand was so disgusted that she felt she was unable, during quite a few sessions, to elaborate the meaning of the dream. Furthermore she began to refuse intimacy and sensuality. Her self-imposed refusal caused her feelings of pain and distress. Then she had another dream in which her house was flooded by water coming from the taps which her partner had left open, and which she anxiously struggled to close, only just succeeding in avoiding being totally flooded. She did manage to perceive her terror in this dream, a terror that was related to the explosion of her own sensuality and from the intense specific pleasure that she was able to experience, but it wasn't enough to reassure her and she therefore continued to keep away from any form of closeness to her own physicality or, more precisely in this case, from "being a woman". The sessions continued and the subjects of gender identity and of claustrophobic and agoraphobic anxieties were discussed until eventually a physical perception, related to the area of femininity, reappeared. Then the analysand had the following dream. Her daughter was on a plane and in great, though unspecified, danger. She "bravely" mounted on board and took her daughter away, out of danger, on firm ground. When her feet touched the earth, she knew she had saved a child that represented the present for her. This dream seemed to express the passage from the prevalence of "seeing" to the prevalence of "touching". Seeing (using sight as the psychic co-ordinator) had been, for the analysand, a kind of dam against the flood of emotions perceived as uncontrollable and devastating, the consequence had been a kind of "de-materialisation" of physicality, achieved by not bothering about proper feeding and by refusing medical care when suffering from tapeworm. Physicality would have driven her to face some long avoided subjects – individuation/differentiation, her conflict with her mother (a mother which she described as very lovely and almost coarse in her femininity), hatred and uncertainty. When, activated by analytic work, her "tactile sensual" senses emerged, she perceived them as a kind of cataclysm, in relation to her limited capacity to establish a net of significant correspondences. She therefore temporarily pushed the senses behind a thick stiff defensive barrier. But her mind was registering the experience and she continued to search for meanings that could contain the emotions originating from the physical sphere. The meanings seemed to become manifest through dreams. The dream of the plane indicated the need to transfer herself into more solid, steadier grounds. Sight is of all senses the nearer to the organisation of abstract thought and can therefore become the medium of an exit from reality. Feeding oneself out of film movies, indulging in phantasies sometimes introduces the subject into a kind of "make believe" world and hinders the opportunity of learning from the experience of living. When this analysand began to rely also on her sense of touch, the latter seemed to actually foster the manifestation and almost a kind of materialisation of her femininity.

As for the availability of the contact net one could say that, not only does this function enable and favour, as we have seen, the establishment of significant correspondences but it also fosters the production of dreams, of phantasies, of day-dreams, and of any other manifestation in which the vertical dimension dominantly prevails.

Using Bion's grid as a metaphor, one could say that the grounds and origin of the functioning of contact net are in the predominance of the vertical dimension which gradually makes space for the horizontal dimension. It is thanks to the latter that the function of thought is eventually reached and established.

The Freudian hypothesis about dream-work describes the production of the dream, its transformation into the manifest content, the associated processes of condensation, displacement, consideration of representability (the passage from a sensation to a sensory image tending towards potential representation) and secondary elaboration which Freud believes to be in many ways similar to rationalisation.

I don't feel that I can add any further clarification to the discussion about the nature of any of these processes and it isn't my aim to do so but rather to emphasise their complexity by introducing the concept of contact net and by examining the development of the flow of sensations and observing its effects.

On the other hand, though I am somehow circumscribing the aims of my research, I don't feel that I can accept Freud's opinion about the lack of "creativity" in dream work or at least I cannot accept it unconditionally. If one assumes that dreams can't be regarded as being ruled by the laws that regulate rational abstract thought processes and that would turn them into intellectual operations, the only other possible solution is to regard them as manifestations of a specific language register. A very intense register at that, highly significant, evocative of many ferments and impulses that closely relate it to the turbulent world of the entropic area, the actual point of departure of all human creative possibilities.

A very specific language register is produced, as it has been formerly mentioned, by the activity of dreaming. Furthermore the mental area which provides the foundations for the functioning of the contact net doesn't, as yet, host language but just the potentiality for language. As the distancing takes place sensations are turned into emotions and emotions can then characterise individual experience. Without this process language couldn't emerge as its development is actually achieved by the establishment of such a distance.

The comments that follow bear an inevitable simplification for which I wish to make excuses, both with specialists and with all the other non-specialist readers. Yet I am introducing them because I feel that they might prove a useful synthesis in functional support of my hypothesis.

As we have seen dream-work develops through two operations:

a) The production of dream-thoughts (latent contents, the actual grounds on which the contact net is founded)

b) The transformation of dream-thoughts into manifest content.

According to Freud there are five main mechanisms involved in the transformation: condensation, displacement, consideration of representability, secondary elaboration and perception. I will discuss later the characteristic functions of such mechanisms as I would rather begin by describing the mode in which dream-work develops.

The primary process is like the engine that puts in motion the five mechanisms mentioned above as well as regression, repression, symbols, representations and the Conscious system. All these mechanisms together provide the raw material for further manifestations going from sensations to emotions, feelings and finally thoughts.

The primary process isn't concerned with logical connections, with contradictory elements, with the complete or almost complete absence of the space-time co-ordinates. It rather relies upon indirect representations (images rather than processes of abstraction) and upon concretisation. Obviously such operations shouldn't in themselves be regarded as disharmonious.

I hope I will be able to clarify my opinion about the notion of regression in the following pages. The notion of repression is a fundamental and universal discovery as repression is the psychic process which originates the production of the unconscious and of its use. It is also a dominant characteristic of ordinary psychological processes.

The knots in the contact net can become active as points of attraction for unpleasant or threatening representations or in similar modes they can become points of convergence and harbour pleasant experiences that may therefore put in motion secondary processes. The latter then enable the formation of symbols originated by the relation between different modes and stages of conscious thinking.

I feel that I am in some kind of consonance with Lacan's theories and that I actually agree with his hypothetical assertion that significance can't be connected by a unique fixed relation to just one meaning. I think that Lacan's proposition really emphasises the prevalence of the vertical dimension and that the hypothesis can't have any value whenever the horizontal dimension prevails as in the case of myth, folklore, religion etc.

In *The Interpretation of Dreams* Freud stated that symbolism includes all forms of indirect interpretation deriving from different defence mechanisms such as displacement, condensation, representation etc. It is in fact sufficient to attribute two or more meanings to any behaviour. The ensuing connection may be regarded as immediately symbolic.

It is nevertheless a very complex matter to descriptively represent the activity of such mechanisms. Freud thought there might be two possible descriptions. The first, defined as "thing presentation" belongs to the primary processes and is essentially visual. The second, defined as "word presentation" is the passage from perceptual identity to thought identity and belongs to secondary processes. To the first, one might relate, for instance, the capacity for hallucinatory language, to the second the normal faculties of thought. I have already stated that I believe that self-observation, by continuously producing and modifying empirical perceptions enables the individual to learn to become an individual even before self-consciousness does its job.

If one refers to the system preconscious-conscious a specific point should be immediately made about the concept of consciousness. Consciousness, a sensory organ for the perception of psychic qualities, can elaborate the above qualities using thought in form of awareness, integration, discriminating capacity, capacity to recognise data of reality both of the internal and of the external world and furthermore, synthesis, abstraction and the extremely important capacity to learn from experience.

The preconscious-conscious system also operates in the modes of a secondary process. According to Freud it has the characteristics of logical thinking and the form of verbal language.

I wish to introduce a new notion here. Verbal language shouldn't be regarded in itself as a prerequisite of logical thinking, "logical" meaning rational, coherent, careful, making sense. One could therefore drop the term "logical" and just use "thinking", verbal and also not verbal. I have mentioned that delusional thinking should also be included in thinking processes and should therefore be characterised by the assumptions which – as we have seen – characterise many other forms of thinking. Thinking that takes place in dreams as well as phobic, paranoid, psychotic, obsessional thinking etc. but also hypnoid states as anything that is latent may, at any moment, become manifest or in other words enter consciousness.

AE. was a thirty year old woman who had a pre-eminently disharmonious mental functioning. After a year of analysis she managed to contain her anxiety to some extent and to express her thoughts and delusional language (of which there had been just traces up to that moment): "They found out that I hadn't passed any exams at the University (by "they" she meant her teachers but this had also been found out by her family after it had been going on for four years). So a teacher helped me with one exam and was punished for it. He was summoned by the court of justice. Just now I have seen one of the tutors in order to propose a subject for my Dissertation. He says that I am doing well with it. Now children are dressing in orange and women are touching their hair (this means she feels that she is considered responsible for the abortion of her brother's ex-fiancée. She is convinced that she had incestuous sexual intercourse with her brother when she was a child). According to them I shouldn't be alive, because of my abortion and because I have received some help with my exam. The tutor was sending in messages by TV. Some say they are on my side and others send in warnings (she names a very well known theatre actor), some want to send me away from University but I have my life to think of and will not do as they say. Then there are the shoves and the ones who make the little cough behind the door of the swimming pool. But maybe I am just thinking all these things. They had stopped because they had succeeded in blocking me by failing my exam, but now that I have passed it everything is starting again. The girl that has been shot, I feel I have something to do with but I don't know how." Eventually the patient's sister was put in the place of the murdered girl. The sister had finished University and the patient felt that she meant to destroy her. "This morning the newspaper said eight people have been arrested. One of them looks like the person who is helping me. It is a message for me to continue with my life. Maybe I will go and visit that girl to encourage her to live and to tell her that I am very sorry . . . I suffer from a delusion of omnipotence and think that I can save her! When I was initially accused of the abortion everything went badly in my family. My father wasn't a father as he should have been. He got into trouble at his work. He asked for my advice, but I couldn't or maybe wouldn't help him! I didn't love him in those days (she means her delusional crisis and the moment she gave up university, two events which weren't noticed at home). My father acted as a father with me, he expected that I would study but he didn't say a word to my brother who did nothing at all. I felt responsible for the abortion and for the suffering and tension in my family. If I do not endorse their expectation that I should look after them, I feel that I am out and that I can't control anything. I control and direct others to overcome my guilty feeling by directing others to goodness". The achievement of a postgraduate diploma in law seemed to express an identification with masculinity and with father's expectations, while care and encouragement of her own femininity had to be put aside and she actually attacked it and deprived it of its value. Intelligence was a masculine characteristic while for her femininity was equal to being "stupid and a whore". AE. was unable to limit the conflict in the vertical relation between mind and body, between basic masculinity and femininity. She was unable to contain the anxiety that was provoked by such a state of mind. This was one of the reasons she expressed her conflict in such a delusional language, a language that was unfit for the establishment of significant correspondences and could only just contain anxiety. Still there was a difference. In the past her anxiety used to overflow beyond these weak boundaries and it became violent and self attacking. Thus the analysand used to violently aggress her own physicality (she used to burn her skin by taking boiling baths, excoriate her vagina internally, bite her lips until they would bleed). By now it had become possible to help her to begin to decode some meanings.

I would like to clarify better my hypothesis. I have stated that anything that is latent can become manifest at any moment therefore becoming conscious. I will use as an example of such state of affairs the analysis of the five mechanisms that are specifically active in dream work. I have already discussed the notions of displacement and condensation when referring to the Freudian distinction between representation and the quality of excitement (sensations). Condensation is regarded by Freud as a "nodal point" that may give strength and vigour to aspects that a person wishes to emphasise as they are representative of his or her psychic world. Freud, furthermore, regarded this process, as well as others even more specifically related to the elaboration of dreams, as closely related and partly similar to thought processes, and he included in the latter jokes, lapsus linguae, neologisms etc. I believe furthermore that I can specifically assign to condensation another peculiar characteristic. It facilitates the representability of the sensations and the emotions through the contact net.

I think we are all familiar with the great impact and "pictorial" vivacity of some dream images, representations and referred condensations present in artistic creations. All these phenomena may well be considered as the result of all the specific processes which Freud ascribed to dreams but they may also be regarded as the effect of the initial activity of the contact net, closer *to living than to perceiving*.

Condensation is adjacent to unconscious thought and its modes of functioning clarify and partly specify, the modes of functioning of the world of sensations. Condensation operates upon sensations, synthesising their common aspects and stressing the impact of the latter, thus enabling their

165

arrival to the area of emotions where a more intense colouring and a thicker meaning are then added.

One might say that, at least in its secondary effects, something similar happens in the displacement that extracts the sensations-emotions from the area of turbulence, which is when sensations-emotions emerge and their main characteristic – of expressing something that is actually felt – becomes apparent. This displacement is quite different from the displacement which takes place in any form of unconscious and which belongs to the entropic area, for the latter may express some degree of independence between the sensation and its representative. Furthermore this mechanism facilitates representability whenever it is necessary to move from the formulation of an abstract idea to the equivalent which may be visualised or vice-versa.

Again and again one may observe that sensory aspects are continuously transformed into explicit psychic aspects.

R. Jakobson, the linguist, connected the Freudian concepts of condensation and displacement with Rethoric's metaphor and metonymy, two procedures which he regarded as the fundamental poles in any language. He suggested a parallel between displacement and metonymy, pointing that the latter is characterised by the link of contiguity, and between symbolism and the metaphorical condition since, in this case, the association by resemblance is dominant. Lacan seemed to be of the same opinion insofar as the expression of desire was concerned. Any language is – according to Lacan – structured by the laws of the unconscious and based mainly upon metonymy, sineddoque and transposed elements. Such processes partly define the representability of dream work which mainly comes to the surface through visual images. In the dream we again have the passage from abstract concepts to images and sensations, basically formed of sensations-emotions.

Freud described, confining them to the area of dreams, the remarkable possibilities of secondary elaboration. The introduction of such changes and arrangements that may render understandable the apparently absurd and incoherent modes in which psychic products appear to the conscious system. He specifically regarded secondary elaboration as a kind of transformer of systems of thought, especially in delusional states, in phobic states, in obsessional thoughts, in paranoid states etc. It is easily demonstrated that, in such cases, the material only becomes comprehensible if one enters the system of the specific language register which is in use.

In conclusion I would like to mention perception which Freud regarded as related to consciousness. The latter he defined with great simplicity: ". . . a fact without parallel, which defies all explanation or description – the fact of consciousness. Nevertheless, if anyone speaks of consciousness we know immediately and from our most personal experience what is meant by it"[83]. Consciousness can therefore be regarded as part of a physical process that is mainly concerned with the perception of the external world (relating to the horizontal dimension). Perception of qualities obviously relates to consciousness of psychic phenomena, including the economical perspective Freud stated that, though consciousness is a quality-related phenomenon, produced by the perception of sensory qualities, it necessarily has to transform the quantity-related phenomena of tension and dis-tension into qualitative forms in order to acquire them for conscious elaboration.

I believe therefore that dream-production should be regarded as a kind of paradigm or model that one may then extend to other expressive capacities such as delusional, phobic, paranoid, psychotic, obsessional states and also hypnoid states. Each of these conditions may be characteristically recognised as one specific, possible kind of language register.

LANGUAGE REGISTERS

From the point of view of technique, analysts should continuously aim at progressively improving their capacities. Furthermore the latter should include understanding of language registers and being able to speak them. It would be useless to compare such registers to any kind of specialist language – scientifical, aesthetical or other – or to examine the "natural-historical language" in relation to any such others. It is far more useful to stress the importance of the function of language registers (rather than just mentioning their existence). Furthermore, the "natural-historical" language and all specialist languages have characteristic colourings in common with the language registers I am suggesting. Even in scientific language which should be the most abstract and universal of all, we can still find some nuances belonging to several different language registers. The scientific language doesn't in fact owe its specificity to definition or to clarification but rather to its throwing a shadow over anything that might disturb the meaning of its constellation of primary terms. This activity certainly impoverishes the riches of actual reality but it is the only mode in which, to this date, man can come to know about reality and about himself.

In analysis the main problem related with language has to do with identifying and distinguishing every kind of language register and with defining the function of each in the analytic setting. Language registers shouldn't therefore be observed as if they were equivalent or comparable to language but as something that relates to language in such a way that language can't exist without them. In other words not similar to language but connected with it.

An example of this can be found in these excerpts of a session with AE.:

AE.: "I didn't want to come today, I was afraid I couldn't manage. Yesterday I went for a swim and was unable to swim the crawl, to co-ordinate my movements and the breathing."

Analyst: "What is this caused by?"

AE.: "I am not happy with my life."

A.: "What is it that disturbs you or annoys you?"

AE.: "The way I eat is all wrong, I can't leave the table and stuff myself with food. I should leave some emptiness and instead I fill myself to the brim. Then I can't swim. I don't want things to happen as last summer. I felt lonely and that everyone was abandoning me, I stuffed myself with food and did nothing".

A.: "You leave yourself alone. The key is in your mode of eating. Do you mean to say that you fill yourself up with food instead of perceiving yourself? As when you fill yourself up with voices of judgements or when you suppress your sensations by scratching your skin?"

AE.: "The problem is in my anxiety."

A.: "Is your anxiety related to your perceiving your limits? Do you feel anxious that you may not do it, like yesterday at the swimming-pool or today in coming here?"

AE.: "I feel dejected, I would like to do a bit better. Sometimes I believe I can do it and that things could be quite different. Yesterday the swimming instructor was too aggressive, he kept harassing and teasing me in front of everyone else. It makes me nervous going to the swimming pool."

A.: "Do you think your teacher is 'for' you or 'against' you?"

AE.: "Instructors aren't hostile. The problem is with the other people who come to the swimming pool. But I don't care anymore. I want to live now."

A.: "What has changed? How come you have stopped caring 'now' and not 'before'?"

AE.: "Initially they were the ones who were more similar to me and it hurt. Then I felt vengeful. Now the best revenge is to let them burst with anger, envy and jealousy."

A.: "Do you perceive all this against you?"

AE.: "They don't want me to improve at University or in friendships. They don't want me to have a happy life. They say I will not come out of depression."

A.: "As in an anathema or in a conjuration?"

AE.: "I am the daughter of nobody. The daughter of a man who worked in the railways. I am not a princess! I can only succumb."

A.: "So, you are saying that when you perceive that you have limits, when you see that your potentialities have limits, you are confronted with the anxiety of not managing, you are stuck with the emergence of hatred, envy and jealousy. You feel overwhelmed and you fear you will succumb. Is it like that?"

AE.: "I don't care now! I suffered in analysis for a year and won't let anyone comment or make remarks on me. Why should I be afraid of University? If anyone is hostile I can answer."

A.: "When you are afraid that you might not manage do you perceive yourself as alone against the world?"

AE.: "It has always been like that for me. I felt calm because I had passed my exam then everything started again. (She means the voices, hints, signs by which she feels surrounded that are either 'for' or 'against' her.) The chaos started again."

A.: "You seem to be accompanied by a sort of ancient Greek tragedy "choir" that makes itself heard whenever you activate your intellectual resources and which is envious of your successes and happy with your failures. Do you think this fits?"

AE.: "I feel tired!"

A.: "It seems that you are working half for yourself and half against all these forces which you perceive to be hostile."

AE.: "They are against me whenever I begin to live."

A.: "Do you mean to say that whenever you 'begin to live' you have to struggle with your anxiety of not managing and with the antagonist's envy?"

AE.: "I sometimes feel disoriented and don't know what to do or where to go."

A.: "The thing about the rose! Could that help?" (In a session of some time before AE. told about the following episode: as a child she drew a rose and painted it blue. Her mother scolded her as roses aren't blue. The comment in telling the analyst about the episode was that there was no place for creativity.)

AE.: "I know that I can only live being myself. Otherwise one loses more and more ground and experiences aren't adequate to one's age anymore!"

A.: "This is important. You might have made yourself feel confused and lost because of envy[84]. What do you think of that?"

AE.: "I have always felt envious but never acknowledged it. Now I think it is normal."

A.: "The less you recognise and acknowledge your envy the more you feel suffocated by the envy of others."

AE.: "But there has been meanness! The question is that if I acknowledge my feelings I can then recognise other people's feelings. It isn't that I am a saint and the others are devils! One can't live with this kind of assumption! When I have a child I won't stop him from hating. It was my parents' mistake to silence everything, I disagree with them now. I have always been suspicious of becoming the mother of a girl, I always thought I would become the mother of a boy. Now I understand that having a girl would mean accepting my own femininity. With a boy there is more solidarity, with a girl one would be almost looking at oneself in the mirror."

In presenting this clinical material I am offering an example of the analyst's technique in adopting specific language registers. In this case the language register is unmistakably delusional. One may easily see that the analyst's verbal capacities foster the analytic dialogue as they enable him to 'momentarily' communicate in the same language register in which the analysand is forced to communicate at that moment – the delusional language register.

In the following excerpt the analyst attends and supports the analysand in trying to establish significant links between the fragments of experiences and of emotions scattered in her mind. The analyst attunes to the language register which the analysand seems to choose at each moment and the analysand can then change from a delusional to a historical language. Through this variation she manages to organise some thoughts about her Oedipal constellation: "I am thinking that I am quite similar to my mother and to my father".

Fragments of a session with AF.

A young woman comes in on time wearing a t-shirt and tights as usual. She sits down and looks at the analyst with a smiling but slightly distant expression on her face.

Analyst: "What are your thoughts?"

AF.: "I am thinking that when I see that there are great problems ... when I read the papers or watch TV, things that concern me as a person ... referring to me ... I am the most important person ... they are mentioning the greatest points."

A.: "What points?"

AF.: "Not quite points of reference ... rather truths ... problems."

A.: "Which?"

AF.: "I feel so responsible ... as a consequence ... because ... I was there ... I stayed there, as a consequence ... things happen sometimes ... fear or occurrences, great suffering causing ... how can I put it? very serious things".

A.: "What is it that is very serious?"

AF.: "The last thing happening, it shouldn't happen ... Nothing can be done about it ... "

A.: "Irreparable then."

AF.: "Something can be done but things get worse and worse up to the moment in which there is something right or true or healthy that can be done about it."

A.: "It is possible to do something then."

AF.: "No reparation can take place because of me."

A.: "It is your presence then that favours terrible happenings."

170

"Up to now there have been continuous severe and accidental happenings".

A.: "Things became worse because of you! Because when you were there . . . " (AF. interrupts)

AF.: "Three years ago, and they were the last."

A.: "What happened three years ago?"

AF.: "Something strange, very strange, strange things could be seen."

A.: "What?"

AF.: "In passing . . . "

Her gaze was distant. The analyst talked to her, saying that speaking of the past was maybe bringing in emotions and thoughts of today. Then the analyst stopped because AF. was far away. After a moment the analyst called AF. by her name, asking where she was, adding that she seemed to be distant.

AF.: "I haven' listened, I was thinking of an answer."

The analyst hadn't asked any question.

A.: "What answer?"

AF.: "I was thinking . . . " (She yawns)

A.: "You are far away, is it difficult to come back here?"

AF.: "I was thinking of a moment ago . . . I was looking at your eyes . . . They are like my cousin's eyes . . . She is a teacher for handicapped children . . . She is capable and very kind."

A.: "Why is it that you are telling me about this cousin?"

AF.: "She is my godmother and my mother's godchild from confirmation, she is a bit thin, she is like me, I am thin everywhere . . . she is a nice girl."

The analyst said that she brought out her destructive aspects first and now she was mentioning a possibility of helping and looking after people in difficulty, like her cousin, dealing with handicapped people.

She was silent a few minutes and then said: "I am thinking that I am so much like my father and my mother, if I look at my cousin I can't remember anything at times".

The analyst suggested that one aspect of her recognised familiar connections while another hid and then forgot them, stealing them away from memory.

AF. said that she had decided to register for the swimming course at the swimming pool. Her language was fluent as she described the bathing suit and cap that she intended to buy and the different swimming styles that she hoped to learn.

Language isn't in this case just a simple code, obeying to its rules as it can be found in the language of grammar or of dictionaries, the latter have little to do with the real spoken everyday language. The spoken language is rich with internal historical, personal experiences, relating to the past, to childhood, to last minute experiences. It is a strongly conditioned experience as it expresses our deep or superficial desires, including the ones which one ignores at the moment. Language obviously relates to the vertical dimension. Everything that comes before language is a condition for actual language to be developed, and language couldn't appear without all its prerequisites and it couldn't be what we understand by language. The essential features aren't therefore similitude or resemblance, as language implies all this. No language is in itself expressed by images. There can only be the experience of images and we can't know it separately from language itself. This is why I am not talking of languages but of language registers, which are primitive forms of language. Language is therefore a unique entity, a kind of continuum, differentiating and expanding in different ways, originating in different contexts and needs.

This kind of formulation enables me to isolate different registers, in language, relating to psychosis, to hallucination, to paranoia etc.

Rhetoric, I would like to add, seems to have somehow officially recognised such a possibility, since all rhetorical figures, like most other parts of speech, necessarily require diversified modes of expression.

Isn't the graphic, figurative expression hallucinatory? Thought also might be regarded in this way. Bion had much to say about that, both on the theoretical and technical levels. He admitted that intuition of psychic reality and hallucination are both separated from the sensory context (and therefore don't take place on a sensory basis), even though they may lead to a sensory experience. He highlighted nevertheless that, while intuition may only take place if there is a tolerance of the lack, or even of the total absence of a sensory experience, on the contrary, hallucination develops. When there is such an intolerance for the absence of the object, then the object has to be made forcibly present.

In the first case (intuition) the capacity to bear the absence of the object and of the sensory flood, favours the establishment of the necessary grounds for a psychic event, or mental experience to take place thus enabling the establishment of conditions necessary for the perceptions to be stimulated and for the acquisition of knowledge through sensory channels. In the second case (hallucination) there is no tolerance of the absence and therefore, there is no attempt to find a meaning that might enlarge the horizons of thought, enabling evaluation of possible choices. There is just an inclination towards obtaining pain or pleasure and this happens through a direct transformation of ideas into action, an aimless action that is a pure search of sensory gratification.

I would like to discuss briefly the matter of rhetoric and of incoherence of speech. Examples will clarify that rhetoric has no interest in the logical coherence of language as it mainly aims at persuasion, not so much at argumentation. An attempt at persuasion may, as it is well known, use the channels of emotion or even of paradox in order to hit on the imagination[85].

A very interesting case is provided by the rhetorical figure of "distinctio" used in the negative sense. The negative use is "obviously a paradox" in which the same thing is stated and denied at the same time, at least as far as the word goes: *Una salus victis nullam sperare salutem* (The only hope for those who have been defeated is in not having any hope) Virgil, *Aeneid*: *Mon unique espérance est dans mon désespoir* (My only hope is being hopeless) Racine, *Bajazet*. These seem to be very interesting quotations, especially for psychoanalysts, because there aren't here just words but reality data and the strong impact of the latter upon the internal world of the individual. There may seem to be great despair and total lack of hope, and this is just what it is about, but there is also the insuperable strength of the actual moment and a healthy limit to the human wish for omnipotence on the one hand and, on the other, a pessimistic but realistic vision of man's capacity for destruction.

This kind of paradox originating in the negative "distinctio" was used by E. Garroni to clarify, in part, his understanding of the notion of paradox in *Senso e Paradosso*[86] as something which is intermediate between rhetoric paradox and logical contradiction owning the qualities of both but not just being one or the other.

We have another similar case with "antithesis" or "contentio" in which sentences, groups of words or single words are counterpoised in co-ordination. Co-ordination may be implicit, that is without the conjunction, it is, in this case, a most interesting rhetoric figure, the well known "oxymoron" as with *concordia discors* (discordant concord) Horace, *Epistles*: or with *etiam si taceant, satis dicunt* (though they may be silent they are saying enough) Cicero, *Divinatio in Q.Caecilium*, or *darkness visible* Milton, *Paradise Lost*.

There are many rhetorical figures expressing inconsistencies, contrasts, actual or apparent contradictions and the language can't in any case be regarded as identical to truth. Some examples are the "hyperbole", the "irony", some kinds of "allegory" (when there is an *inconsequentia rerum*) the "equivoque", the "ambiguity", the "adversative asyndeton" (expressing antithetical thoughts) and so forth.

Rhetoric certainly doesn't express in detail the concepts which I am discussing here but it does focus upon the contradictions of language, either in order to use them to obtain persuasion or to advise against their use. Some of the rationalist thinkers of the past, such as Leibniz, actually used to believe reality to be originated out of logical principles and contradictions in language out of subjective defects in its use, while, on the other hand, language itself was regarded as essentially and ideally non-contradictory. Cartesian Linguistics were grounded on a fundamental homology between language and logic. Coherence was seen as the main model for language and any incoherence was regarded as a temporary deviation of its use. Contemporary logicians, on the contrary, start from the inverse presupposition. Logic is for them an instrument for the creation and description of coherent languages, beyond common language which is never coherent. Logic is therefore concerned with formalised languages and the latter may be appropriately described as object-languages, described by means of a "meta-language" which can be regarded, between other things, as more powerful than the languages it describes just because it can describe them.

A. Tarski contributed this theoretical model by opposing formalised languages to a "universal common language" which is supposedly adequate to express any kind of subject, including the language itself, and as it isn't in fact adequate for any specific matter, it actually originates all kinds of difficulties, paradoxes and antinomies. An interesting example of this can be found in Tarski's analysis of the famous antinomy of the liar[87]. Wittgenstein also, in his mature years, maintained that logic and formalised languages are late and somehow peripheral forms of language and shouldn't therefore be enabled to act backwards upon language in general. Wittgenstein employs a beautiful description: "Our language can be seen as an ancient city, a maze of little streets and squares, of old and new houses."[88]

Several linguists, T. De Mauro[89] between others, regard language as a kind of semiological code, characterised by its semantic indeterminateness and creativity. This definition reminds one of Tarski's notion of "universal common language". De Mauro suggests that *a language that is so close to an original state of confusion might well originate several more refined formalised codes of speech*. This hypothesis is of extreme relevance for the subject I am discussing in this book as there is a significant coincidence between De Mauro's former contribution and my hypothesis of the contact net – the dawn of thought – that impels language, through language registers, towards its realisation and completeness in the forms of thought. Furthermore, if linguists describe language as it is, rather than as it should be, how could they avoid regarding its manifold, variable, sometimes even paradoxical and contradictory appearance as an element of its intrinsical characterisation?

The predominant or even exclusive use of one language register should therefore be regarded as the sign of an actual state of disharmony. Here is an example:

> An analysand predominantly used an image-producing language register. One of these images – she said – appeared obsessionally. She saw herself climbing on the windowsill or on a very tall smooth

pinnacle and then letting herself fall without meeting any obstacles. The material was analysed as her being in an unsteady balance between a psychic emptiness and a saturated area of turmoiling sensations and emotions.

As far as language is concerned, one shouldn't regard as disharmonious the conditions in which different language registers are used in alternation but only the states in which any one register is chosen and used most of the time. In such situations it becomes very difficult for a person to use other registers and to find some help in them while trying to adapt adequately to the incessant challenges of life.

As it is, the incapacity to use dynamically the potentiality of the different language registers doesn't at all alter or condition the individual's *belief* in his or her own skills to use verbal expression and in the *capacity for representation*. But it does create difficulties in analytic work if the analysand chooses to use, as a defence, any one of the above mentioned languages.

The person who chooses to use a language at the disadvantage of all the others is obviously regarding the chosen language as omni-comprehensive and universal – the only valid language. Because he is convinced of this he reinforces it. In other words when the disharmony relates to an inadequate use of the personal modes of expression, a kind of radicalisation of such modes of expression is seen as useful and therefore takes place. Thus regarded, the language doesn't express a request for isolation but rather an attempt at emphasising something.

The registers which come apart from the "natural-historical" language may well be regarded as *emergency languages* in that the contact net facilitates their appearance under the drive of the special needs of specific emotional conditions. They do therefore disappear, together with the states of mind which require them, when a person can revert to his or her everyday language. Obviously, though most people use a language that bears analogies with "natural-historical" language (as it appears in its formal aspects) the essence of every specific language corresponds to the dominant psychic structures of the person who uses the language and sometimes even qualifies the personality of the user. It is therefore possible to distinguish the structure and colouring of a delusional, phobic, paranoid, obsessional (etc.) kind of language, in the use of "natural-historical" languages without it bearing or meaning any kind of disharmony.

Finally, the risk and the limit of such emergency languages is in their being devoid of any contact and comparison between psychic and external realities or, in other words, of any synthesis between the vertical and horizontal dimensions. They lack a flexible functioning contact net, capable of continuous adaptation to different circumstances. Obviously the cases of lack of contact between psychic and external reality are extreme cases.

The comparison is in most situations somehow present, even when there is severe disharmony, but it is often quite unilateral, as it lacks any possibility of being tested. When only one register has been selected for absolute exclusive use, there is no possibility for control of the language left. An actual barrier is formed and it may well be the last defence against a blind automatic functioning originated by the intense continuous pressure of sensations and emotions that can't be hosted and provided with shape in the contact net. This is the only real drama in disharmonious states.

The functioning of the contact net originates in the reciprocally fostered harmonious development of the two dimensions, vertical and horizontal, without any overwhelming influence of one upon the other.

This isn't so much a hypothesis as a phenomenological notation. Thought doesn't come from somewhere, it rather forms itself. Furthermore, the concept of vertical dimension doesn't explain thought, it doesn't even aim at trying to do so. We have to start from the mental area, but what is a mental area or space apart from being a potential capacity for thought?

And what is thought? That is something else. I don't feel I have the capacities to answer this question, nor am I interested in trying to do so. I try to understand its functioning, mine is a sufficiently immodest aim as it is.

All my investigations are based upon a conception of language as a non-autonomous area that isn't just based on consciousness or on what is explicit. Language couldn't in any way be limited to such boundaries. Consciousness and explicitness exist of course in language but there are also elements from our internal experience, which relate language to other aspects of experience and to other modes of representation or expression. For this reason in some passages of this book I have substituted the term language with "capacity for expression". By this term I am referring to a very initial moment, to the first prerequisites for the establishment of a linguistic communication. This is relevant also for the structuring of personality as if a person doesn't get the opportunity to reach some mode of expression of experiences (be it just of the mere emotional states) there will be no structuring of the personality, no existence.

The capacity for expression is therefore a most important and significant feature. The verbal-linguistic capacity isn't but an aspect of it and it can become a common or a formalised language, still showing, nevertheless, everything that it implies and everything that comes before it. One could say that it is an expressive wholeness of which language isn't but a facet or a kind of final step of a process that can't be grasped just by its result. No language is or may be regarded as an independent sphere. One would be totally unable to communicate if the things that are being told weren't related to one's personal history, personal and group history. One wouldn't be at all oriented and wouldn't even know the meaning of pointing at something. The first difficulty which every person meets is that of bringing to life the representations as distinct references to some specific meaning. The process isn't at all simple or obvious.

NOTES

70 Elsewhere also defined as "psychic"(T.N.).
71 The terms "relation" "dimension" "area" "relationship" have all been used in turn to go with the concepts of vertical and horizontal. It may be useful to specify that such terms respectively refer, depending on the specific context, to the position occupied in the individual's mental world, to the actual range presented and to the dynamic and therefore relational link with other systems.
72 "Deviations from this psychical period that is specific for them (the neurones) come to consciousness as qualities" Freud S. (1895) *Project for a Scientific Psychology*, SE, Vol.I, p.310.
73 One can think of the passage, described by M. Klein, from the Paranoid-Schizoid to the Depressive Position.
74 Freud S. (1917) "Mourning and Melancholia", SE, London: Hogarth Press, vol. XIV, p. 239.
75 Cf. the relation between bulimia/ agoraphobia and anorexia/claustrophobia.
76 Bion W. R.(1962), *Learning from Experience* London: Karnac Books, 1984, p. 36.
77 Bion W. R. (1962), *Learning from Experience* London: Karnac Books, 1984 p. 35.
78 I use "prevail" for, as I have already mentioned, I think the concept of regression is inapplicable here. In pregnancy and in child-bearing. same as in adolescence the corporeal stimuli cause the COO to emerge anew. The COO bears in each case specific characteristics functional to the actual need which shouldn't be mistaken with the characteristics of the newly born baby.
79 The concept of "distance" used in linguistics may be regarded as equivalent to the concept of "mental space" ("mental area" (T.N.)) used in the psychological field.
80 SE, London: Hogarth Press, vol. V, p.579–580 n.1.
81 Ferrari A. B.(1983), "Relazione Analitica sistema o processo?" *Rivista di Psicoanalisi*, 29, 4, 476–496.
82 Bion W. R.(1962), *Learning from Experience* London: Karnac Books, p.79.
82 Freud S. (1940) *An Outline of Psycho-Analysis*, SE, London: Hogarth Press, vol. XXIII, p.157.
84 The meaning of "feeling envious" was clarified with the analysand in recent sessions.
85 I am grateful to Prof. Emilio Garroni for helping me with this subject and for providing an essential reference: H. Lausberg (1949), *Elemente der Literarischen Rhetorik*, Hueber, München 1967.
86 E. Garroni (1986) *Senso e Paradosso. L'Estetica, filosofia non speciale*, Biblioteca di Cultura Moderna, Laterza, Bari 1986.
87 Tarski A. (1944), "The Semantic Concept of Truth", *Philosophy and Phenomenological Research*, IV, 1944.
88 Wittgenstein L. (1953) *Philosophical Investigations*, Blackwell, Oxford, p.8.
89 T. De Mauro (1982) *Minisemantica*, Bari: Laterza.

7

ANALYTIC APPLICATIONS
F. Romano[90] and A. B. Ferrari

INTRODUCING THE CLINICAL CASES

The hypotheses which have been presented above can, in our opinion, actually provide a compound of analytic tools. The notions of vertical and horizontal dimension, of ego configuration, of Oedipal constellation, of contact net etc. have been formulated with the help of observations and analytic experience and derive from our understanding of mental functioning as an essentially dynamic process.

We regard the Analytic Relationship as a self-interpreting framework[91] characterised by a double movement, the analysand "proceeds towards himself" and the analyst "returns towards himself" in the "here and now" of the development of the work, and, thanks to these movements, the mental resources – in other words the processes of thought of the individual – are activated.

The framework is an observable datum. It is actually the compound of all the elements that make up the Analytic Relationship. Each of them actually represents the Analytic Relationship with a definite level of meaning and pertinence and concurs in creating a progressively widening framework, that can then re-interpret the minor frameworks which it contains. The notion of "self-interpreting framework"[92] refers to a quite specific characteristic. The analyst doesn't ever count on any external reference for interpretation, for all elements are internal to the framework and to the relation as the single elements of a wider frame, the latter gradually coming together with the help of definite and conditioning theoretical supports.

Obviously such a position implies a criticism of the notion of "interpretation" which we have therefore long since substituted with the notion of "analytic proposition"[93].

We think it is extremely important for every Analytic Relationship to focus on the vertical dimension, especially in what concerns the Onefold-Twofold system and the influence of the latter in the relation between physicality and the psychic functioning. A process is thus originated in which significant correspondences between sensations and emotions on the one hand and the thinking apparatus on the other may be established. The analysand can then progressively substitute the newly formed contact net to the stiff defensive barriers which he had erected against an emotional flood that was perceived as overwhelming.

The Analytic Relationship thus supports the analysand's activation of the capacity for self-observation (this process of activation is described in the section "The Contact Net: a hypothesis"). At the beginning of analysis the analysand is often mainly a "participant" as the absence of a contact net causes an almost complete saturation of the mental area. The capacity for self-observation necessary for the formulation of thoughts is in such cases greatly hindered or even completely inhibited. By focusing the attention on the vertical dimension it becomes possible to reach an actual confrontation with oneself and a specific individuation both of the anxiety and of the inefficacy of the defences which were formerly employed. It also becomes possible to evaluate realistically one's own responsibility in trying to find ways towards new equilibria.

We would also like to add that focusing on the vertical dimension doesn't mean forgetting transference, for the latter continues being one of the main points of reference of analytic research.

At this stage transference is intrinsic to the internal system of the analysand. Speaking is, in other words, always something that has to do with transference. As a consequence of this the analyst is invested of the analysand's conflicts and becomes part of the analysand's problems. The mode in which the analysand uses the analyst is of fundamental importance for the observation and evaluation of the seriousness of the analysand's conflicts and problems. In the vertical dimension the analyst supports the more integrated features of the analysand and enables him to explore other possible modes of approaching reality. In so doing the analyst becomes a kind of "mental area" inside the analysand's own potential mental area, as the analysand is so participant that he is unable to make himself some mental space. When there is a condition of strong emotional tension, the analysand's anxiety tends to include the analyst in the analysand's system, in order to contrast the frustration experienced in still having such a dependent mind. The analyst thus functions as a kind of negotiator between the conflicts of the analysand rather than as a helper for his problems.

Here is an example. An analysand may ask the analyst to just listen to him. The analyst might then ask how long it is since the analysand has stopped listening to himself or what thoughts or emotions he doesn't want to hear. If the analyst were to accept the request and just listen, the analysand would establish a dangerous dependence. But the analyst needs to work in order to develop and eventually abandon his function, a function that may in such circumstances be compared to the function of the mother towards the newly born baby. As it has been said on "The Contact Net: an hypothesis" the matter has the function of anticipating and of catalysing the baby's contact net which is then necessarily formed and developed further by the baby itself.

We have observed that the initial focus on the vertical dimension engenders feelings of comfort in analysands and encourages them to perceive themselves as capable of a mental functioning which they may have felt was seriously damaged at the moment in which they asked for help. As a consequence of this, anxiety seems to become more easily contained.

This renewed faith in one's own capacities easily turns into a kind of manic state in the more disharmonious conditions, as, like it has been stated before, manic manipulation is easiest in the Onefold-Twofold system when external reality is somewhat distant. It is the analyst's task to draw the horizontal dimension (Oedipal constellation, ego configuration and the representation of the relationship with the external world) nearer and, as a consequence, the vivid perception of limits produced by the impact of external reality.

Analytic experience has shown us that the use of the above mentioned concepts as active instruments in the Analytic Relationship rather quickly puts in motion many of the analysand's resources. Thus the analysand can find, in the vertical dimension, the focal points round which he has structured his rigid and impenetrable defensive barriers, made of restrictive theories about himself and about the world, and his automatic behaviours and prejudices capable of seriously hindering or at least of reducing his possibility of learning from his own experience. This doesn't happen easily when the vertical and horizontal dimensions intersect incessantly.

We have often observed that by focusing on the vertical dimension it becomes possible to shorten the analytic treatment even in very disharmonious situations[94]. It is well known that Freud investigated questions related to the ending of analysis[95], our question nevertheless is: when and on what evidence should an analytic treatment be regarded as concluded? And furthermore, can any analysis ever be regarded as concluded?

One might say that the end of an analytic experience may be seen as the conclusion of a relationship in which it has been possible to get thought processes started. If one regards analysis, in a wide sense, as a process in which one seeks and structures the person one really is, analysis could then never end but, on the contrary, it could last to the end of one's life.

This is especially true of the analysts and one could well say that their analysis never ends.

The process which, on the contrary, may and should come to an end is the actual historical Analytic Relationship. It should be terminated in the modes and times of the analyst, measured nevertheless on the distinctive modes and times of each analysand.

We do believe that the specific approach suggested in this book brings as a consequence a shortening of the analytic process, though the shortening certainly isn't its principal aim. The approach mainly aims at investigating the modes in which the analysand's mind may be activated in the analytic context. Thus we suggest that the main objective in analytic work might be to promote a maximum of mental resources in the minimum possible time compatible with such an objective. This approach is therefore characterised by the central importance of the experience in the analytic relationship and by the consequent shortening of the analytic work. A shorter analytic experience that shouldn't in any way be regarded or qualified as a new or specific branch of psychoanalysis[96].

In the hypothesis presented here, the psychoanalytic approach is deeply modified by the disavowal of the concept of pathology, in favour of the notions of mental harmony and disharmony. The presence of the variable "time" influences significantly the length of the analytic experience. As the space-time variables are the fundamental axes on which most things, mental functioning among others, are based.

Time is especially important in working with adolescents. Their transformations, psychic and physical, are so rapid and meaningful that anxiety easily saturates their minds. They need to think of the future (unknown) for the first time and experience limits. Furthermore, when all this happens they are alone, alone for the first time, like all adult human beings. One can easily understand then, that it is important to show the young analysand how he may, on each specific occasion, alter his or her point of view, how their eyes can become different and see things that couldn't be seen before.

A majority of analysands can advantageously receive help in this way as many problems originate in an attempt to "by-pass" the anxiety lying in this vital moment of change and growth (either nestling in an infantile mode of functioning or passively "borrowing" from the external world an imitation of the image of some adult functioning). The time variable may be used by the analyst in all these cases to promote an activation of the potentialities of the analysand instead of just waiting for events of life to do as much. When the actual ending of analysis is established, for instance, one may observe that analysands put in action the same defence mechanisms which they had employed at the beginning of the process. The initial state of turmoil is again present, the emotional impact is experienced as so powerful that it doesn't seem to allow for the transformation of the perception into experience. This sequence is so typical that if an analysand didn't show any signs of "disharmony" at such a moment the analyst might well fear that something in the process has gone wrong.

When emotions are extremely powerful and uncontainable everybody, even the most creative person may revert to the original defences. Everyone can become the prey of anxiety and seek protection from the threat of distress and extreme tension. When this is the case in analysis, the analyst may then show the analysand how the latter, because of his emotions, tends to ignore or even dispose of the experience he has done during the whole process in the analytic relationship. The work that is done at that moment, "reviewing and resetting", can count on an extremely important ally – time. At the end of analysis analysands again tend to become participant instead of being observers of themselves and forget or suspend anything that they have learned in the initial period of analysis. They cannot count on the help of their mental area or space as it is again saturated by the emotional pressure.

> An analysand who was working towards the end of her analysis said she often surprised herself by using ancient modes of functioning but added that she felt she did it almost on purpose, so that she could see such modes and compare them with her new acquisitions, she said she did this so as to be able to choose. In so doing she brought evidence of the establishment of a function of self observation.

A sensitive analyst is capable of making adequate arrangements for a timely ending of analysis. In so doing he "gives the tree of the certainties a good shake" when anxiety compels the analysand to cling to his old modes of functioning. It is easy at such times for the analyst to show the analysand what is happening in his internal world, to help him become conscious of his old disharmonious modes and of what he has acquired. It isn't a discovery or an insight anymore at this point, it is rather a kind of revision.

The meaning and the acquisition of this phase of the experience is in the self-observation, inside the analytic framework, of one's mechanisms and in the conscious development of a sense of responsibility for one's being, by means of the activation of the horizontal dimension. The capacity to communicate with oneself, which the analysand acquired in the initial stages of the analytic process, is now made more complex by interaction with others. At this stage of analysis transference assumes its most well-known and common form.

From this point onwards all psychic achievements are worked on by the analysand, they are nevertheless made more complex by the need to keep in mind the presence of the other, the analyst. Things are different from the beginning as in situations of extreme internal conflict the analysand actually *was* the other. After the conflict has been clarified by analytic work, the analysand can finally take responsibility for his actions. It is unnecessary for the analyst to deal with the conflict, it is sufficient that he mentions it to the analysand clarifying that he has to respond for himself to himself and to take responsibility for the consequences of his actions, gestures and even thoughts about the world around him.

In this new situation, with the analyst clearly another person from himself, the analysand verifies whether and what he has acquired and metabolised in his work in the vertical dimension and if the acquisitions are functional to his individual needs. The transference is meanwhile in existence in the horizontal dimension.

One can think that a capacity to think should have come to existence by now and that the analyst should respect its freedom and let it function with its own resources towards the world and towards the individual himself. The individual needs at this moment to experiment, to find out, to investigate the functionality of what he has just conquered, of his new capacities.

In the initial part of analysis the analyst becomes a part of the analysand's mental system. He is in direct contact with the material and with the modes of defence including the most hindering ones, and may, at any moment, intervene in the vertical dimension highlighting the analysand's senses, meaning, and the direction given to his choices.

Later, when an ending of the analytic experience has been agreed upon and established, the analysand may easily, as a consequence of this decision, be the person he really is, without having to wait for the perception of his own mode of being to be awakened by the actual impact with specific events. It isn't therefore necessary to wait for significant events to actually take place or for changes in the life of the analysand to happen concretely influencing his situation. As we have said at the beginning of the section we regard the Analytic Relationship as a self-interpreting framework, and when the subject of its ending is historically introduced by the analyst, the analysand is often stimulated to a confrontation with the experience of an end, and therefore with the perception of limits but also of vulnerability and solitude. When death anxieties are understandably evoked it is impossible to push away or deny such a perception. The perception is therefore faced and helps the analysand to enrich his experience in life. The experience of ending the Analytic Relationship actually makes the perception of its presence more vivid because the absence is somehow made present as well.

A bulimic adolescent girl had been in analysis for three years. A few months after the end of analysis had been decided she was able to experience death anxieties for the first time. Initially she reverted to her old modes. Bulimic behaviour appeared once more and the habit of vomiting increased as a defence against the anxiety of losing control of her actions and of the movements of food inside her body. When such events were discussed in analysis and there was pain and anxiety related to fear for the fragility of the acquisition, she then became able to perceive the rigid defensive barrier which she had always erected against such anxieties and against focusing her attention on "ends". "I used to fill in all spaces when something ended – she said – my grandfather died? Never mind there was my grandmother! My childhood ended? I stuffed myself with food! I used to occupy all spaces when something ended. I furiously tried to put something or someone in my place. So there never were ends for me or things missing, there wasn't even life. Now I begin to have memories. Before, I used to know that I was in the place but I had no memories about the happenings".

The choice of the moment in which to promote the beginning of the final phase of analysis depends only partially on the "analyst's tactfulness", it rather relates to his capacity to lead the analysand "to reach the lowest layers" of his disharmonious modes (reach the deepest point of his internal experience) and progressively establish new significant links between the emotional flood and the thought processes.

Finally we believe that the analytic situations that follow may illustrate adequately how the hypotheses presented above may be applied as analytic instruments.

CASE S.

During the first year of analysis this analysand appeared to be absolutely unable to recognise or name her emotions and feelings. Eventually she perceived something which she described as a persistent sadness but which she was unable to place. Before that, in the sessions, all emotions and feelings were expressed by her as visual, olfactory or synesthetic sensations.

The phenomena which the analyst observed in the session seemed to represent the results of a kind of explosion of her mental system which interrupted the communication between physicality and the psychic. Her body continued to be present, as well as its stimuli, and continued to transmit but found no correspondence in the mind. There was only a kind of bodily mind, still active, substituting the functions of the mind which, on the contrary, were blocked. She maintained that she could better control her emotions if they stayed in her body, because she could control what she saw but couldn't see and therefore control, her mind or her emotions. So, if she had some psychic pain she tried to control it (to give it a form and a meaning) by transforming it into a physical pain, biting her lips or scratching her skin.

185

In one of the first sessions her anxiety about silence emerged. She spoke about herself going to sleep at night. If there was a total silence she felt she had to make a noise with her fingers on her pillow to reduce the anxiety of "not existing". The analyst then said: "It seems that you are checking whether there is something to listen to, it is like a kind of code, someone is trying to transmit something to someone else and asks: 'Are you there? Are you listening?'".

S.: "I am thinking of a scream. I feel like screaming"(in a former session when she had a painful sensation like a catch in her stomach she said it was like catching a scream, wordlessly as in Munch's painting).

A.: "What does the scream express? Is it anxiety? Despair?"

S.: "I don't know. It's a scream".

The anxiety to which S. couldn't give a meaning could have been related to two different and distinct emotions, the anxiety of the "transmitting end" and therefore the terrified scream that there might be nobody there "to" listen (the distress of being alone and deaf to a part of herself) and the anxiety of the "receiving end" fearing that there is no one to listen to (the distress of being alone and dumb to a part of herself).

The analyst employed here the model of the significant correspondences and tried to foster the development of communication in the vertical dimension, especially between the area of physicality and the area of psychic functioning.

When the feeling of sadness appeared, the analysand described a sensation which she defined as the wish to gain distance from everybody. She experienced contact with other people as intolerable for she realised that "she wasn't as others thought she was". She actually tended to appear very efficient in interpersonal relationships and this didn't correspond to the feeling of inadequacy which she hid deep in herself.

Two widely split and non-communicating aspects were beginning to emerge, one internal, so to speak, which appeared to be mute, closed, isolated, unable to articulate any words or thoughts. The other external, supplying concrete organisational capacities, maybe imitative. Thanks to this second aspect S. staged a kind of parody of "normal life" but remained deaf to all sensations and emotions.

The analysand's massive defence was splitting, she never had an idea of what she looked like as she excluded her physical aspect from her perception. As it has been mentioned in the section "Identity and the Ego" she couldn't remember what she didn't know that she had forgotten.

"Yesterday I felt terrible, I suffered an immense anxiety and it wouldn't pass! I chatted with someone I knew, at the shop, and I felt ill. I saw myself . . . It actually happened inside me . . . I saw myself oscillating my head from left to right, I would have liked someone to catch my head and stop it, but no one could see that I was doing it, I couldn't have told anyone, no one could have understood how I was feeling."

Though she now managed to recognise the feeling which she called anxiety, she couldn't link it to any kind of meaning or thought, and when something like that happened the only thing she could do was "wait until it would pass". It was a kind of turmoiling state of anxiety, perceived in a condition of total isolation and withdrawal.

On the plan of the vertical dimension this analysand was characterised by a deep and violent conflict. As analytic work proceeded it enabled her intense feelings of inadequacy and impotence to emerge and the conflict therefore became more and more obvious up to the moment in which an almost total blockage of the mental functioning was highlighted. During a few sessions she said nothing except that it was useless to continue with analytic work, that it was too late, that she never knew what to say, that she forgot whatever was said in the session, or experienced in her life. The emotional atmosphere during these communications oscillated between intense hatred and a pervasive feeling of impotence – the anxiety was at its utmost.

The analyst began to fear that the analysand's life might be in danger, as she seemed, at least this was the analyst's opinion, to have totally hindered her own mental functioning. One could feel that there was a total absence of an internal echo of the external world, while from the internal world nothing came towards the external, except these feeling of extreme and "dumb" hatred.

The analyst felt that from this immobility some very violent uncontrollable instincts could emerge and that the analysand might become a prey to such instincts and kill herself.

The feeling of hatred which the analysand nurtured in the vertical dimension wasn't concerned with any real matter. It wasn't a reaction, but rather a kind of "active" hatred. It seemed to have its roots in the Oedipal constellation. An idealised father figure and a mother which she represented as unable to recognise her or distinguish her from her sister, unable to welcome, to give attention and love, a kind of rag-doll mother, cold and inanimate.S. had tried to identify with the masculinity of her father's figure but had only succeeded in precociously and violently attacking her basic femininity.

The construction of her psychic scenery was made slow and difficult because of her tendency to cancel all the traces of her experiences to a point in which she was left with no memories. Actually she did register the experiences in her mind but only as an encumbering compound of meaningless traces, as she would become very destructive as soon as a significant correspondence was about to be formed, and left her mind in a state of despairing poverty.

One can think that splitting might have become the fundamental characteristic of her psychic apparatus, regardless of the contents. Her aim was that of preserving an active splitting in regard of any kind of perception, even of pleasurable perceptions which were immediately experienced as threatening, since they were potential sources of frustration. From this the despairing poverty of her mind ensued. On one occasion she appeared to be especially pleased during a session as her husband had given her a racing bicycle, a present which she had wanted since childhood. No one had known about this in those days and the bicycle had been given to her brother. She expressly mentioned that her happiness didn't relate to the present itself but to her husband's attention in listening to her and in wanting to satisfy her wish. In the following session there seemed to be nothing of that, she said instead that she wanted to disappear physically, to let herself die though she didn't have the courage really.

It was possible to show her the sequence of internal events and she recognised that in her "wanting to disappear" there was the illusion of an attempt to anticipate any possible future disappointment she was terrified she might suffer from her feeling of pleasure. In the session she tried incessantly to put splitting in motion and always started by stating that she had nothing to say, didn't have anything in mind, didn't know how to start. She couldn't remember what she didn't know she had forgotten.

During quite a long time analytic work developed with the help of bodily sensations which the analysand spoke about and which revealed that her mental functioning was quite archaic. It was possible to trace in the analytic relationship some significant correspondences between sensations, emotions and thoughts. The analyst preserved all useful traces and tried to put in motion the analysand's processes of thought. By means of a kind of function of reverie he managed to by-pass the chasm which S. kept excavating in the vertical dimension.

It was thus possible to preserve the analytic relationship's capacity to construct each time the meanings and significant correspondences with the bodily sensations which the analysand spoke about – a catch in her stomach, a lack of breath, the anxiety of silence, the little cough which expressed the need to "hear that she existed"(she actually meant "hear" with her ears) etc. sensations which were translated into emotions, often violent, or in meaningful thoughts, or again into traces of experiences registered by her mind. If, on the other hand, the meaning was just stripped off, the analysand was left with an encumbering burden.

Thus the analytic relationship was a sort of antidote for the analysand's incessant splitting. The latter then gradually gave space to a state of deep conflict, as mentioned above, between different needs felt to be incompatible. During a particular session in which the tension between opposites had been severe most of the time, in a state of extreme anxiety she whispered: "I must go, I must go away, it is useless, I must stop". Still she stayed where she was as if unable to move. The analyst after repeatedly but unsuccessfully trying to help her by giving a meaning to her anxiety and trying to contain it, eventually managed to establish an atmosphere of closeness. This helped the analysand to state the following words:

"Often if I am driving my car along a straight road and the road turns I have the impulse to continue straight and crash the car and myself against the wall".

It seemed to be the consequence of the protracted use of splitting, the mind's chosen mode of functioning as the analysand herself had stated in other sessions: "that black mark on the wall is a kind of point of reference for me but in touching it I have realised that it sticks out and that it might come away. I can't bear that it can come away and that in coming back I may not find it in its place. I have a strong impulse to take it away now, to scratch it off!".

The perception of the end of things, of the impossibility to control the passing of time, the anxiety originated by separation, which she experienced as desertion, and finally the anxiety of dying were felt by the analysand as being so pervasive and indigestible that she "had the impulse" (a kind of compulsion) to suspend, to pull off the contact, to anticipate an ending which she felt as a betrayal or as a desertion: "I have the impulse to crash against the wall".

The analysand's conflict was discussed once more by the analyst in one of the sessions that followed. While the analyst was speaking S. said she was in deep pain as she saw herself huddled down by the couch, hugging her knees and pulling them close to her breast, her head bent, totally shutting herself away. She identified this posture with her closed, hidden aspect that had no communication with her other aspect, the aspect which she used to show to others and which she now compared to a knight enclosed in his armour. She saw the two aspects as two characters – two S. – opposed to each other and with no communication whatsoever between them. For a moment she said that she wanted to offer herself a hand to help herself out of the state of isolation in which she had seen herself but after a second she shut off and hid behind her usual statement: "Never mind, it is useless, it is too late. All this means that I am worse since I come here, I'd better stop".

Her getting worse had, in her opinion, another facet: "Not quite voices, but sentences flow in my mind without my thinking them. They are nasty and violent. I can't control this phenomenon, it doesn't depend on me". She felt the sentences were somehow projected by someone on the screen of her mind and, though the analyst asked what they were about, she didn't want to say initially. Some time later she said the 'sentences' said she was ridiculous, that she was exaggerating, that she was inventing it all. It wasn't therefore true that she was suffering and she should stop thinking all that nonsense. She described this as "two people fighting inside me a terrible fight, one says the sentences, the other tries to make the first shut up".

Everything was violent in her psychic scenery. The aggressive sentences, the attempt at suppressing them, the isolation and the refusal of communication. In this condition all sensory or emotional perceptions were felt as devastating and unexplainable.

"This night I felt horrible ... I can't explain ... I woke up and my husband wasn't there. I felt my heart was bursting, it was beating so strongly, my head was spinning, I began to cry ... as he ... I can't say it ... he was dead".

One can understand such phenomena as the sign of an initial activation of a vital area since up to now the analysand's psychic scenery had been similar to a lunar landscape, frozen, desert and lifeless. This initial liveliness was nevertheless experienced as dramatic by the analysand and it was difficult for her to accept it. Hence the intensification of the attempts at detaching herself and at extinguishing the vitality.

Everything that appeared in the sessions she soon lost trace of and it was up to the analyst to pick up the thread again. Eventually she would find her way and recall her own significant correspondences. If S. had to count only on what happened at the beginning of each session she would certainly have stopped coming to analysis.

"Thinking is very hard work for me. I get tired and give up. That is why I would like to stop coming."

In other cases the analyst could encourage the analysand to take responsibility for having expressed him or herself in a certain way. In this case, nevertheless, asking, for instance, why the analysand continued to come when she was actually expressing the intention of stopping, would have been like implicitly reinforcing one of the two aspects of the analysand's conflict, that is the refusing aspect, and this would have been unwise as the other aspect related to the wish for life, was still very weak, almost inconsistent.

One year of analytic work enabled her to bring the two aspects (the two characters) close to one another. She could therefore think that "she didn't know how to think" and at the same time that "she didn't want to think". She "didn't know" because she continuously aborted all significant correspondences and didn't therefore have the words to express what she felt. She had her sensations and emotions but couldn't name them. On the other hand she "didn't want" because when a significant link appeared, her hatred (the active hatred which has been initially hypothesised), made her cut off the connections and thus annul the capacity to create significant correspondences. She therefore couldn't hold on to the presence of physical perceptions, such as being cold or hot when the season changed, and would continue wearing sandals with no stockings on as winter came by or keep her woollen things on when summer arrived. It wasn't that she didn't perceive the cold or the heat but because she couldn't establish any significant relation or correspondence between such perceptions and thus value them. If someone suggested that she should wear a warmer jacket she would wear it but wouldn't change her trousers or shoes accordingly, just because no one had said she should.

She didn't realise how severe her situation was: "When I try to think my thoughts just oppose one another".

One could have said that when a thought appeared the "I don't know" disappeared and the "I don't want" came into being. She wasn't anymore annulling the condition in which she could "know" but soon re-established the "I don't know" condition.

"Then – she said – I feel anxious and stop because I just can't do it."

A.: "Do you think this is a good solution? this is what you do whenever you are in pain or in sorrow. You pull off the contacts."

S.: "It isn't pain, it is fear".

A.: "When facing fear you pull off. When you were ten you stopped eating, when you were fifteen you stopped studying. Now you consider stopping coming to analysis. Do you think it works?"

S.: "If I have done it for such a long time it must have worked."

A.: "Do you realise that you aren't protecting but rather exposing yourself to each one of your perceptions pleasant or unpleasant that they may be?"

S.: "If I were to decide to proceed I should face all this. I can do it here. But when I get away from here I am alone and I can't do it. It has already happened. I try to think and then I have to stop ... but ... it is also like this: 'everything' is true and the 'contrary of everything' as well!".

A.: "If you are totally rational and detach yourself from feeling, if you have to choose between two dishes that are identical in nutritional and caloric value you can't do it just by rationality. The taste or your wish at that moment can help you."

S.: "With thoughts it is different, because taste can't help there".

A.: "You can only say this because you detach your head from your feet! As in the dream in which you took away the head of the big insect. When you do this, even if your feet are freezing you can't do anything with that sensation. Your head is full of meanings but you can't use them because they are "detached" from your feet. So wearing or not wearing stockings is the same, because anything and the contrary of anything are just equivalent."

S.: "I am sick."

A.: "What is in your stomach, do you discern an emotion?"

S.: "I feel as if someone had taken up a barrier and everything that is in one part of my head is pouring into the other! Things must be put in order or everything will be mixed."

She is frightened, her communication reveals a state of alarm and anxiety.

A.: "What mixes with what?"

S.: "I can't say but it is a terrible sensation!"

A.: "Let's look together at what is so terrible. What do you think of that?"

191

S.: (Her tone of voice shows suffering) "My head feels very big, too full of things ... but I feel someone is putting things in the right place."

A.: "Wait, don't be afraid. In this disarray there are your potential qualities. Didn't you notice that in this disarray you have formulated a thought for the first time? You have found a mental meaning for you sickness. Up to a short time ago was just an incomprehensible bodily sickness."

The function of analysis was above all to try and stop, and/or to put a limit to, the analysand's compulsive mechanism of expulsion which aimed at keeping the splitting in action and only brought impoverishment as a result. This objective was attainable through a containing and a regulating function, more like a dam than like a barrier, that could regulate and slowly balance the feeding system of the analysand's mental functioning.

This could be done initially because the analyst used the hypothesis of the sensory organs as psychic co-ordinators. In so doing, as we have seen, the analyst helped the analysand to trace the emotions, feelings and thoughts that corresponded to the sensations which the analysand had perceived, initially, as belonging exclusively to her body.

CASE AC.

A thirty-eight year old female analysand, AC., after about one year of analysis tried, for the second time, to become pregnant by artificial insemination. Her attempt was unsuccessful, she aborted a fortnight after the insemination.

During that fortnight she had several dreams. One felt that she was trying to find a form and a meaning to many intense and specific sensations and emotions related to her wish to become a mother, as well as to her actual attempt at becoming pregnant. Possibly her dreams related also to the problem of the assumption of a gender identity, something about which she still felt very doubtful.

The analysand understood the manifest content of the dreams as a progression representing the initial phases of the pregnancy and its failure. The analyst understood the dreams as a communication between AC. and AC. about the problems she had in trying to find her own identity, her feminine identity in particular (latent content). The message contained in this communication emerged from the unconscious in the form of dreams and was decoded and understood by the analysand with the help of the analytic dialogue. She had to take into her mental area the question of her femininity together with the related emotions.

The night before the implant of the embryo she dreamt that she had sexual intercourse with a black waiter and associated the dream with her using her husband to become a mother: "I can only use a man if he is a servant". In the following dream she celebrated buying flowers for herself. Her association was about celebrating the implant. She was pleased at the idea of giving life but her pleasure was somewhat omnipotent. Possibly the actual birth was her birth as a woman, rather than her birth as a mother. The following dream was about differentiation: "Pieces of brightly coloured crisp paper, like the paper that florists use, danced in couples on my analyst's writing-desk, under her benign eye". She associated this image with the process of differentiation of the cells in her uterus. In the following dream she was bringing a present to a matriarchal figure – a tray with a gelatinous substance very much like a jelly. Her comment was: "Now the fight for survival begins, I am coping with the matriarch". If one puts the two dreams together one can imagine that the analysand was thinking of the implications of the process of differentiation/individuation, the need to oppose a more adult and powerful figure – her mother.

On the following night she had another dream but this time a masculine figure appeared, older than her. "A bright little old man, dressed in black, but his face was young". She came out of an apartment, arm in arm with him and walked to a crowded square. Another image appeared in the dream. Something like the necessity of constructing a net of significant links capable of containing the intense specific emotional wave of the present moment. "I am in a square, facing the sea, there are big waves and they come into the land, covering the pavement. On the left one can see the shape of a big passenger-ship. The sea is full of little boats, on the boats there are people from the civic service wearing fluorescent jackets, they have the task of keeping the sea at bay".

This dream indicated the initial presence of an attempt at containment, though still inadequate in comparison with her extremely intense emotions – motherhood/sea[97].

One might then think of the men from the civil service. They were not the dreamer, they were other people (the analyst, the husband etc.), the containment was therefore inadequate. The analysand had to take responsibility for herself. The civil servants were a picturesque image but inadequate to this aim.

The problem of gender identity was much in evidence in the following dream: "I was wearing grey flannels, and a jacket and I was standing in front of the mirror. I passed my hand on my head and my hair became very short, a man's cut. I heard myself saying – You are as lovely as your father – then again my hair was as it is now, untidy, excessively long so that it becomes untidy and indefinite. Then I pull my hair to give it a feminine style. I am not lovely but I am feminine. I think there is a conflict in me and it gets stronger and stronger. The parts are separate, in total opposition. It's becoming more and more difficult".

In commenting her dream AC. referred to the splitting of the embryo which she felt was becoming detached and spoke of a fight, meaning the fight of the embryo in her uterus between life and death. We believe the fight was between aspects of basic masculinity and femininity and the message of the dream was an indicator of the deep difficulty in assuming a personal position and a definition of identity. We can expect that as long as the contrast between the two components prevails there will be a condition of paralysis, not of choice, and that all possible creative opportunities will be lost.

Subsequently she dreamt of a singer with androgynous features, dressed in white and who was carried in triumph. The lack of differentiation still prevailed (one might say it triumphed). The main anxiety which the analysand was facing was therefore the anxiety of individuation.

There were two other dreams (before the abortion). Iin the dream before the last there was a woman alone, no man near her, with a little girl, her daughter. An anxiety about solitude, associated to the individuation of becoming a woman. In the last dream a little girl was alone in a hospital and looked for her mother. She only found a little dog: "a little whitish mongrel, a bit dirty". Femininity was regarded by the analysand as something of very poor value – a little girl, naked, alone, impotent, needy and in the company of a dog!

This sequence of dreams was produced, in our opinion, under the emotional drive related to the wish for maternity, it was the first emergence of anxieties related to the problem of the relation with femininity. The abortion in the physical area might well have corresponded to a birth in the psychic area. A little girl was born and she had to cope with a definite mother and father in the development of a process of differentiation and individuation. AC. had probably fought against this event with all her strength and opposed it as much as she could. But eventually she had to integrate herself in her own identity and to accept it. Initially masculinity prevailed and the pleasant sensation of being male – the lovely man in the grey flannel suit. Then the fight for differentiation and the attempt at taking refuge in a undifferentiated situation (the androgynous man) with progressive modifications until the moment in which she became a naked little girl with her mother's dog.

For a period of a month and ten days after the abortion she couldn't dream or cry. Then she had this dream: "The churches in Rome had been partially destroyed. This had been well known for quite a time, but in a kind of hidden way. An architect, who was a powerful man, had carried out the destruction. I go and see one of the churches and out comes a funeral. There are no flowers or flags but it is an important funeral. My father's funeral! I am there on one side with two friends, my husband's employees. Then I understand that it is my husband's funeral. One man is young and handsome the other is depressed all the time and cries on my shoulder".

There seems to be no doubt that when femininity manifests itself it is experienced by AC. as catastrophic and it makes it necessary for her to distance herself from masculinity, represented by her father in the horizontal dimension.

The sequence of dreams of this analysand has been presented to give an example of how one can understand the language of dreams in the presence of a contact net which links together emotions, yet in the physical turmoiling state, with meaningful thoughts from the psychic area, represented as dream material.

It is an attempt at establishing significant correspondences, in the vertical dimension, between the contents of the entropic area and the projects of thought through the "royal path" of the dream. It is a process of refined creativity which the analysand persistently superimposed to, and therefore confused with, her wish to become a mother but which, above all, concerned the creative potentialities of her actual mental functioning.

CASE AA.

"I feel I am unaware of anything that happens inside me. I feel I can't put myself in touch with my emotions and can't therefore understand them. If I don't feel and discern what happens in me, how on earth can I feel and discern what happens in other people?

Things that are painful for others seem indifferent to me. I am thinking of when you called to say that we wouldn't be seeing each other for two sessions. My wife was there and told me that I had gone pale, but I thought I wasn't feeling anything in particular! I feel uncertain about a world that belongs to me but which I can't reach or be aware of. I wonder why I feel so detached. I am beginning to think that there might be a rich, varied nucleus in me ... but the emotions just don't filter, except when they are clarified in the sessions.

I am afraid that all this may be an intellectualisation as well. I tend to make a rule out of everything and trying to understand all the time is really quite a hamper. Seen from outside, because I am so calm I may appear serene, solid and trustworthy but I feel that there are intense emotions in me and that I am pushing them away. I pick up some valuable truth but then it contrasts with some other impulse".

The mind of this analysand couldn't transform the sensations and the emotions into experience. Both were therefore expressed only through physicality – he turned pale. In his speech one could detect the presence of a rigid barrier instead of the flexible contact net. Very little of his emotional world could therefore gain access to his mind and form thoughts. He suffered from panic attacks and this was the reason of his seeking analysis.

One morning, while he was driving his car, he felt happy at the thought that he had had a pleasant time with his wife the evening before, something which was unusual. Thoughts about death immediately crowded his mind. He might suffer cardiac arrest, his father might die, his son's school bus might have an accident, his daughter's future might be unhappy.

Suddenly AA. found himself stuck in a traffic jam and was immediately overtaken by a panic attack.

The traffic jam seemed to represent the situation in his mind. Without the activation of the contact net allowing impetuous and confused circulation of emotions in the direction of thought AA. was unable to give harbour to his own happiness and pleasure. An arrest of the communication between himself and himself followed and the pleasure was immediately transformed into its contrary – death.

Since the beginning of analysis AA. showed a strong refusal for the emotions which he felt to be primitive and dangerous – hatred meant destructiveness to him, love meant possession. It was impossible for him to tolerate the emergence of whatever feeling or need both in himself and in others, and therefore tended to repress any such emotion in a violent and sadistic manner. He used to suffocate his emotions in himself and suffered panic attacks when they re-emerged. Similarly he felt intense anxiety when others, his beloved ones or other significant people, expressed their emotions and he behaved repressively towards them as well.

At the beginning of analysis he had a dream in which his emotionality was represented by a frozen baby. He was in a desert and a baby in a pram was being taken away by some hostile entity. He knew that it would be very cold at night and warmer during the day, he eventually found the pram but feared before seeing the baby that it might not have survived.

On other occasions he represented his emotionality as a naked fragile child, smashed down by a rational, strong and sadistic adult.

As analytic work proceeded one could observe the development of links to form the contact net. Initially the only significant links could be traced by the analysand in dreams.

The Oedipal scenery presented a mother who was unable to take care of his needs and which he hated deeply and felt rancorous towards. AA. didn't seem to feel that anything might change, not even in time. He used to ask himself: "How can I accept my emotions and be fond of myself when I feel that others don't appear to accept me?"

Sometimes his hatred seemed to extend to the analyst and on those occasions he seemed to regard her as a prostitute since she asked to be paid in order to receive him.

Analogously he despised his father from whom he had tried to differentiate himself by developing culturally and intellectually, but he felt nevertheless close to this father figure when he perseverantly adhered to authoritarian figures. Though his ideal was to be a rebel, he once dreamt he had turned into an ally of the nazi, to avoid being arrested.

In this situation he perceived himself as desperate and impotent, incessantly knocking against a kind of wall, the impossibility of communicating and being understood.

The analysand obviously attributed to the external world the situation of incomprehension and lack of communication which was actually taking place in his internal system and of which he was unaware. He did realise that he hated violently and deeply, out of proportion with real facts when he met in others that kind of shutting up, which was mirroring his shutting to himself. Such hatred and violence seemed to originate in the impossibility of demolishing the wall, therefore in the perception of his absolute impotence.

In the Oedipal scenery, a mother figure unable to respond to his needs and emotions, contributed to the development of a feeling of inadequacy and fostered the painful and dangerous condition of non-communication that was internal to his system.

He suffered because his feelings didn't seem to be able to find a gap in which to filter. He spoke of a gap towards the external world, but the barrier was actually installed in his internal system and the emotions couldn't therefore find their way to thought.

He mentioned that he painfully perceived the presence of a barrier between himself and others, maybe made of other people's skins and of his own as well, but he mentioned also that he was afraid of being swallowed away by others and therefore of becoming fused, losing his boundaries. He feared, and at the same time desired, the fusion in order to annul the barrier which he erected not only against others but also, and predominantly in himself, against his emotional world. One might have said that the wall which he perceived between himself and others was the reflex of the barrier which he had erected in himself, against his emotions, and that the lack of communication which characterised the mode in which he represented himself in the relation with others in the horizontal dimension was the reflex of a fracture in the vertical dimension, of which he could only see a shadow, projected in the external world.

The analysand tried incessantly to avoid situations which would put him (in the vertical dimension) in contact with his intense hatred and violence which he feared he couldn't control and couldn't anyway understand.

By uniforming to the majority, therefore to the stronger characters, he avoided contrasts that might originate intense emotions and violent shocks for him: "I am scared of very heated discussions, I am scared of the violence that circulates everywhere, one might go beyond the limit of words and reach the level of physical confrontation. Each discussion leaves a trace in me that is difficult to heal. I am left with the hatred, with the hostility".

Whenever feelings of pleasure or love emerged AA. immediately and automatically opposed a barrier to prevent their development. He maintained that he never missed anyone after separations and that he forgot people, or couldn't even remember what they looked like. A woman with whom he had a love affair during several years seemed to have disappeared from his memory as if she had never existed. If he realised that he liked some woman or that he could become fond of someone, he annulled any feeling of attraction or interest and avoided any occasion of meeting such a person. When a friend of his school years, one of his "best friends", repeatedly tried to establish a contact, AA. accurately avoided every possible occasion to meet until the old school-mate was eventually discouraged and gave up.

"Everything is going fine now. My work, the pleasure of being with my wife and children, I should be living a happy life but I feel there are some nasty counter-forces that keep me from feeling fine as I live. I seem to be repeating a kind of pattern in my functioning. Each nice thing must be spoiled, while all dramatic, difficult and tiring events are emphasised. This night I had a lovely dream, rich and enticing, now I can't even remember what it was about".

The analysand tried in all possible ways to distance the perception of desire and of pleasure as, in the absence of a contact net, they evoked emotions that where uncontainable for him, being as they were, somehow closed in themselves. He seemed to put in action a massive negation, almost a sort of denial, but didn't, in our opinion, actually resort to splitting. He did, in fact, hold on to a kind of awareness of emotional experiences and couldn't therefore totally forget them.

"Is mine a superficial kind of love then? Am I capable of loving? I do feel that there is love in me but it doesn't seem to have any propulsive force. It is like this with my wife. I say I have a good opinion of her but I feel a kind of indifference ... The other night in a dream there was a sentence which said 'AA. is dead', as I woke up I recognised a sexual desire. I got close to my wife and eventually woke her up to make love with her".

The perception of his own state of death was so acute and intolerable that he had tried to convince himself that he was alive, hopelessly trying to contrast his death anxieties.

"I had one sentence of the dream in mind, something like 'there must be three of us'. So, as soon as I woke my wife up I got a kind of obsessional mechanism in my mind. I had to remember what came before that sentence. The obsession occupied my mind to a point in which I experienced a strong anxiety. I lost my erection and couldn't have the intercourse that I had wanted. This hadn't happened for quite a long time. With a girl-friend I had in the past it used to happen and my thoughts used to get stuck in a very peculiar manner, something like having to wear the shirt in a special way etc.

After the death of my sister and until the time I went to high school there was always the same hindrance ... the desire was strong but through this obsessional mechanism I stopped myself from ..."

When he started analysis AA. mentioned he was obsessed by the doubt that he may have provoked the death of his sister, which took place when he was twelve. The sister was crossing the road when a car came along and provoked the fatal accident. AA. was prey of the thought that he might have pushed her and that he was likely to be her murderer.

One can imagine that because of the death of his sister AA. may have stopped facing the subject of his own life and identity. Thus he began to die whenever life emerged, as he had placed "death in himself and life in his sister" passing on his identity to her and making himself non-existent. His identity was founded on his sense of guilt and if he were to take off his "tragedy costume" he wouldn't have known who he was anymore. To keep this construction going, he had to "die" incessantly as in so doing he somehow kept his dead sister alive. This analysand had lived without having the experience of searching for an identity. He couldn't "bury" his sister because he would then have to deal with a totally unknown himself. When he left aside the screen of his persecutory sense of guilt he suddenly faced the dramatic problem of knowing nothing of his own identity. One can imagine that the sister had been, and somehow still was, a well beloved, idealised and envied object, representing sensitiveness and balance and that the comparison with her made him feel extremely ambivalent. He was never able to harmonise in himself his wish to 'be the sister' and his hatred at perceiving himself different from her. In his mind he definitely pushed his sister towards the car that killed her. By "killing" his sister AA. "killed" his own sensitiveness, he lost himself and was bound to live in the nostalgia of a relationship based on gentleness, not on rough violence. Then he had to die at every moment of his life so that his sister could live and found himself in a really paradoxical situation. He came to think that it was much more dangerous to "go backwards and not kill his sister rather than kill her".

For a very long time he had used this protective screen as an identity to be invested when he had the life so that he could then be killed, especially when he experienced pleasure or joy. The anxiety had been so great that it had provoked death, death had then turned into a defence and the primary anxiety was believed – an illusion – to be controlled by dying at each moment.

Thus, the analysand couldn't elaborate his mourning or his anxiety and guilt. He persevered to avoid facing a quest for the person he actually was. When he was about to become an adult, in the delicate turning point between childhood and adolescence, the death of his sister had violently introduced in his internal world the perception of endings and of vulnerability. The modes which he adopted to contrast the overwhelming anxiety which the event had originated – as described above – besides being grossly inadequate, hindered severely the process of research of his sense of identity. For one thing he never really faced the question of gender identity, alternating images of femininity and masculinity both contrasting and ambiguous. Sometimes there were images of refined women, lovely and mysterious but also untrustworthy and unfaithful, icy and incapable of making themselves available, other times there were images of contradictory and incompatible men. On the one hand a stubborn and vulgar masculinity using women exclusively for sexual appetites, regarded as similar to the father figure, on the other, a gentler and more affectionate masculinity, capable of a dialogue with femininity. The aspect of violent masculinity equipped sexuality with fierce and sadistic phantasies in order to reach the necessary excitement and defeat any anxiety about impotence-death. AA. ignored therefore whether the excitement was related to imagining himself as a raper or to identifying himself with the woman victim, but was compelled, in any case, to either roughly thrust away the femininity, or the basic masculinity. The aspect of gentler masculinity was, on the contrary, feared and kept at a distance, as like all affects, it was regarded as belonging to a subordinate category, somewhat inferior in hierarchy.

There was also a third model of masculinity, again partial and unintegrated in respect of the others, and it was the one to which the analysand thought he was referring most of the time – a man with a mind, who controls to exasperation everything that has to do with feelings or emotions, pursuing his aims and asserting his ideal goals at all costs, without any qualm, of any sort. This model of masculinity tackled the others and kept them at bay.

"Feelings are terrifying, they distort reality, they are a hierarchically inferior entity, they should be dominated".

Sexuality could have been an area in which these contradictions might have met at some point. It was refused and excluded from the psychic area as too painful to experience. How could the ideal and idyllic completeness of the relationship with his sister enter his system, if he was convinced that he had been compelled to suppress her by killing her? "I feel that I am divided – he said – like a centaur alternatively using his head or his body, but it can't go on like this, as I am a whole person and furthermore I have the terrible feeling that I can't love concretely because of the split and lack of harmony between the two states. Thus it is my mind that stops me from actually making love".

The block was against a feeling of dumb and deep hatred, related to a sense of deep disillusion in regards of reality. It probably originated in an archaic mode of mental functioning, endeavouring to find in illusion, that is in the construction of a fantastic reality, a kind of antidote to the pain of frustration.

His desire to join up with his sister's life showed that something was missing in his system. There was no place for basic femininity. Thus he had an unreachable objective: "My wife's refusal and withdrawal, her carelessness in looks, her lack of attention towards me really disappoint me. . . ."

The disappointment was inevitable since he projected the image of his sister, that is of femininity, upon his wife.

"I feel I am hostile towards her . . . well, the sexual relationship between us maybe is an instrument of my hostility . . . I sometimes have sadistic phantasies, but it doesn't work with her . . . I think it might be easier with other women, but I am afraid of becoming impotent at the moment of intercourse! The desire is present but it is kind of asleep."

One might have said that his desire wasn't practical given the situation and that this explained his perception/sensation of being dead as represented in the formerly analysed dream.

His aggressiveness was expressed, sometimes sadistically, against other people and seemed to originate in a reaction against a feeling of inadequacy, he was apparently unaware of, in an incapacity to feel his own emotions and therefore to tune in with other people's emotions. He didn't accept his own fear and didn't understand it, he just crushed it by means of aggressive behaviour.

"Do you want to know what I feel in myself? Fear!

I feel frightened. The fright makes me ill. I feel like a man who has lived for a long time in a dark cave and suddenly comes out to the light . . . It hurts the eyes and for this reason the man might want to go back to darkness. Others have always seen me as wise and trustworthy . . . This is my identity . . . this is how others see me".

One may see here the kind of fear and dismay which many analysands express when they realise that they can't anymore rely on their sense of identity upon stereotypes, idealisations or theories, when they have been using them for a long time in the past, in order to avoid the overwhelming anxiety of "not knowing".

NOTES

90 Fausta Romano has University Degrees in Philosophy and Psychology. She worked as a psychologist in a National Health Service Unit in Rome from 1979 to 1997. She teaches at I.F.R.E.P. (Institute of Research and Training for Educators and Psychotherapists) and at the "Scuola di Specializzazione in Psicologia Clinica dell'Università Pontificia Salesiana" (Advanced Training in Clinical Psychology). Since 1989 she has attended Prof. Ferrari's groups of Clinical Supervision.

91 Ferrari(A. B. 1983), "Relazione Analitica: sistema o processo?" *Rivista di Psicoanalisi*, 29, 4, 476–496.

92 Ferrari A. B., Garroni E. (1979), "Schema di Progetto per uno Studio della Relazione Analitica" *Rivista di Psicoanalisi*, 25, 2, 282–322.

93 I am suggesting the use of this term because I understand the analytic relationship as a relation in which «the word that the analyst says to the analysand

isn't the description of something but rather the making of a *relationship*. I believe this clarifies my reasons for choosing analytic proposition instead of interpretation. It is worthwhile underlining that I understand this term as communicative interaction rather than as *description of*». A.B. Ferrari (1986) "La proposizione analitica" in *Atti del Convegno della Società Italiana di Psioanalisi di Gruppo*, Bulzoni, Roma.

94 This isn't true of training analysis as the latter necessarily requires special continuance and specific attention.

95 Freud S. (1937) *Analysis Terminable and Interminable*, SE, London: Hogarth Press, vol. XXIII

96 This approach is different from the approach of short psychoanalytic psychotherapy: the latter is a specific technique, still related to psychoanalysis, but employed in cases in which – as stated by D. Bolelli – there isn't actually a severe pathology of the self. In the more serious cases short psychoanalytic psychotherapy may only be employed as a preparatory tool for a subsequent analytic treatment, not as a specific treatment in itself.(Cf. Bolelli D. (1996) *Andare a tempo*, Roma: Borla)

97 In italian there is a similarity between the word mother: *madre* and the word sea: *mare* (T.N.)

SECTION III

Adolescence: The Second Challenge

8

PSYCHOANALYTIC NOTES ON ADOLESCENCE

Adolescents suffer intense mental pain due to an acute sensitiveness about their internal world, about the clamour of the external world and about the compound of sensations and emotions which they are hardly capable of controlling.

Adolescence is for several reasons the most turbulent age of life. The main reason is that adolescents know very little about their own potentialities and that such ignorance generates panic. Adolescents try to face their panic by referring to models which usually originate in ideal worlds.

An adolescent may come to terms with experience or refuse it. The price he then has to pay in adult life is extremely high, both in terms of his quality of life and of the waste of his potential. A child may recur to an endless capacity to invent theories, which he may then use to observe and fantastically manipulate his surroundings with the help of his supposed magical "powers". An adolescent, on the contrary has to face his "phantasies" and can only do so when they grow more and more difficult to produce continuously and to nourish. For phantasies to exist, in fact, a really encumbering ideal world is required.

Furthermore, adolescents are heavily conditioned by their own projections and therefore vulnerable to ideological tenets. Only gradually can they substitute their personal experience with their phantasies as in adolescence *doing* and *learning* necessarily coincide.

Furthermore, while a child can count on his own capacities to form some hypotheses about life and to protect himself by using defined spaces (the boundaries of the playroom or other boundaries set up by adults) in which he can feel contained and sheltered, an adolescent necessarily has to attend to and control a kind of huge unpredictable seismic event.

First of all adolescents have to cope with sudden and overwhelming physical modifications implying a deep and structural change – which turns them into strangers, nearly unknown to themselves. Such modifications then originate responses which, in their turn, cause problems – noisy modes of behaviour, extreme choices in clothing, hectic manners, strange looks, adhesion to peculiar groups etc.

Adolescent boundaries lack the quality of children's boundaries, they don't provide rules or containment as in the case of children, and the adult world gradually infiltrates them. Because the area of experience is thus expanded, manic attitudes often appear together with a *distortion of the perception* of time. It is a defence against the anxiety related to the discovery that living is a complex, dangerous adventure.

The clinical problem, when working with adolescents, is therefore of no easy solution. It is necessary to understand what level of manic behaviour is tolerable or, in other words, functional to the young analysand so that the analyst won't, by tackling excessively the manic defence, cause a renewal of the infantile defensive behaviours. Childhood is in fact still quite present in the memory of the adolescent, as a well-known safe refuge, and childish modes are still quite desirable, but the truth is that they then reveal themselves inadequate or even burlesque.

Attempts at escaping in the past or even in the future cause the adolescent to believe that his thoughts and notions of life are commonplace, since they are obviously inadequate to actual needs. But an adolescent may also, on the contrary, manically feel that he already detains every possible knowledge. Common language is therefore often scorned, since it is regarded as an adult code that doesn't answer adolescent needs, while cryptic languages are introduced, with the aim of creating new areas of experience in which many adolescents feel that they can have a try at moving more freely. Such stratagems often have the function of preserving new perceptions and experiences which provoke intense anxiety and which the adolescents therefore try to disguise as they feel thoroughly embarrassed about them.

The appearance of embarrassment characterises pre-adolescence and requires great sensitivity and respect both from the analyst and in general from adults. It is related to the timid appearance of the initial features of a personality in formation. An adolescent has to deal with the reality which attracts him strongly but whose boundaries he can't recognise or even situate. As a result he often feels lost and at times inevitably confused.

Since I believe that doing and learning are for the adolescent expressions of one same complex operation, I am convinced that it is necessary to formulate anew, both theoretically and clinically, the notion of *acting* in adolescence. Acting is obviously always a kind of communication, but in adolescence the *doing* often has the specific meaning of a communicative interaction directed towards the analyst. An adult person *acts* to attack either self or others. An adolescent, on the contrary, expresses a request that he may share something. The adolescent and the analyst then have to understand whether it is a *proposal* or a *protest* that was contained in the action, and they can also understand and establish together whether doing is useful or useless in cases in which the *acting* doesn't convey the possibility of learning or acquiring experience. Doing and learning may therefore introduce an opportunity for elaboration of specific emotions and experience of self. The experience carries great interest and attraction for adolescents as they usually tend to think that, besides including doing and learning, experience brings power. Still, adolescents are usually ambivalent towards experience as, if feelings of inadequacy prevail, fear compels them to become isolated, and they therefore immediately respond by seeking situations in which they can share things, either in a group or in an institution. If they can't respond to their necessities in this way (this may happen for reasons that have to do with the incipient formation of their identity) they then develop an exaggerated self-esteem. This is a condition that, far from helping them to develop further, tends to bring about a *disdainful isolation* which adolescents usually ascribe to the world's, specifically the adult world's, lack of understanding.

Analysts who work with adolescents should mobilise and employ all their resources to deal with states of harsh isolation. Behaviours relating to such states are described in this book and often found in clinical work. They require analytic propositions to be formulated with an appropriately assertive and incisive tone, as adolescents do experience intensely both their sensations and their emotions but lack the psychic structure necessary to contain them. On the *technical plan the urgency of their needs demands the use of the vertical relation* for the latter facilitates an immediate relief of anxiety, by enabling the attribution of a name and a function to the experienced emotions. The horizontal relation is consequently implicit in the proposition formulated by the analyst. If the latter, especially in the initial stages, focuses his work on the horizontal relation, he risks being regarded as representing the adult world and may therefore interfere with the possibility of establishing contact, turning the transference into something even more precarious than usual.

Some analysts prefer working just with adolescent boys or just with girls. Their choice doesn't necessarily depend on their identity but rather on their specific sensitivity, enabling them to understand better either one or the other. This is a quite important aspect of working with adolescents, since they need to search for, and work upon, their own identity, including sexual identity. The analyst's sensitive understanding may facilitate the appearance of feminine or masculine aspects in the adolescent analysand and foster their acceptance and integration in this extremely complex and significant period of life.

ANOREXIA – CLAUSTROPHOBIA – CLAUSTROPHILIA
BULIMIA – AGORAPHOBIA – AGORAPHILIA

Clinical practice with anorexic adolescent girls often reveals a claustrophobic substratum over which anorexia obviously detains a defensive function. If the analyst suggests, as a vertex for observation, a focus on
claustrophobic aspects, the anorexic girl understands that she is the pris-
oner of a theory according to which her body must be imprisoned, shut up
and controlled, as it is a very dangerous subversive element.

Nothing, or almost nothing, can in fact prevent the transformation that
takes place between childhood and adolescence, and even more so in girls.
Girls seem to experience a conflict. They can only observe their physical
transformation, as the latter takes place under their eyes, and can do very
little, or even nothing, about it. At such moments most girls choose, understandably, a specific female stereotype as their aesthetic point of reference,
but this doesn't prevent them from incessantly undergoing, for quite some
time, unforeseen changes. Sometimes they might experience their body as
if it didn't belong to them, as a source of anxiety, almost a persecutor.
Claustrophobic aspects may then be supplanted by claustrophilic aspects,
as a kind of grant that the body may be somehow hidden or shut off.

A similar model, applied to cases of bulimia, has thrown evidence on the
relation between the latter and agoraphobia. At its roots there is the lack
of limits or even a desire to occupy a "limitless" limit – death. For anorexic
girls dying is part of the game, they want to kill themselves, and their body's
imprisonment has this meaning. Bulimic girls, on the contrary, want to
expand to occupy space and make "limitless" space limited, so that they
can then exercise their omnipotent control. This distinction between
bulimia and anorexia as well as between claustrophobia and agoraphobia,
doesn't really correspond to psychic reality, as the different aspects and their
contraries aren't all present at the same time, but rather undergo modifications, according to different defensive needs and underlying anxieties.
Technically, by introducing the subject of claustrophobic and agoraphobic
aspects, it becomes possible to reduce or even avoid anorexic and bulimic
defences and to open a dialogue which enables the formulation of adequate
analytic propositions. In the body-mind relationship there is, in these cases,
a kind of physical pole – the body – that undergoes a transformation and
becomes the area of conflict, and there is also a psychic pole that tries to
lead the game, sometimes in a very perverse fashion. Sometimes anorexic
girls seem to have a very clear perception of their "own anorexic space"
or, in other words, believe that they can omnipotently control both their
mental functioning and their physical essence, by alternatively recurring to
claustrophilic and claustrophobic functions.

THE CASE OF AG.

AG. was about twenty. She had been severely anorexic for three years and was now in an intensely bulimic phase. In the last few days she had been vomiting immediately after taking food. She thought this was happening because her boy- friend had left her a few months earlier. She mentioned her sexual experiences and added: "When I have a minimum relationship . . . *my body swells up so much* that when I am asked to go out I answer, 'I can't!'"

"Yes, I do know that I express myself through my body, all these years I did nothing else but let my body speak. I don't think I have anything else".

Here again one may see anorexic and bulimic features of adolescence intertwined with claustrophobic and agoraphobic features, generally relating to a kind of specific personal project. Such project has the characteristics of what is usually named an illusion. The illusion is a detailed plan, projected in time, aiming at magically responding to all needs but whose unique mathematical certainty is disappointment. This may appear senseless but in reality it isn't as the disappointment actually originates the whole process, establishing a kind of perverse circle. In the case of AG. the illusion and subsequent disappointment related to the swallowing of food, and the act of throwing it up created a kind of permanent movement, as the ever present disappointment fostered the illusion, which then turned into a new disappointment, without ever allowing for a way out.

From the point of view of technique it is necessary to alternate, depending on the emotional characteristic of each situation, the use of claustrophobia when in the presence of anorexia and of agoraphobia when in the presence of bulimia. The *phobic* feature shouldn't always prevail in the formulation of the analytic proposition, since the *philic* aspect is also sometimes extremely important in the actual choice of the defence.

In the case of AG. it was necessary to determine what kind of illusion might have originated the disappointment – a fear of the boundaries, or a fear of no boundaries at all, or, on the contrary, a feeling of being imprisoned, of suffocating, of being left with no place to be in . . .

"At some point I felt I was swelling and swelling and that I couldn't . . . come out!"

There was a conjunction anorexia-claustrophobia in the in-take of food and subsequent vomiting and, furthermore, in her difficulty in accepting her femininity. When young men invited her to go out, she was compelled to deal with her actual feminine sexual identity, something which she experienced as a prison and therefore refused, just as she vomited her food.

One can observe that the anorexic defence (as any other defence) is based on the assumption that one shouldn't, ever, depend on others. Adolescents don't tolerate dependency, as, in any state of dependence, they tend to feel intensely and ineluctably imprisoned.

It is important to highlight that, though the situation of AG. was quite disharmonious, the actual *claustro-agoraphobic conjunction is common in adolescents, as a continuous alternative movement 'from' and 'towards' that has the function of making growth possible.* Adolescents necessarily have to make space in themselves for new experiences but also feel that the internal space in themselves is small and insufficient. For this reason, from their internal space, they long for an external space, a place, or theatre, for them to live in and make their experiences. The risk they are then exposed to, at that point, is of getting lost in a kind of unlimited space. Those are the functions and meanings of the claustro-agoraphobic process in adolescence.

Just one more point about the notion of *illusion.* Adolescents easily become preys of illusions because they tend to be so extreme and intolerant of any kind of modulation in thinking, of anything that has to do with modification, with the gradual reaching of one's aims, with partial developments and progressions etc. Technically, a good way for analysts to deal with illusions is by transforming them into something that has to do with the adolescent's 'hopes'.

THOUGHTS ON A POSSIBLE THERAPEUTIC APPROACH AND ON GENDER IDENTITY

The structuring of identity fosters, in both sexes, an increase in aggressiveness and destructiveness. One might think of anorexia, which seems to relate to an attempt to destroy the feminine image, as a function and as a personal destiny, *rather* than with an attack on the maternal object. Or again one might think of anti-social attitudes in both sexes (such as theft) as a sort of complex circular request for affectionate attention and a need for punishment.

Aggressive and destructive behaviour are often evident in the children of divorced couples. The conflict might here establish as in a kind of spiral, as adolescents continuously tend to create relationships which they may then compulsively break. It is a kind of punishment when they feel they are responsible for their parents' divorce. They feel they are condemned to bear endless separation themselves.

Sons and daughters of divorced parents have to face the sense of guilt and persecution related to the Oedipal Constellation which is increased where a single-parent family is concerned. The definition of identity becomes in such cases an even more complex affair than usual.

Generally speaking, when the sexual identity is about to be defined, a kind of escape from such definition is possible with homosexual behaviour. The boy who once suddenly said: "I realised that I only had two possible choices, either to kill my father or to mimic my mother". The young man who described himself as homosexual and came to the sessions with his boy friend, the young girl who dressed like a boy, these situations all evoke distorted parental images, related to phantasies of phallic mothers or of fathers somehow mistaken for huge penises. In analysis, such situations turn into a peculiar touchiness in respect of the analyst, whose manners are often seen as either frustrating or seductive. Such a state of affairs may be made even more complex by elements relating to sensuousness, an aspect of fundamental importance for the definition of identity in general and of sexual identity in particular.

Since the phantasies and fears of adolescents, as opposed to children's phantasies and fears, closely relate to elements of real life, it may well be necessary to adopt an attitude of utter flexibility, preserving both the seriousness of the analytic contract and the possibility for a gradual approach, when discussing analysis with adolescents. An important peculiarity of work with adolescents is that they are often encouraged to begin analysis by someone other than themselves. This engenders a sense of annoyance and constraint in the young person. In such cases it is important to modify the analytic contract, allowing the adolescent to chose when and how he is going to come to analysis, but at the same time encouraging him to take responsibility for himself and for his analysis. This requires clear and detailed agreements on the mode and form of the analysis, or such freedom might well be used in perverse and unprejudiced ways. The young person should be informed clearly of his or her psychic conditions, urgencies and needs, and may therefore decide, within the limits of a personal capacity for perception, whether the analytic experience is a possible path towards the resolution of inner anxieties. Such procedure enables young patients to get to know themselves and their own resources and therefore to start acting, thinking, in one word, living more functionally.

If on the other hand, adolescents feel they are forced to work analytically against their wish, the activity will have no significant effect on them and they might even experience it as nothing more than a kind of noisy interference.

During the initial approach it is sometimes necessary to agree to begin work with just one session per week, explicitly stating that this is a preparatory introduction to actual analytic work. I think such an attitude may prove functional as it somehow feeds the area of the personality that most needs help. Analysts know well that this is a very fragile area, if compared to destructive, anarchic, protesting, vindicating aspects of the personality of adolescents. The function of fortifying, as it is usually done in very severe cases, the introspective, thoughtful and constructive features, is therefore an actual pre-analytic function. There are instead adolescents who come regularly to their sessions as they have a commitment with their parents or with adults in general. It is wise to ask oneself whether this kind of analysand always imposes something upon himself and if, by forcing himself to the sessions, he is doing the only thing he can do, or thinks he can do, in order to obtain and own something (love, attention, benevolence), to succeed in something, to get to know about something . . .

This is a rather provisional state and may relate to the mode in which adolescents have been brought up, to family vicissitudes, or to deep personal anxieties that cause the adolescent to avoid situations or decisions in which he would necessarily be in touch with himself. Such behaviour usually relates to an impressive lack of confidence in one's own resources and to a strong sense of inadequacy.

Life drives adolescents to take up their stand, dragging them into a circle of relationships, affects, emotions, commitments of study and work and so forth. In order to live, facing every day's pledges, they need to control the perception of their own inadequacy and to get rid of the responsibility of their actions by blaming others for them. Many adolescents manage to live thus, quite effortlessly, "cunningly" avoiding all situations in which they might be testing themselves. The result depends on the amount of their splitting or on their capacity to perceive what is happening. If an adolescent has a capacity for perception he may then approach his own resources, if he hasn't that capacity, not only can he not use it but he often also fears its appearance and avoids it altogether. Often, in such cases, adolescents are captured by something the family calls "consistency". *Families often expect the adolescent to start from consistency as a point of departure instead of reaching it as a difficult goal and often tend to forget that inconsistency is a fundamental aspect of the adolescent's actual development.* If the family therefore "imposes" analysis on the adolescent it is indirectly imposing consistency as well. Thus the situation is exasperated and the adolescent can't be free and acknowledge a dialogue with himself (as it immediately becomes "psychoanalysis") or even an inconsistency which enables him to reach and recognise, later, his own specific consistency. One should nevertheless also keep in mind that in adolescence, because of the difficult task of construction of identity, the capacity of looking after oneself is sometimes only "preserved" thanks to the help of "others" (family group, parents etc.).

When resistances to the analytic treatment are obvious and encumbering, the analyst may agree, with older adolescents, to start work with one session per week, then proceeding towards the full number of sessions that have been agreed to in the analytic contract, at the same time encouraging analysands to become constantly and responsibly involved in analytic work.

Technical aspects, such as sitting *vis a vis* or using the couch, should be decided case by case, as, unlike the adult, the adolescent "grows up" and might change his place in the consulting room, thanks to a development due not so much to his actual age but rather to the analytic stimuli. Generally speaking, when the analyst can be perceived as an *other* – instead of as a persecutory object – one may say that anxiety is decreasing and that confidence both in oneself and in the analyst is increasing.

A new and different manifestation of the Eclipse of the Concrete Original Object can be observed in adolescence. Here the process is the exact opposite of the one that took place at the beginning of mental life. Then, *the mind presented itself to the body* and now, it is *the body which presents itself to the mind,* thanks to the inevitable push of biological development. The push is sometimes so extreme that the body becomes a stranger and the adolescent feels panicky that he cannot foresee the transformations. The body of adolescents "becomes" and "is" at the same time. At some point it is an object of knowledge but then undergoes further incessant modifications and becomes again unknown and embarrassing.

I believe that during adolescence most of future life structures itself through acceptance or refusal of an integration of physical and mental aspects. It is a kind of *"Second Birth"* or speaking more realistically, a *Second Challenge* necessary and constructive as it creates the foundations of the *first conscious elaboration of the mind-body conflict.* A conflict that can either lead to harmonious or to severely disturbed or disharmonious results.

Adolescents encounter and recognise the image of their body projected in the future, things here are quite different for boys and for girls. Girls encounter a concave body, boys encounter a convex body that seems to close in itself. Girls seem, among other things, more willing to attend their intrapsychic essence (vertical relationship) while boys, because they constantly tend to measure themselves with the external world seem more attuned to horizontal relationships. Furthermore, girls' natural developmental process seems to start from the body and then reach the mind while with boys, though the developmental trend is similar, the mind seems to move towards the body, a movement that relates also to cultural conditioning. A common prejudice regards the body as impotent and feminine and the mind as powerful and masculine. The consequences of this attitude are dangerous distortions in pre-adolescent and adolescent intuitive visions of the differences between the masculine and feminine mental functioning. The result is often a negative opinion of femininity and an unjustified exaltation of masculinity.

These differences are to some extent significant as they relate to attitudes and behaviours of adolescents in the general background of western culture. They may be considered relevant to the mode in which girls and/or boys are what they are but they don't extend beyond the basic difference in gender identity.

How should one then regard, in one's clinical work, the difference between boys and girls, relating to their specific psycho-physical characteristics? *Biological aspects do of course create a difference, besides that, experience shows that boys privilege the muscular aspects and the "doing" rather than the capacity for reflection and thus they deeply condition both the form and the quality of their thinking.* The difference is clearly revealed in the divergent modes of development of the analytic relationship. With boys the development seems to be somewhat episodic, relying upon isolated segments of work and upon a kind of fragmented irregular pace. Anxieties may appear suddenly, in the analytic relationship itself, as unforeseen explosions of unknown entity. With girls, on the contrary, the development of the process is mainly homogeneous and the areas of urgency appear in an almost regular sequence.

There is another substantial difference between male and female adolescents, it has to do with being capable of accomplishment and with accomplishment itself. Boys – this might prove a useful clarification – often involuntarily miss the distinction between the two states. Attitudes of negation or denial often express the fear that their actual accomplishment might be taken away or destroyed. Boys don't know that their capacity to accomplish isn't in any way at risk together with their accomplishment. *The inhibition of many male adolescents and adults is often associated with a confusion between actual accomplishment and potential capacity to accomplish.* In girls this anxiety is neutralised or at least softened by an unconscious awareness of a potential capacity to generate.

When in analysis, adolescents manage to refer to memories, a significant development takes place. By remembering they actually make space for a psychic area in which they become able to begin to *exist historically.* Furthermore, remembering enables them to become actors in an experience which they recognise as their own. One might say that the appearance of memories actually marks the beginning of adolescence. In clinical work one can usually see that adolescents try to "link" together events from different sessions, thus attempting at supplying a meaning to what is said or done. The emergence of memories, far from being an accumulation of data, comes as the reappearance of memories from childhood, in an endeavour to provide them with sense, situating them in time with a ''before' and an 'afterwards'. Thus, remembering significantly participates in the organisation of identity (an adolescent might remember: "this is the smell of last year's glue") and consolidates the recognition of space and time. At this stage, theories eluding reality-data (the wish and the quest for perfection that so torment the adolescent) are abandoned in favour of discrimination and of the capacity to create a distance from the things that are discriminated. *Discriminating means creating a hypothesis.* It is important to underline this change. It is the change *from an utopian model to a hypothetical model.*

A difficulty for the analyst lies of course in finding right modes of intervention, as adolescents often experience analytic propositions as an undue interference with their own problems, and the analyst's abstention or silence as a sign of indifference. A question may be asked in many ways. If in a direct form it could hurt the adolescent's susceptibility, it may still be formulated indirectly. Adolescents are very sensitive, it is therefore necessary for the analyst to care and to establish an accurate, precise communication attentive to an appropriate language.

The analyst who is working with adolescents should, hopefully, have an internal asset that can enable him to establish and preserve a state of genuine empathy and an unwavering emotional tone. He ought to be able to stay, at the same time, with himself and with the adolescent, especially in the presence of the two features that are characteristic of work with adolescents – "*provocation*" and "*invention*". Provocation could be said to be almost a game. Adolescents often provoke to keep the analyst's attention away from something which they wish to hide but, more often, to verify the therapist's behaviour and capacity for containment and his degree of interest. Invention, on the contrary, relates to small children's inclination to exaggeration and lies, something children have fun with and which at the same time softens their anxieties, creating a magic "paradoxical" world. Adolescent "inventions" are the residue of the magic world of childhood and have the same aim. They reduce the anxieties produced by the contact with reality. Clinical practice encourages me to name such states of the mind *delusional unsaturated states*. The latter are employed by adolescents in order to substitute an experience tainted by persecutory aspects of reality to former infantile theories. Adolescents seem to need to *invent* in order to *contain*. "Invention" is an attempt to *construct* "reality" starting from a very small available fragment. It is somehow an answer. When adolescents do have an answer they then can think something like: "I have nothing to do with this problem" or "I am not afraid of this problem" and so forth.

Often the phantasies which drive adolescents to "invent" relate to hatred or to internal destructiveness, to death wishes about killing and/or being killed. When "inventions" are perceived as disharmonious mental constructions they may be faced straight out in analytic work by asking the adolescent patient: "What is it that you fear?" or "What are you afraid of?".

Children just own a body, adolescents on the contrary observe the construction of theirs. The physical drives in adolescence are so quick, powerful and revolutionary that they almost equal a second birth. At the beginning of life, the mind starts functioning to contain the bio-vital drives of the body and to provide them with a direction. In adolescence the mind observes the transformations of the body, not undifferentiated as in the infant, but endowed with a specific masculine or feminine physicality. Adolescents become a body or in other words "assume a corporeal form" in a process which requires an acquisition of knowledge and implies intense suffering. Analysts should be internally prepared for this condition. They should be ready to reduce to the minimum their own personal wishes, their memory and, consequently, their capacity to "understand", as only in this way they might perceive what originates in the adolescent from his five senses, physical senses, but founding for the psyche. In so doing they may become able to introduce the analysand to aspects of himself which he ignores, though they might not yet exist, unfortunately, an adequate language for all the sensory and maybe also non-sensory features of human psyche.

KNOWLEDGE – PAIN – DESTRUCTIVENESS

Because adolescents have little capacity for control of their emotions, they tend to protect themselves by enacting different mechanisms, ranging from negation to activation. These defensive forces give origin to different psychic events in the sessions but also to action, such as threatening to interrupt the session or leaving the consulting room. Such events do require extensive analytic examination before going for the sensations and the emotions which have caused them.

One should always keep in mind that adolescents need to make experiences and that analysts should be able to make such experiences thinkable. If the emotional state of an adolescent is too intense it is necessary to reduce that intensity so that the emotion can then be thought about. Threatening to leave the session, for instance, is something that can be thought about while the analysand's actual departure isn't. Experience suggests that the best thing is perhaps to encourage the adolescent to participate, as much as possible, in the formulation of the analytic proposition, so that it might be elaborated together by analyst and analysand with *the analyst allowing the analysand to understand the modes and forms by which his, the analyst's, mind operates thus showing the analysand how one may think about things.*

On one occasion a young girl asked her analyst: "Are you absolutely sure of what you are saying or are you just thinking it in this moment and we can discuss it?". This question is really an answer to the analyst's proposition and reminds us that analysts need to understand the mode in which adolescents experience the presence of an adult, especially of their parents. It is functionally important to pay attention to the place and role an adolescent gives to his parents and to follow the evolution which the parental images undergo in the young person's mind as the analytic process brings about new changes. Observation reveals a correspondence between the transformation of parental images on the one hand and the development of peer-relationships on the other. Initially, the presence of a "best friend" allows the opposition against parental figures, enabling the expression of the strong feelings adolescents feel can't possibly be shared with adults. Having a best friend is therefore functional to the needs of adolescents, to everything they want or would like to be. Absolute relationships are therefore established and everything is comprised in them, including aspects connected with sexuality such as identification or comparison. Later on, when the opposition to parents becomes less extreme, adolescents start having more than one friend and establish more realistic relationships.

Boys and girls, I would like to point out, are different also in the mode in which they make friends. Girls may – for cultural reasons or other – continue having a "best friend" for longer than boys, while the latter are more inclined, after some time, to fear their inclinations might be misunderstood or they might even feel personally uncomfortable about such relationships.

Becoming an adolescent, experiencing adolescence is inevitably painful. "Being" an adolescent is painful. Adolescents often try to avoid pain by taking refuge in defensive states such as denial or sublimation or, in some cases, they might even try to rush forwards in search of painful experiences as they feel attracted by them and perceive them as special and unique aspects of life.

During the adventure of adolescence there are also great differences, between boys and girls, in the field of physicality. Becoming a man, for instance, doesn't create many problems. The physical transformations aren't painful for boys, but rather pleasant or exciting, as in the case of masturbation. Some of such experiences may be similar in girls as well, but the process goes further in their case. Girls have to deal with physical pain (caused by the menstrual cycle) and this isn't a pleasant or satisfying experience at all. Girl's childhood precocity in learning seems to halt at the time of the first menstruation, when the latter signals that they may potentially, or even virtually, become mothers.

When girls undergo states of violent internal conflict they may influence or even measure their bio-physical development (i.e. they sometimes temporarily arrest their menstrual cycle) opposing physical transformations which are felt to be premature and therefore dangerous to their psychic resources. They are trying to get the time they need to be able to change, so that they won't have to oppose and fight their own development anymore.

When the menstrual cycle starts, it originates acute expectations that greatly stimulate sensitiveness but may also sometimes generate anxiety. Girls may deal with such an anxiety by accepting it but they may also try to slow down or accelerate the process that is provoking it. The painful experience is wholly internal just as their physical pain is internal. It is essentially related to the vertical axis.

Boys have a less traumatic experience and their "here and now" is less involved and less conflictive. The painful experience is *displaced on the world*. Boys experience a painful world (the fight for supremacy). Their pain relates, in other words, to the horizontal axis.

In adolescence pain relates to knowledge. It is a process in which time is, as we all know, of fundamental importance. *In boys*, nevertheless, *the painful process of getting to know themselves and the world seems to be more devoid of any temporal-historical characteristics*. This may depend on the absence of very precise physical signals and on the consequent inclination to avoid the awareness of owning and of being responsible for one's own specific physicality. One might see an expression of this difference in the statistic data which indicate that, in urban and suburban areas of western countries, the male drug-addicts are a much higher percentage than the female ones (about 80% of the whole population). These and other problems have been explored, up to now, using the concept of regression. I believe, in fact, that this concept isn't really applicable in adolescence, when the experience takes a form and the form involves the reliability of the whole psycho-physical system.

In my hypothesis there are two areas of the personality and the activity of both areas is connected with the functions and disturbances of the processes of thought. The two areas, which I have named entropic and negentropic, are in close relation to each other and the quality and state of their relationship influences significantly the system of thought.

I describe the entropic area as the area dominated by the turmoiling flow of sensations and the archaic matrices of emotions which have their natural seat there but which might nevertheless easily reach states of instability. It is the area of creative potentialities and of potential structures of thought and needs to be contained for life to be possible. The function of containment is developed dynamically by the negentropic area, which originates from the entropic, and creates the foundations of the capacity for relationships from its first initial mode – the mother-infant relationship.

The entropic area is viable to any kind of process. Its unstable dynamic equilibrium may, and often does, originate harmonious situations but it is also open to the risk of being overwhelmed by internal or external events and of manifesting itself in states of great turmoil and chaos – such as depersonalisation, loss of identity etc – states which I generally name disharmonious but that have nothing to do with regression. The vertical (intrapsychic) dimension is supposed to respond to the motions of the entropic area by syntonising with the negentropic area that may consequently include the single individual and life-experience, in the horizontal (interpersonal) dimension.

The functional convergence of entropic and negentropic aspects enables individuals to contain and deal with internal resources as well as enabling them to accept, modify or even transform reality.

Freud believed that mankind reaches adulthood passing through momentous steps which are developmentally described as "stages" and which imply, as a consequence, the concept of regression. The progress of psychoanalysis then produced the concept of splitting – a concept that was described with utmost richness and accuracy by M. Klein – a mechanism that is responsible for the subtraction of substantial aspects of experience from the personal developmental course. Splitting seems to be an important point during adolescence *as there is certainly a difference between being a child, an adolescent or an adult and containing a child, an adolescent or an adult.* Aspects of childhood continue to exist in everyone but aren't the actual childhood. So do aspects of adolescence but not the adolescent. Everybody has aspects of childhood and adolescence in adult life. If it were possible to accept the concept of regression, one should then also propose the use of the concept of "progression" but because psychic life is founded on a constantly unstable dynamic equilibrium, the use of concepts such as regression or progression seems to be devoid of any sense. *It is on the contrary necessary to evaluate if and how, in everyday life, one is using adequate or inadequate instruments for the functional challenges which are required from life.*

Regression, furthermore, closely relates to and requires, as an inevitable corollary, the concept of "dependence". Again in disagreement, I believe, on the contrary, that the possibilities of accepting and metabolising the progressively integrating aspects of personality actually rely on the gradual development of autonomy and therefore on the capacity to take responsibility for oneself, obviously within the limits of one's actual potential.

This process only acquires a meaning if it develops in time. If, in other words, it is experienced temporally. In female adolescents the passing of time is even more significant than in the male as the body that becomes the body of a woman expresses itself very loudly and is perceived in a way that really introduces the understanding of the passing of time. Observations determine in observers a specific individual vision, a kind of personal Gestalt. Several Gestalts may appear in a sequence, specific for each individual and a kind of global vision moves, circularly, almost as in an orbit. The person may freely use defences, either archaic or refined or *always, as many would say, archaic* for defences are thought to be present since birth. *I am on the contrary hypothesising that other defences may appear at the beginning of adolescence,* for bodily modifications must necessarily be followed by psychic adjustment and, also, that without an adequate elaboration, defensive aspects from the period of adolescence may easily be transformed into disharmonious aspects. Some disharmonious aspects may therefore be regarded as relating to the first years of life while others – as accurate observation seems to point out – could well relate to adolescence.

I believe it is advisable to avoid the medical model which refers to the body in its mere physical sense. Obviously degenerative or pathological phenomena of the body have to be either cured or removed. It isn't so for the mind and this model appears therefore insufficient or even misleading. Psychic disharmonies shouldn't be compared to physical ailments, though they might produce analogous effects and leave analogous traces, because they usually have stronger potentialities for compensation. As opposed to biological disorders, psychic disharmonies tend to fortify the mind by increasing the strength of psychic experience. It is highly unlikely for instance to see relapses or processes which repeatedly follow the same course. Something similar also happens to the body (an increase of the immune defences after a specific pathological event, for instance) but the physical responses seem to pertain to the field of direct answers rather than being further elaborations or even creations as is the case of the psyche. This statement doesn't really contradict the formulation of the concept of corporeality (mind of the body) as it describes situations in which there is a physical urgency and the body, without being able to rely on the mind, "desperately" tries to survive by endeavouring to reach a state of sufficient containment and cohesion.

I have stated earlier that such disharmonies give origin to many disturbances related to the area of depression. I believe such a statement to be quite coherent with my hypothesis as one sees, in adolescence, a sort of "second challenge" – a new body appears (Onefold) symmetrically with the appearance of the mind (Twofold) at birth.

Because there is no experience if there is no perception a child can't obviously make all the experiences that are necessary for his whole life, he may at the best, make all the experience he needs in order to be a child. The infantile horizon is confined within its own characteristic limits. Even the Oedipal Constellation, though it might be connected with the relationship with the parents, virtually horizontal, is initially experienced in the vertical dimension as it is fed by the child's phantasies about father and mother, not the actual historical father and mother, but a father and mother experienced in an internal world. Later, one might hypothesise, the child moves on from the vertical to the horizontal dimensions thanks to the Oedipal experience.

Finally, children, particularly in Latin cultures, are seen in a very protective light and are the focus of extreme attention. They therefore inevitably feel important, somewhat dazzled and maybe even excessively stimulated. Moreover their surroundings contribute, since the beginning, to form, inform or even deform them, as the intense inducements shape up their minds and things happen around them only with that aim. At that time the mind alone develops, as the body of the child follows the child, it grows up but just in physical measures, it bears no significant changes.

Later, when the time of adolescence rushes in, there is sudden change. The intense light of extreme protection and attention disappears and there is just the light of reality left. Adolescents are suddenly alone. Thus they realise that they are adolescents, that they are alone.

At that moment there are three possibilities:

a) Ask for help in order to remain a child.

b) Try to avoid adolescence, paying a very high price – the loss of the quality of life, as clinical experience has shown us.

c) Face adolescence and fight with all possible resources and with the help of the group of peers.

Events and meanings change, depending on the possibility that has been chosen, and reality then influences all possible characters of each life, in all their possible roles – concrete and fantastic, real, tangible, dreamlike, hated or even desired.

Strong intense conflicts may at this time of life provoke destructive acts such as attempts of suicide, which may or may not result in actual death. Such self-destructive acts express an utter refusal of reality, caused by the feeling that one's resources are inadequate, by states of panic and by a consequent closure of the mental horizon.

Suicide may be carried out in different ways, from the actual direct attacks on life to the more subtle and silent modes of self-destruction such as the fatal Saturday-night challenges, drug-addiction and so forth.

PROTO-DEPRESSION

Many specific disharmonies in adolescence are connected with states of isolation. The latter is frequent in drug-addiction, anorexia, bulimia, claustro and agoraphobia, deviance and delinquency, in the common and complex states of learning difficulties and, finally, in the whole range of depressive disturbances which are nowadays causing an increasing number of suicides. The main initial conflict in adolescence is originated by the existence of intense expectations, contrasted by the deep belief that it will be impossible to satisfy them. The latter relates to an inadequate analysis of one's own resources and of the personal capacities necessary to face the challenges imposed by the environment and by the world of adults. Isolation can be the expression of a narcissistic sensitivity and it certainly relates to the conflicts originated by the acquisition of knowledge as well as to the testing and employment of personal resources.

I name proto-depression the psychic configuration connected to such conflicting experiences. It may have different causes and characteristics but it should, nevertheless, be considered a significant warning as it may become the nucleus of a future manic-depressive syndrome, or cyclothymic disorder as it is often called. *Proto-depression appears when the adolescent mind has in itself the characteristics that are necessary for the actual experience of life.* In other words when the child's phantasies disappear, making space for a new mode of living, when adolescents become the directors of their own life and consequently experience the existence of limits. Finally, I am using the term proto-depression as I wish to differentiate the depressive state of adolescents from the depressive condition experienced by infants in the first year of life.

Adolescents have to deal with the problem of getting to know themselves. They are simultaneously pressed by internal and external demands and they develop specific defences, aiming at lowering the emotional weight. When their actual contemporary problems reach a sufficient stage of elaboration and integration, adolescents can deal again with their still active infantile conflicts including possible unelaborated aspects of the depressive position.

If the signals of alarm aren't recognised, and possible presence of a proto-depression isn't faced, an actual depression may then develop in adult age, as an adult person may revert to depression when facing situations apparently similar to adolescent conflicts. There is, nevertheless, a substantial difference. While proto-depression in adolescence still has a life-promoting function, actual depression developing in adult age is usually saturated with a sense of death.

The proto-depressive configuration has, once again, different characteristics in male and in female adolescents. This happens because the body has a fundamental role in adolescence and actually detonates this second challenge. For instance one might think of some young ex drug-addicts who have attempted suicide several times. Obviously their relation with drugs was characterised by the idea that it might be possible to control their use of the substance. The "illusion" was the result of a challenge originating in adolescence, as the result of a uni-lateral decision, devoid of any reality-testing. Something that had to do with an adolescent attempt at actually "fooling" life. Such choices reveal a strong self-destructive feature which has been empowered by the use of drugs, and has thus become an over-whelming force.

The initial conflict in adolescence is mainly caused by expectations which are, in the young person's opinion, impossible to satisfy but also by the lack of actual adequate resources. Adolescents operate a peculiar splitting, and thus originate two diverse, somehow autonomous, psychic structures. The first harbours omnipotence, the second impotence. By handling the two structures as two entities, they preserve their double role but reinforce the sense of scarcity of their resources. As a consequence they sometimes become persecuted by their impotent aspect and try to displace themselves eventually committing suicide. When they feel that they are fully incapable, their ambivalence determines a self-destructive capacity. Their obvious inca-pacity then contrasts with their, again obvious, capacity to destroy their own life.

In other situations suicide is the answer to an expectation followed by disappointment. It has been seen to happen recently, with worrying fre-quency, to young people in the military service and to students who haven't passed their exams, high-school final examinations particularly. The social group also has some responsibility in these cases, for it tends to disregard the *initiatory* importance of such moments of passage. By disregarding such importance the social group implicitly condemns the adolescents who, for one reason or another, fail such ordeals.

The discontent of civilisation, extensively quoted, should be regarded as the "discontent of adolescence", as many of the disharmonies of adults, particularly depressive disorders, originate and consolidate in adolescence. Our civilisation doesn't seem to acknowledge the capital importance of ado-lescence for future life and for the inclusion in the group. It requires its members to enter the productive cycle as soon as possible. Does anyone really pay attention to the experience and meaning of being an adolescent? How long does it take to become an adolescent? Will there be enough time to become an adult or will society expect and demand premature inclusions into its fierce whirlpool?

Adolescent girls, thanks to their bodies' rhythm and necessities, seem to be better anchored to reality data as well as to all aspects related to the pass-ing of time. Clinical work shows us the mode in which the two sexes expe-rience and interpret time. Girls seem to mature and psychically integrate sooner and more easily than boys. The difference relates not only to their metabolism and to their specific endocrine development but also to the definite changes in their body, and to the importance they give to the moment in which their body becomes potentially adult. Boys, on the contrary, cannot rely on their processes of growth to develop and adjust psychically and their evaluation of time isn't therefore as pressing or as conditioning as it is in girls. Different rhythms in growth cause different perceptions of the passage of time, i.e. time is seen as "shorter" and more urgent by girls than by boys. The two sexes therefore seem to have different modes of elaborating their understanding of time, a difference which again originates at the biological developmental level but which eventually becomes a fundamental feature of adolescence as a whole.

INCOMMUNICABILITY AND LEARNING

The question of acquisition of knowledge in adolescence relates to the problems of incommunicability and of school progress and introduces the subjects of how such matters might be dealt with in analysis. *Almost paradoxically adolescent incommunicability can be said to be, for many adolescents, the first form of communication.* Adolescents believe that no one can understand them, especially their parents who are thought of as having no adequate resources to do so. There is a kind of ambiguous consistency in this hypothesis. Adolescents think that no one can understand them because no one has experienced their own specific very personal experience, which is of course true, but at the same time if anyone tries to approach them and tries to understand them, they immediately feel upset and sometimes almost robbed of their experience.

It is sometimes useful to point out such a process during the session *while it is actually taking place* in order to endeavour to reduce the distance and re-establish a dialogue.

It is also necessary to make a differentiation in the session between incommunicability and other forms of direct communication. We will have an example of this later in the case of AH., a case in which a kind of shameful reticence, expressed in different forms, was quite evident, as is the case with many other adolescents. The problem of doing badly at school (which shouldn't be related too closely to the problem of acquiring knowledge) is also somehow connected to adolescent reticence. Because we live in a society in which "successful or unsuccessful" scholastic results have enormous importance, adolescents tend to feel they have failed or on the contrary succeeded, just because of this and nothing else. School difficulties may well be the expression of a strong narcissistic structure which hampers the development of an interest on anything else but oneself. It is therefore technically important to understand the function of such defences. Unsuccessful results may well be a defence, expressing also the adolescent's capacity for tolerance, or even preserving vital space. Adolescents have their limits and sometimes express them by their defences. The latter should be understood and respected, never forced.

School failure may sometimes paradoxically represent a kind of psychic rescue for adolescents. In order to become concerned with studying and learning it is necessary to count on a psychic area free and available for that function. When studying appears to be actually impossible the psychic area may well be occupied by anxiety and therefore not accessible, but the anxiety may, nevertheless, supply useful elements which help to throw light and bring to the surface significant features of the adolescent's psychic condition. The analytic session supplies the analyst with information about possible learning disabilities. If an adolescent appears to be curious and interested, his difficulties in learning probably do not relate to a disability but are just functional to his internal system. Such a difference appears even more obviously when an adolescent mentions, in the session, that knowledge doesn't just belong to parents or to the analyst but to the common potentiality of getting to know about things. *Such a capacity to understand oneself and the world is also relevant for decisions about how to end analysis.*

When one refers to adolescence one usually means the age going from 11 to 20. It would be in my opinion desirable to accurately research and understand the sociological and strictly psychological reasons which originated this record. Common clinical experience shows that the beginning and ending of adolescence are much more elastic than that. It shows furthermore that it sometimes begins and ends later. The above mentioned limits could only continue to prove correct if one were just to describe the *"significant psycho-physical development"* relating to age. I believe that the Twofold (psychic) essence may well be regarded as autonomous in respect to physical time. Once the chronological developmental drive is exhausted, something may be left behind and become a kind of *a constant of the mental functioning*, sometimes significant for the whole individual life, configuring the qualities and nature either of a child, of an adolescent or of an adult as the privileged characteristic of the person's mental functioning. Only if the three specific modes of functioning are harmoniously integrated can there be a real woman or a real man. There is nothing new in such a statement. Poets have long since written that each human being is at the same time a child, an adolescent and an adult.

This is to say that adolescence doesn't just precisely correspond to a very definite period of time. Most analysts nevertheless (unfortunately) tend to visualise adolescence on the basis of their own personal experience. Speaking in general, the categories 'child', 'adolescent', 'adult' inevitably stir very strong emotional responses while personal experiences easily distort and limit analytic capacities. In working with analysands who have the conventional ages of children and adolescents, analysts should hence focus, and be exclusively concerned about, their real or potential capacities or the lack of same. Personal experience has convinced me that in childhood and adolescence the range of individual behaviour tends to oscillate between two extreme situations. An area of almost autistic orientation, on the one hand, and manic attempts at flights into adulthood on the other.

Childhood and adolescence are dramatically characterised by the Onefold-Twofold confrontation. In adolescence there is a degree of awareness that is of course impossible at the beginning of life when the physicality requires the mind and not vice-versa. The beginning of life is a time of intense turmoil. For some kind of equilibrium to be established, the Onefold-Twofold relation has to reach some sort of consistency in relation to the external world, initially constituted by the primary figures of father and mother. Thanks to an intense interaction with such figures a more stabilised period, which Freud understood and for which he indicated by the concept of "latency", is eventually reached. It is a kind of *gentlemen's agreement* between physicality and the psychic individual essence (a silent agreement, scarcely conflictive, as one of those quiet moments that sometimes introduce storms) announcing the new dramatic storm of *adolescence*. Here the psyche is forced to face a new unknown physicality, it is the beginning of the second challenge.

Thus regarded the scenery created by the beginning of adolescence originates further thoughts and hypotheses. The first hypothesis, it is only more of an analogy for the moment, should enable us to conceive a completely new and different situation as far as the personal vertical relation is concerned. The second hypothesis addresses more adequate or even just tentative modes and forms of mental functioning in the new situation which creates tensions and conflicts just as the beginning of life does, but which needs new hypotheses to explain it. I am in fact hypothesising that adolescence – though of course connected with childhood – should be understood as a completely different event. The hypothesis could, in my opinion, prove sound. Children use reality to feed their phantasies while adolescents are unable to deny the reality principle. The realistic – or almost realistic – perception of the world they will live in, is the very poignant difference between adolescents and the children they used to be. Such a perception doesn't exist in the mind of children, but does exist in adolescents and furthermore originates new conflicts, such as the so called adolescent depression. Close observation of the mental functioning of adolescents reveals that pathological categories can't be compared with the common or generally accepted rules of psychic functioning (which in Kleinian theory relate to the infant's mental functioning) but are on the contrary characterised by new dynamic features, suggesting the presence of specific defences typical of adolescence.

Development in adolescents is, in my opinion, sometimes characterised by the presence of disharmonious features commonly named psychotic. Such features may sometimes turn into actual psychotic states. I believe that analysts shouldn't nevertheless regard them as such – which would on the contrary be the case with children and adults – but should analyse them in relation with the wider context of *experience-knowledge* which the young person is encountering. The clinical observation should in other words be focused on the possible growth-promoting function of such episodes.

A most interesting phase is, in this respect, the initial passage from childhood to adolescence, the period called latency. I understand this phase to be characterised by information, both conscious and unconscious. The information should prepare formation, that is the period of experience-knowledge. It is the most dangerous moment. The appearance of the temporal dimension makes things all the more difficult, confused and apparently unreachable, the young person understands that things can be different, unknown as yet, but different. If information is functional and abundant, if the process of formation of experience isn't excessively hindered (hard, menacing external obstacles), if there is a sufficient capacity to deal with the emotional world, it is then possible, for pre-adolescents, to attend the task of creating themselves. Creating is the alternative to deforming, as deformation is, alas, the unique response which the young persons can give to themselves if they don't find adequate help.

Growth is a multifaceted process. The passage from latency to pre-adolescence is, in my hypothesis – a kind of concrete research, through experience, of individual founding characteristics. There is a stage of *differentiation* from others and the world, preparing the conditions for *individuation*, a very important step for the *vicissitudes of future identity*.

Latency children play and discover their characteristics of similarity and difference from others, mainly peers, as well as their attitudes, physical strength, tastes, interpersonal inclinations, future choices, modes of relationship with younger children, adults, the group etc.

The infantile drive tends to be modified. Children appear to be more silent, sometimes empty or bored or even isolated from their environment. They contrast and remark the differences, comparing their parents with a friend's parents, their mother with their best playmate's mother and establishing some initially approximate differences in economical, aesthetical, social characteristics. They recognise and accept status symbols, understand differences, learn to discern reality data.

The child's investigation isn't carried along on purpose. It is a process of discrimination and differentiation that eventually leads him to a sense of existing if not to an actual understanding of meanings. It is an initial individuation which establishes, in my opinion, the foundations for the research of identity.

As a consequence of this process adolescence becomes less dramatic in its beginnings. When there hasn't been time for this infantile experience, pre-adolescence often comes in as a kind of emotional shock. One often sees in analytic practice and supervision that with some pre-adolescents there seems to be very little consistency between the past and the difficulties of the present.

By keeping one's attention focused on such processes the analyst may adequately foster, for instance, innumerable solutions of the Oedipal constellation, or deal with the child's attempts at blocking growth, or again the young person's endeavour at almost by-passing adolescence by means of a massive assumption of the horizontal dimension which would permanently hinder the foundations of identity.

Clinical work with latency children often tends to deal mainly with the fantastic world of the first years of life. I believe that such focus mainly leads to frustration, and that by highlighting, on the contrary, the processes of differentiation and individuation analysts can improve their understanding both of latency and adolescence.

Having initiated my research from the formulations of Freud, Klein and Bion I have come to the conclusion that the structuring of the Ego, relating to the quest for identity, takes place under the influence of the Oedipal constellation and is strongly influenced, in the first years of life by phylogenesis. The archaic infantile Oedipus is characterised and somehow exhausted in a total desire for possession, responsible for the activation of children's phantasies. The activation is originated in children's need to survive by structuring the foundations of their Oedipal constellation. When the desire for possession is lacking there is a risk of primitive autistic situations.

Later, just before latency, the phylogenetic drive diminishes and children start harbouring precise identificatory movements which, in turn, diminish the violence of their phantasies. Freud believed that at this point the Oedipal situation could be thought of as concluded. My hypothesis is rooted in Freud's conceptualisation and extends it by asserting that the search for identity, including gender identity, begins at this point. This is the beginning of a process which goes from identification to personalisation of the Oedipal conflict, through the contribution of each single experience, throughout life and until death.

Freud one must say once more, offered an extremely incisive and coherent comprehension of the Oedipus complex and couldn't have avoided regarding it as concluded rather than as continuing. His phallo-centric vision and consequent exclusion of the feminine component, as well as the importance attributed to sexual aspects, were relevant in regarding his investigation as concluded at that point. According to Freud the phylogenetic drive influenced the choice of the object and therefore the establishment of gender identity, which was in its turn relevant for the conclusion of the Oedipus complex.

My hypothesis is that the passage takes place during a longer period of time during latency and adolescence when the phylogenetic response is absorbed by and included into ontogenesis. Thus adolescents take responsibility for their perpetual quest for identity and gender identity.

I differ from Freud when I assign different competencies to phylogenesis and to ontogenesis in the structuring of identity and because I oppose

Freud's deterministic vision with a notion of responsibility, highlighting its decisive importance in the choice of the object.

Finally, I believe the whole process to be strictly related to the appearance and elaboration of a gestaltic vision of one's own personal physicality.

THE CASE OF AH.[98]

AH. was an eleven year old pre-adolescent. At the beginning of analysis he could only experience and accept the perception of his own existence through the concrete possession of objects. He was unable to access symbolic processes as he was saturated by the anxiety of not existing. He felt all adults were criminals he should fight against, as they had power and things, and limited his space. He felt he had to conquer his space fighting a kind of 'war'.

In one of the initial sessions he drew children holding hands and wearing a mask. He picked up the scissors and started cutting them but when he couldn't do it with absolute precision he destroyed them all. When the analyst said that if he couldn't tolerate imprecision he couldn't protect his own creations either, or even his creative capacity he answered: "I destroy them. The world doesn't belong to adults. I turn them into dust!".

The child in AH. felt the threat of the adolescent he was becoming and tried to protect his identity through the power of destroying his own creations.

It is technically important to help adolescents, when they experiment themselves in doing, by supplying them with instruments enabling them to discern and differentiate their capacity from their actual production, in order to prevent their dissatisfaction from extending from the latter to the former.

In one of the following sessions AH. brought some extraterrestrial monsters with him and employed them to represent an attack on his parents and later on his sister. The analyst made some propositions about the attacks having the aim of conquering anew the space which his sister was occupying and AH. answered that the toys in the box were his, and that everything in his house belonged to him: "Don't I have a room? Is it that only others own things? Don't I exist then? The square down by my house is also mine". The analyst then remarked that the square belonged to the city as well and that it was his square when he went to play there. AH. contrasted the analyst initially but then burst into tears for quite a while.

AH. was linking his identity to concrete possessions. The analyst was trying to suggest the possibility of founding his identity on the notion of belonging and therefore on the use of things rather than on possession but didn't succeed, in so doing, in reducing the anxiety of existing which supported AH.'s possessiveness.

The formulation of analytic propositions is a delicate affair in the work with adolescents, as the magic-omnipotent world of childhood is still present, the movements of the mind ranging from infantile to adolescent modes are quick and sometimes imperceptible. In leaving the world of childhood behind, adolescents reach an unknown territory and sometimes experience agoraphobic anxieties. They then withdraw from the new and unknown perceptions and seek the narrow "reassuring" space of their infantile phantasies enacting a kind of defence.

The world beyond the familiar square generates anxiety in adolescents as they perceive an internal pressure and the external limits of the new reality they approach by growing up. Their familiar square is well known to them and therefore most reassuring.

The analytic proposition has the function of harbouring the concreteness of adolescent communications, and of taking some of that same concreteness away so that the symbolic aspect may be privileged, highlighting the variety of configurations that are contained in the communication – possessiveness, sadism, the impulse to learn. The analyst should foster the adolescent's perceptive and discerning functions, enabling the development of a capacity for abstraction, for thought and knowledge; highlighting in other words the young person's epistemophilic potential.

Children, one could say, cling to possession as a remedy against the pain and anxiety caused by the loss of initial certainties. Adolescents, on the contrary, refer to a sense of belonging, more related to processes of symbolisation, and therefore begin to structure their ego configuration.

Children manipulate reality with their omnipotent phantasies and in so doing they reassure themselves in respect of the adults. Adolescents accumulate experiences and enlarge their perception, therefore necessarily leaving behind omniscience and omnipotence in order to preserve their new capacities of contacting the world. The world imposes on the pre-adolescents and adolescents the necessity to examine their hypotheses and compare them with reality. Adolescents are spectators of the change which takes place in them. Children, on the contrary, "own" their body and count on the stability and continuity of the perceptions that derives from it.

Adolescents don't get any benefit from the illusion of concretely possessing something but rather take advantage from developing a personal mode of perceiving their experience in life. Their initial ego configuration somehow influences their experience of life. Life, in its turn, reinforces specific features of their ego configuration.

AH. about to end analysis, became able to start inhabiting his house, his body and emotions not perceived as threat anymore. He also became able to use a mental area or space, a kind of "square in his mind", for symbolic meanings and for thought. In one session he was able to discern clearly between his capacities and magics: "First the magics, as a child . . . not true; then capacities, as a grown up and true".

"Don't you know? I was down at the square and I was thinking . . . I used my abilities and thought that my aunt was at home . . . It was true, I went to visit her and she was there . . . It was afternoon, it was Sunday. My aunt was not at work, she was at home. This was "capacity" not "magics" . . ."

THE POINT OF MAXIMUM URGENCY IN ANALYTIC PRACTICE

Adolescents either "choose" to face their adolescence or are tempted to avoid it. Innumerable arrangements take place between a young person and his or her internal world but also with the environment's liability and potentialities. Analysts who have worked in this field know well that a thorough experience of adolescence proves most structuring for the whole adult life. Clinical practice with adults shows that, in many cases, an experience was avoided or even ignored (Peter Pan is an example of this) or maybe just restricted by so many adjustments that severe disturbances consequently developed especially in the management of emotions. Adolescents find it most difficult to deal with their turbulent emotional world and their difficulty influences their sense of identity so that they eventually pose questions such as: *"Who am I? What am I?"*.

Clinical observations have convinced me, in agreement with other specialists, that many psychic disharmonies originate exclusively in adolescence. In clinical work one should keep in mind that adolescents need all the characters which are part of their life to be present, hypothetically or concretely, analyst included. The analyst is one of the active co-protagonists of the analytic relationship and this explains, in part, why the setting needs to be so different from the setting used with adults.

Children and adolescents tell things (which they can't say in words) with their mimic, the position of their body, etc. Their movements inform the analyst about their anxieties and about the point of urgency. It is like a luminous sign describing their position, the state of their mind. It is up to the analyst to be capable and sensitive enough to register and understand the meaning of the message.

The point of maximum urgency is obviously extremely important for any analysand but more than ever for adolescents, since their urgencies don't just generate anxiety but also invest the question of time. So the analyst should keep track of the urgency which is temporally present and this introduces a significant difference from work with adults.

The appearance of a sense of *Time* is quite a specific mental feature in adolescence. Adolescents are curious and interested in contrasting existence with non-existence, the latter as a kind of empty unknown state reminding of the question which children so often pose: "Where was I when I wasn't there?".

It isn't by coincidence that all cultures have some sort of "paradise" a kind of play-space, a sound answer to the infantile fear of not existing.

The sudden irruptive appearance of the perception of the passing of time (latency period) is the first fundamental passage from childhood to pre-adolescence and from the latter to adolescence. Then, the child one has known won't be recognisable anymore.

In childhood space is circumscribed to the family area. It is an area of free movement for the child, it is his territory. Outside this area the child is contained by his father and mother. His territory is thus sometimes projected into the world. The pre-adolescent on the contrary faces something unknown. If time exists then there must be *space* also, wider then the family area, signifying something as yet unknown.

Children relate to other children but their world of experiences can't be really communicated, nor are they interested in doing so. Their world is closed in itself. Children function mainly, or even solely, in the vertical dimension. They talk to invent the theories they need, sometimes refined theories, almost hypotheses about life. The answers they give themselves are satisfying and functional to their vision of the world. They are also soothing to their worries about the incomprehensible projects and behaviours of adults.

Pre-adolescents can't anymore use infantile theories because the external world forces them to test its own theories by the horizontal dimension. Magics, not suitable to satisfy the real-experience-test, are therefore, in pre-adolescence, sometimes substituted by rituals. Pre-adolescents oscillate between infantile positions (when anxiety grips them) and pre-adolescent positions when they feel supported.

Curiosity supplies another helpful and powerful impulse towards the exploration of unknown areas of experience. Things aren't in anyway easy for the analyst since he needs to have a competence in both ages. When the child is mainly a child he needs to accept the child's theories about life and help him understand that the anxiety about emotions isn't related to the latter's quality but rather to its intensity. When, on the contrary, the more pre-adolescent features are present, the analyst should modify his technique accordingly.

Both pre-adolescence and adolescence are characterised by turbulent and disharmonious behaviour not relating to pathology but rather to the process of learning from experience. Theories are weak at this time and confrontation with life therefore incessant. There is no knowledge of what is requested and such ignorance generates intense anxiety. If, on the contrary, experiences are refused, wholly or partially, severe consequences may ensue in adult age, both in terms of the quality of life and of the waste of potential resources. The disharmonious features eventually tend to progress towards a solution as the capacity for containment develops. The behaviour becomes more functional to personal needs and resources.

It is really a second occasion for challenge. Adolescents have minds, often good, lively, attentive, curious minds but their minds know nothing about their bodies. The body imposes itself upon the mind usually between the ages of eleven and thirteen. From then onwards the mind has to take care of the body.

It is a problem for boys, but one can imagine what a problem it is for girls since they tend to feel more conditioned aesthetically, culturally, socially etc. For both sexes the analytic relationship is sometimes characterised by eroticism because of the young person's insecurity. It is therefore important that the analytic propositions should be formulated highlighting the experience which adolescents have of the presence of their analyst, in order to reduce the intensity of the feelings and the correspondent levels of anxiety.

Anxiety as the product of a search for identity is the main problem of adolescents. Analysts should therefore help them to understand the necessities of life and the possible useful adjustments. It is like accompanying or following them but without any confusion of competencies or of responsibilities. Such areas must be kept perfectly clear for the analytic relationship to be able to function in generating experience.

The analyst's presence and commitment may also assume a pedagogical value since doing and knowing coincide with experience. There is no point in denying this aspect for just being there, waiting to begin a session at a given time as agreed, has a pedagogical value. On the other hand adolescents may quite likely not come to their sessions. Their absence has the aim of testing the analyst's interest and tolerance, it is also the young person's manoeuvring area in the presence of intolerable feelings such as hatred. If hatred is used to absorb the frustration deriving from limits and from comparison with others, the analyst figure may easily be destroyed. The aggression reinforces the reasons for absence and feeds persecutory guilt, keeping the analysand away from the sessions. If the analyst can endure the state of affairs, and elaborate on it, he may then interrupt the vicious circle, bringing the adolescent back to the session and helping him to understand that his phantasies *aren't lethal*.

To reach this aim it is necessary, for the analyst, to use single facts as general models of behaviour, leaving out all persecutory guilt which makes adolescents feel abandoned, persecuted and full of anxiety for what has happened. It is another pedagogical aspect of the formulation of analytic propositions as adolescents have to learn through themselves and through their experiences. Our Monday adolescent isn't the same on Wednesday. Analysts need therefore a great mobility in their mental states.

THE CASE OF AI.

This is the first meeting with an eleven year old boy. It is presented with the aim of discussing several important features such as:

a) the point of maximum urgency,

b) its function,

c) the theories upon which the boy founded his thoughts and actions,

d) the construction and formulation of the analytic proposition.

The analyst met AI. before meeting anyone else in the family. She also met, separately, AI.'s mother and then his father, but only after meeting AI. . . . This method helped the analyst to avoid the interference of mother's opinion on AI., his father's opinion etc. It was therefore easier for her to form her own free opinion as she was requested to do.

Another advantage of this procedure is, in my opinion, greater freedom for the child or adolescent. Though one may have the greatest respect for families in general, it is necessary to keep in mind that when a young person is suffering any difficulties or disharmonies in the vertical or horizontal areas (relationship with the parents) the parents can't possibly be able to offer all the necessary help.

Mothers often feel even more fragile than fathers about this, since they tend to become, more than fathers, convinced that they have in some way harmed their children. They love them all the more for this reason and tend to lose some of their capacity for perception, therefore further increasing their "love". As a result of this they sometimes lose track of their children's necessities and also of their own capacities and needs.

By meeting the young person before the mother and father the therapist can gain better understanding of the specific areas of competence of each of the members of the family and therefore more successfully help mother and father to re-establish their actual parental functions. Furthermore the analyst can hope to be able to help the young person to feel more protected during the new experience, a sort of special care that is particularly important in cases in which the consultation results in a recommendation for analysis.

This procedure, it should be said, is sometimes worrying for parents, or mainly for mothers, especially when the children are still quite young. A lot depends on how it is presented. One should keep in mind the pain mothers feel, in particular when it is their first child that comes for consultation, and the anxiety related to the effort of becoming a mother.

The beginnings are important. The risk is that mothers may experience each session of their children's analytic experience as a kind of memento of what they have been "unable to do for their children". Analytic work with children and adolescents often comes to an abrupt end because parents, more frequently mothers, are overwhelmed by their emotions – possessiveness, competitiveness, jealousy. This happens unfortunately even though they may have been warned of such risks, informed of the dangers of sudden ruptures, or even when they are themselves in analysis, or meeting regularly, monthly or fortnightly another therapist.

Another dangerous attitude in the family (once again especially in mothers) is the opposite attitude, that is of leaving the young person totally in the care of the analyst. What happens in such cases is that whatever function is expressed or mobilised in analysis doesn't have any echo in family life. The young person learns about himself but receives no emotional support outside the session. He then becomes inclined to observe and coldly judge his family. Consequently he tends to detach himself. In so doing he also tends to become detached from his own affects, a really difficult situation for which there seems to be no solution. A really dangerous fracture between his experience in the consulting room and his life in his house or, better, in his own room in the house.

AI. came to the consultation accompanied by an understandably very nervous mother. She was extremely thin while the boy was quite fat. One felt she just couldn't deal with aspects of physicality, either in herself or in the boy.

The analyst asked AI. what his difficulties were: "Everybody teases me. My friends ban me, they call me stinky and chubby".

The analyst commented that it was very painful to feel isolated, ill treated and teased. AI. said that his father had problems like that and this made him, AI., suffer a lot. When asked to explain better he added: "He drank a lot. His friends drank, so he drank also or they would tease him".

The boy seemed to be again talking of his problems. He used the same tone in talking of his friends and of his father's friends. One could begin to understand that AI. was using fat as a protection against many things. One could maybe have a glimpse of mother's projections as well.

AI. continued to talk – his father's two names – a name and a nickname – and his multiple jobs as a labourer, only enabling him to come home late in the evenings.

The analyst tried to focus on the *point of maximum urgency* for AI. . . . By point of maximum urgency I mean the area of the actual anxiety, apart from the defences. In this case, the statement *my friends ban me*. The rest of the sentence "they call me stinky and chubby" justified the point of anxiety, the sense of being banned, but didn't express it at all. The ban included AI.'s father: "My father had problems and I suffered a lot."

AI.'s communication could be re-written as follows: 1) My anxiety includes the anxiety I am having for my father. My ban is his ban. He pays for it, drinking with his friends so it *won't* happen again. 2) My father's problems rob me of a model which I need to feel psychically adequate. A strong model which I can't find or use: "He drank a lot. His friends drank, so he drank also or they would tease him". It is the description of a catastrophic situation with no way out.

The analyst had to keep in mind the boy's needs, the anxiety about being banned, the lack of an adequate model for identification. In other words what I have named the point of maximum urgency. His attention needed to be directed there.

234

If in cases like this the analyst succeeds in reducing the intensity of the anxiety the young person may then become capable of listening both to the analytic proposition suggested by the analyst and to himself. If this doesn't happen, the anxiety somehow covers the capacity of perception and the mind is unable to think.

Once the area of urgency and the specific anxiety have been defined, the analyst may introduce new elements, or eventually even solicit them from the analysand, to continue the analytic dialogue. In the case of AI. the analyst knew that there was an anxiety but did not know as yet the boy's actual unconscious hypothesis hidden, as it were, behind the anxiety. She ignored in other words the function of AI.'s statement. Understanding *the anxiety and its function* is indispensable to the formulation of the analytic proposition.

AI. continued to talk for a bit about his father's activities and then he went on to tell the analyst about school, the teachers he had known, the ones he knew at the moment, he asked the analyst whether she knew any of them. He was obviously trying to deal with unknown situations, trying to establish links with school or anything else that may help him to understand what was happening in the session, to understand himself.

AI. continued his description: "There's science and maths . . . we're fourteen boys and eleven girls, girls aren't so quarrelsome". When the analyst asked about being quarrelsome AI. immediately answered: "Sometimes I feel that my head is empty".

There seemed to be no doubt. The analyst's question about the meaning of the word "quarrelsome" revealed that the word was related to AI.'s capacity to hate and to express it. But AI. only signalled the final consequence of the process: "Sometimes I feel that my head is empty".

It was a difficult situation for the analyst. AI.'s mind disappeared and there was emptiness instead. Was the emptiness a "fat" emptiness, trying to enclose and retain all the feelings of hatred? What could the analyst do with an empty head?

Thinking was felt by AI. to be difficult and painful – collecting thoughts in such a condition – and the analyst didn't ask why it was so difficult to think. The omission caused AI. to state: "I didn't know you were a woman, men are better at understanding problems". AI. had actually managed to avoid the perception of his feelings of hatred, and with this answer he was declaring that he couldn't communicate his feelings and emotions to a woman – his thin and nervous mother – but that he thought he could tell them to a man, a father if there had been one psychically available.

The difficulty or emptiness was caused by the irruption of a very strong emotion – hatred. The analyst might have highlighted the strength of emotions without specifying, for the moment, what kind of emotion it was. In so doing she would have enabled AI. to separate, and therefore *discern, thoughts from emotions*. This distinction is very important for the development of the analytic dialogue. Some emotions are so intense that they hinder the functioning of the mind, some states of mind, on the other hand, inhibit emotions.

The analyst asked what it was that AI. meant and if he could explain his thoughts better. It wasn't a thought but rather a theory. AI. was enunciating his vision of the world. His thin mother had the task of protecting-preserving his fatty self but his point of reference, though weak, was still his father. This mode of understanding the problem, of grasping as it were the underlying theory, can support the analyst in dealing with technical points and with questions related to the analytic relationship.

"Three kids in my class I am on good terms with. With the others I am not at ease". The analyst commented on the difficulty of being at one's ease with everybody and AI. continued: "In primary school just three of the girls. I felt good then". Memory appears 'then'. Remembering in pre-adolescence is actually like creating a distance from one's childhood. Creating a historical dimension for oneself.

AI. had some personal history behind himself in the past. He had a place where he could put his memories. It was as if he had said that when he was a child he could, after all, do something with his mother. But there is also the need for some kind of restriction of the mother figure 'I didn't know you were a woman' before being able to turn to father.

All the characters that were necessary for the understanding of the formation of identity and of the resolution of the Oedipal constellation were present. AI. showed his rich internal world since his first meeting. The richness and complexity of the material not only committed the analyst to understanding and registering but also to adequate answering or else the anxiety might have overwhelmed the boy.

Suggesting that thinking is difficult and even more so in the presence of emotions is really like supplying a kind of key or clue, or helping to understand the mental functioning. Such help should be provided whatever the age of the analysand, child, adolescent or adult.

AI. had come for consultation and this was his first meeting. I believe that it is possible for the analyst to intervene and supply his proposition even in first meetings and still have the possibility to refer, if necessary, the analysand to another analyst at the end of the same session.

AI. went on: "After school I go to my grandma. Then my mum comes, we eat and she goes back to work. I stay with my grandma. In the evening I go home with my mum. On Wednesdays my Mum doesn't work but sometimes she does. Some days I go to my old school, after school time".

The analyst commented that he went home, back to his things, in the evenings. And that one sometimes misses very much the things one doesn't have anymore and one would like to go back. AI. answered with emphasis "Yes. I felt good there".

The analyst's comment wasn't correct technically.

One can of course understand that a boy might miss something out of the past and that he might try to imagine going back to a place where his life was less harassed by conflicts but one shouldn't, in any way, highlight or encourage the *going back*. In this case one could have said that because he was finding the present difficult he was trying to seek refuge in things that belonged to the past. This comment would have enabled AI. to make an experience of the *temporal dimension* or even of the *space-time co-ordinates*.

Pre-adolescents have great difficulties in accepting the existence of such co-ordinates. The magic world of childhood is still quite present in them. Accepting the co-ordinates compels their mind to discriminate and discern reality data and this is painful and limiting for pre-adolescents. When they begin to discern the rhythm of past, present and anxiety about the future, pre-adolescents slowly and arduously begin to understand and assume the existence of the three space-time points of reference that enable all adequate and functional mental activity.

AI. picked up a sheet of paper saying he wanted to draw. He had, until this moment, used speech to communicate his anxieties and thoughts. The hint at *going back* may have influenced his decision to use a more indirect mode of communication, not really taking responsibility for what was communicated (or is this an adult prejudice?).

"Pteranosaur". One shouldn't be concerned about the name AI. wanted to give to his drawing. It must have had a meaning that he knew and understood and that he should have been asked about. He said it was a mixture of a monster and a scorpion. "The claws . . . it is a pteranosaur . . . the tail . . . it is a prehistoric bird . . . the body is like a man's body . . . a praying mantis . . . the left arm . . ." "The tail is like a steering wheel to find one's way in darkness . . . the face is a devil's face". "When it bites it really bites". "It lives in a cavern on the top of a mountain". "It is a monster eating all living things, people and animals".

The analyst risked a comment: "What a lot of terrible things this pteranosaur is". AI. answered: "I would like to be a monster so that I could defend all ill-treated animals". "Such as?" asked the analyst. "Me" AI. answered promptly.

The answer expressed the vastness of the boy's pain, anxiety and terror.

If one were to consider the horizontal dimension alone, the situation would have appeared to be dramatic and one would have felt that nothing could be done about it since a total massive defence had been activated in the monster. By keeping the vertical dimension in mind, on the contrary, one may find that the possibility for an analytic proposition appears to be quite functional to the boy's anxiety. *What is it of AI. that AI. doesn't like?* AI. had *described the way in which he had tried to protect and defend himself from the world*, projecting everything out of himself and creating a monster. But in fact, as AI. had intuition of, the most important feature of the problem belonged exclusively to his internal world.

This is what one might call the function, the conscious or unconscious reason of one's saying and doing. The function, in its turn, depends on the personal hypotheses at the root of one's vision of the world.

These are the essential elements on which, in my opinion, the analytic proposition may be set up. These were the data on which AI.'s mind functioned. It was a mind that felt excluded and that had neither models nor recognition of itself through a father figure, though an identificatory relationship with the latter may still exist. AI. had no possibility of recognition of himself through mother either, he wasn't a child anymore and couldn't therefore regard himself as such. The only thing he could do was resort to *omnipotence*, as a defence to his extreme impotence, by constructing a monster owning some feminine characteristics as well as masculine, devouring all living things, *all living things*.

The mind of this boy harboured at that time a kind of desert where hatred was a sort of lethal wind, with no obstacles to it. The details of the drawing were dramatically eloquent. AI.'s hatred had taken the form of an animal assembled with parts of other animals. AI.'s defence said that hatred was his weapon and that it could protect him, as long as it had all the characteristics which AI. had assigned to the monster. The monster was isolated on the top of a mountain, signifying AI.'s pain and anxiety and expressing also the price the boy was paying for his defence – utter seclusion.

AI. could only be helped to recuperate AI.'s company if he received help to observe and encounter himself. Thus he could begin to tolerate and soften the aspects of himself which, for the moment, he could only externalise and manage out of himself.

What was there in AI. which AI. didn't like? the answer to this question was given by AI. himself later in the session: "I could kill anyone who kills a hedgehog, or a dog or a cat. I would like those people to feel how painful it is". The analyst suggested something about feeling weak, defenceless or attacked and that it might be necessary to become a monster to defend oneself. She also added that hatred can only generate further hatred.

AI. obviously thought that he could contain what he regarded as the shock coming from the external world by this monster-creating defensive technique. The analyst's contribution was bound to introduce the vertical dimension: "What is there in AI. that AI. doesn't like?" Only in this way the analytic dialogue could begin, founded on AI.'s answers. Up to now there had been a lovely dramatic description, full of pain, hatred, violent emotions, but there hadn't yet been an exchange of mutual experiences – the point in which analyst and analysand meet and share their views.

AI. continued: "Yes. Well it depends. I ill-treat animals. For instance I kill cats".

There the analyst could at last show AI. what it was that he didn't like of AI., indicating the passage from the horizontal to the vertical dimension. One can see that by asking AI. what he didn't like in himself, the analyst was encouraging him to observe and consider himself and his feelings. As it was, AI. "killed cats".

It was an extremely important sequence. Instead of resorting to simple and fixed projections, justifying the use of hatred as the sole possible instrument for the construction of a protective monster, AI. could now take responsibility for something that he could share with the monster. The analyst had succeeded in creating a minimal *psychic area* necessary to allow the boy to confront himself, without being totally overwhelmed by his emotions and feelings.

I name it a psychic area because I believe there is a *functional psychic distance* (like the adjustment of in-focus binoculars) *between living, observing, feeling*. If one succeeds in structuring a minimal psychic area, even in the presence of extremely strong emotions, such as hatred for example, one will be able to think of something, to establish a relation between body and mind, between emotions and thought.

AI. wondered for the first time what it was that he didn't like in himself. It was his first moment of self-observation, the first time he referred to, and used, the only actor who knew about AI . . . AI. had become the monster's first and unique victim when he had constructed his complex monster-theory, the theory of a monster with a name, assembled out of many other animals in such a refined way and so fierce that no one could escape it. Now the analyst's task was to free him from the anxiety that had compelled him to create the monster, free him from such a monstrosity, so that he could recuperate his capacity to love, a capacity which was imprisoned in his capacity to hate.

"I endure and endure. Then I blow up and begin to strike. I endure for one whole school year, then I blow up . . . With one hit I can break a neck". Anyone's neck and head, of course, but AI. didn't know that, when he said this, his head was already quite lost.

The analytic experience could have aimed at bringing AI. nearer to himself, at giving him the chance to understand that he had a mind (a head) and that his mind could operate in modes that were functional to his needs. AI.'s statements and consequent findings in the first session were encouraging. By helping him to recover his capacities for thought it was possible to assist him in reaching a condition of internal tolerance of himself as opposed to his former state of pure hatred. The tolerance could, among other things, enhance his capacity to resist frustration, so that he might begin to think of the future, should the present continue to be too painful.

As the session continued AI. asked for another sheet of paper and started to draw some mountains and a sun that was setting a tree on fire.

As in the other drawing AI. was expressing his enormous difficulty in containing the impact of his emotions. The second drawing was stimulating and somehow symmetrical to the first – hatred killed, love set on fire. The urgency was in finding some containment so that using his emotions could become less dangerous and AI. could make some space for the for-mulation of thoughts. The analyst had at this point a very good opportu-nity to begin a dialogue with AI., suggesting as it were a kind of muzzle for the monster, so that the sun-love might ripen AI.'s mind or fruits, a suit-able metaphor, since AI.'s was a family of farmers.

Something of the sort actually happened since, as the session continued, AI. went near the box of toys and said: "I've seen a fort, I am full-grown may I play?"

The three sentences: I've seen a fort – I am full-grown – may I play? – synthesise the delicate moment of perception-transition reached by AI. through the analytic dialogue.

The first movement in the session belonged to AI. It was his capacity to express and make known the fundamental situation at the root of his psy-chic functioning – the two poles of hatred and love. The second movement pertained to the analyst, it was her capacity to make AI. feel protected and "shielded" so that he could eventually notice the presence of a fort.

The remarkable decrease of AI.'s anxiety eventually made him feel that he could play. It was a kind of rescue of his capacities. Then suddenly the pre-adolescent in AI. appeared with a problem – the passage from child-hood to adolescence. The sentence "I am full-grown" expressed AI.'s doubt whether the new condition could still allow *play*, the play which had dom-inated his life for so many years.

NOTES

98 This case was contributed E. del Greco Psychiatrist, Member of Italian Psychoanalytic Society.

GLOSSARY
F Romano and S. Facchini

Adolescence: Broadly, a condition of the mind aiming at continuously researching one's essence, originating in latency's dynamic processes of differentiation and individuation. It begins with actual adolescence, coinciding with physiological transformations relating to gender identity* (between the ages of ten and fourteen) and lasts for the whole individual life. If at birth one can hypothesise an autonomous beginning of mental functions (COO*) in adolescence one may see the body structuring itself in a way that will last for the whole objective and subjective individual experience. Peculiar defences appear, specifically characterising this age of life. Adolescents dynamically adopt three kinds of defences against the anxieties deriving from such physical and psychic modifications. A) They may tolerate the anxiety of "not knowing" and try to "learn from their own experience" as it takes place (doing .. in order to learn, learning .. in order to do). B) They may take refuge in obstinate repetitions of childish psychic attitudes (refusing reality and extensively resorting to phantasy and daydreaming). C) They may resort to adult models, not correspondent to their actual needs, borrowing them from the external world. In cases B) and C), which are flights into a hypothetical past or future, disharmonious situations may develop (cf. Harmony/Disharmony*), starting during adolescence and expanding as time passes.

Analytic Proposition: Communicative (not descriptive) interaction by which the analyst stimulates the analysand to recognise and assume the modes and forms on which the mind can count. It enables the analyst to use the actual experience of the analytic relationship. The latter can thus be described as a "self interpreting system".

Analytic Relationship: Self interpreting system characterised by two movements. The "going towards himself" of the analysand and the "returning towards himself" of the analyst. In this system the analyst and the analysand equivalently share responsibilities and specific competencies and the development in the "here and now" expresses a creative function aiming at activating, by means of analytic propositions, psychic resources and potential processes of thought in the analyst and in the analysand.

Barrier: Condition of the contact net* when it is made out of knots which don't have significant correspondences*. Consequences, saturation of mental space*, disorderly communication between the two systems Onefold* and Twofold*, turmoiling states*, panic, etc.

Basic masculinity and femininity: Dynamic forces specifically co-existent in the genes of each individual person as masculine or feminine modes of being. They exercise their pressure in the entropic area* and are important for the dynamic structuring of identity and gender identity*.

Concrete Original Object (COO):
A unity composed of:
a) a physical body
b) the sensations originating from this body
c) a mental apparatus responsible for registration and notation.
Concrete as its primary quality is physicality.
Original as it relates intrinsically to the original specific characteristics of each individual person.
Object as it is just the actual body of the individual with no consideration of the results of any developmental process.
The COO is the datum/presence. The Onefold* in relation to which the mind, Twofold* begins to function.

Contact Net: Multidimensional function which becomes active in the Vertical* dimension or axis when the latter intersects with the Horizontal* axis with the aim of facilitating the flood of sensations and emotions towards perception. Thought can then give a name and a meaning to what is present at the moment. The net takes shape through points of contact (cf. knots*) that sometimes originate significant correspondences*.

Denial: Defence mechanism against specific psychic temporary states relating also to psychic qualities of others. Such states can't be really disremembered by the individual. This sort of opposition or defence against them can nevertheless take place.

Eclipse of the body (Eclipse of the COO): a continuous process beginning with birth in which mental activity throws a shade over sensations and emotions. It has the aim of facilitating the emergence of thoughts and actions directed at supplying structuring meaningful forms, functional for the survival of the individual.

Ego Configuration: a concept that indicates a deep sense of identity understood in its solely dynamical essence, that is, regarded as capable of expanding and diminishing, depending on its momentary structuring capacity, in the alternating vicissitudes of the body-mind relationship between Onefold* and Twofold*.

Entropic area: this area is characterised by the presence of sensations and emotions acting in a turmoiling form (cf. turmoil*). It belongs to the vertical* dimension and mainly represents the domain of the Onefold*. It is characterised by an unstable equilibrium as described by Prigogine deriving from the turmoil-commotion.

Envy: A feeling that determines the attribution to the other of resources which a person can't recognise as his own. Thus the other is transformed into an enviable and desirable object. This process originates emulation, competition and gratitude.

Gender Identity: A physiologically defined characteristic modulated during life by the multiple functions of the Oedipal Constellation*.

Harmony/Disharmony: If one thinks of the body-mind dyad as of a dynamic entirety, the concepts of illness and health may well become inadequate or even reductive. More adequately one might think of more or less structured Ego Configurations*, characterised by different levels of cohesion, and of psycho-physical situations in which the physicality and the psychic features alternatively prevail. Such psycho-physical situations can be more or less harmonious or even disharmonious with the necessities of the individual.

Horizontal: A Co-ordinate that intersects the vertical* co-ordinate defining and delimiting the mental space* or area. The horizontal co-ordinate is different from external relationships, it is the expression of the Twofold*, of potential perception of temporality and of all relations with the external world expanding to the extreme confines of knowledge.

Knots: The points of intersection between the vertical co-ordinate* and the horizontal co-ordinate* where a form, or a meaning, is achieved. The knots, when potentially significant (cf. significant correspondences) are essential to the formation of the Contact Net*. By failing to attain a significant and meaningful form they can become the saturating elements of an actual barrier* opposing the flowing of sensations and emotions.

Language Registers: Basic components of the common-historical language which settle, expand and differentiate depending on contexts and necessities. It is possible in common language to isolate different language registers that are in a kind of osmotic relation with each other (delusional, phobic, psychotic, hallucinatory, dream register etc.) and that mainly emerge in the passages from the entropic/turmoiling area* to the negentropic area*.

Mania and Depression: General trends of psychic functioning present in every individual. They supply a kind of emotional tone or colour and may emerge, during the elaboration of experience, in any area that one could define as disharmonious (Harmony/Disharmony*). Depression is mainly present in the horizontal* co-ordinate in which one can find the active presence of the Oedipal Constellation*, the Ego Configuration* and the world. Because it implies features of external reality it may exasperate the feeling of impotence towards it. Mania, on the contrary, is an emotional characteristic of the Vertical co-ordinate* and doesn't imply aspects of external reality but rather enables free and extended manipulations of same.

Mental space or area: The space or area that, in each situation, is made available by the Eclipse of the COO*. It is defined and delimited by the intersection of the Vertical* and Horizontal* co-ordinates and enables the regulation of the distance between emotions and the activity of thought, fostering the focusing of sensations and emotions. It is the necessary condition for the activity of thinking.

Negation: A defence mechanism that comes into action in relation to psychic events. A subject who is unable to forget something that he can't remember may try to oppose such an event and endeavour to disown it in every possible way.

Negentropic area: An area that belongs to the Twofold*, whose dynamic principle relates to life-preservation, as defined by Beavers. In this area there is a prevalence of horizontal-deriving models.

Oedipal Constellation: The constellation expresses the multifaceted aspects which, though quite different from each other, all belong to a common area – the Oedipal scenery. It is the base upon which research and organisation of individual identity, including gender identity*, are founded. On these grounds identity is investigated anew and re-structured with each new experience.

Onefold: The body in its physicality and active presence (see COO*). At birth the Onefold goes into a turmoil* provoked by the intensity of sensations. This condition activates the Twofold* that has the function of containing and re-ordering, through the vertical* relation, the sensory turmoil. The perception of space pertains to the Onefold.

Perversion: Static maintenance of behaviours that aren't functional to the needs of an individual.

Psychic co-ordinator: Sensory organ that eventually emerges from the situation of turmoil as a potential co-ordinating medium to obtain knowledge of self and the world. Any sensory organ may be employed as a psychic co-ordinator.

Selective function: A defence mechanism which, at a given moment, eliminates all unimportant, meaningless, and non-functional data, therefore protecting and regulating mental life. Thus understood the selective function is different from splitting*.

Self-observation: A function of the mind necessary for individuation (latency phase), capable of continuously producing and modifying theories, or better, empirical perceptions in the vertical co-ordinate*. It takes its start in what Bion called "preconceptions" and may progressively become a "condition for knowing". It is different from conscience for the latter implies the presence of morals, an acquisition of later years.

Significant correspondences: The significant correspondences are the knots* of the contact net* on which the possible structures of thought are based.

Splitting: A defence mechanism which operates in disharmonious situations (cf. Harmony/Disharmony*) definitely distancing the psychic event, which is regarded as dangerous for the equilibrium, by the Ego Configuration*. It is an attack on mental functioning and brings impoverishment as its consequence. Once it is established it tends to become the main mode of functioning for it is difficult to dismiss it. A person can't remember what he doesn't know he has forgotten. Splitting therefore differs from denial*, negation* and from the mind's selective function*.

Transference: A condition which is characteristic of all human relations. The mode in which an individual invests another person of his or her capacities, or lack of capacities, for perception and understanding. The analytic setting facilitates such an attitude. Observation of the modes in which analysands use transference, helps analysts to understand and to evaluate, between other things, the modes and forms of their mental functioning.

Turmoil: A temporary state of the individual at birth. It is a condition of derangement in elements which are, on the whole, mainly homogeneous. The state of turmoil is produced by the trauma of birth, it is the initial stage of a state of entropy and of the consequent search for new equilibria.

Turmoiling states: Temporary conditions of derangement, particularly related to phases of transition such as the passage from latency to adolescence, from adolescence to adult age. It relates also to changes from one language register* to another as well as to all disharmonious situations (cf. Harmony/Disharmony*).

Twofold: The initial function of registration, originally activated by the protective mental presence of mother or mother substitute. The Twofold extends to the external world, originating the second primary relationship, the horizontal* relationship. The function of perceiving the passing of time pertains to the Twofold.

Vertical: A Co-ordinate that, intersecting the horizontal* co-ordinate, defines and delimits the formation of the mental space* or area. The vertical co-ordinate enables sensations and emotions to pass from the entropic* state to a state in which they may be expressed, a state that is functionally characteristic of the horizontal co-ordinate*. The mode in which the two co-ordinates articulate in time relates to the modifications of the Oedipal Constellation. In its turn, the articulation between vertical and horizontal both modifies the Ego Configuration* and is modified by it. The vertical co-ordinate is the expression of the Onefold.

INDEX

102, 109 115, 129, 134, 159,
162, 182–183, 189, 206, 217,
219, 222–224, 230–231, 237,
246
Tirelli L. 29
Transference 63, 135–136, 180,
183–184, 207, 245–246
Turmoil 51, 58, 95, 137, 149, 218,
225, 243–246
Turmoiling states 73, 94, 110, 117
140, 146, 175, 182, 187, 195,
242, 246
Tustin F. 55, 68
Twofold 11, 17, 20–21, 31, 38,
44–45, 47–48, 50, 52, 54,
57–64, 66, 74, 80, 84, 86–88,
93–95, 111, 120–122, 136–137,
145–146, 148–149, 151, 153,

180–181, 220, 224–225,
242–246

Vertical 10–12, 20–21, 53, 55, 60,
64, 66, 70, 72, 76, 81, 106, 111,
119–120, 127, 132, 135,
137–140, 148–149, 151–154,
156–157, 159, 161, 163, 165,
172, 175–177, 179–181, 184,
186–188, 195, 197, 207, 213,
217–218, 220, 225, 231, 233,
237–238, 242–246
Virgil 173
von Neumann J. 32

Wigner E. 30, 39
Winnicott D.W. 16–18,25, 55, 68
Wittgenstein L. 174, 178